Theo van Doesburg

Theo

Joost Baljeu

van Doesburg

Macmillan Publishing Co., Inc.
New York

Macmillan Publishing Co., Inc.
866 Third Avenue, New York, N. Y. 10022
First published in the UK by Studio Vista, a division of Cassell and Collier Macmillan Publishers Ltd.

Library of Congress Cataloging in Publication Data

Baljeu, Joost.
    Theo van Doesburg.

    1. Doesburg, Theo van, 1883–1931.
N6953.D57B34   1974   709'.2'4 [B]   74–7400
ISBN 0–02–506440–1

First American Edition

Printed in Great Britain

Contents

Acknowledgements

This book would not have been possible without the kind assistance of Mrs Nelly van Doesburg whose vivid memory for facts concerning both Van Doesburg and several other artists, and her unforgettable anecdotes regarding the Dada movement, helped to build up a colourful picture of this exhilarating period. In all respects I am indebted to her never-failing and stimulating cooperation.

Translation of Theo van Doesburg's texts given here is as literal as possible. The extracts from his poetry and prose were translated by Mrs Esther Z. R. Cohen, whereas I made the translations of his writings dealing with art and architecture. We thought this a sound approach because Van Doesburg attempted to project different personalities in his literature and in his writing on art through his use of language. I wish to thank Esther Cohen for her invaluable help, in particular with compiling the bibliography, as well as her personal encouragement during the years in which this book was produced.

I am also very grateful to Dr Robert Welsh from the Department of Fine Art at the University of Toronto for his accurate help in rendering these translations into the clearest possible English. Dr Welsh was invited to do so through the kind offices of the Rijksbureau voor Kunsthistorische Documentatie, The Hague, and its then director, Dr H. Gerson, at present professor of art history at the University of Groningen, the Netherlands. In this connection I should also like to thank Mr Stephen Adamson for his editing the final phrasing of these texts.

I am also indebted to the late Mrs H. Milius for kindly providing me with information concerning Van Doesburg's activity before his first trip to Germany; Professor C. van Eesteren for information about his collaboration with Van Doesburg on the De Stijl models of private and studio houses made in Paris; Mr A. Elzas for explaining his part in making some drawings for Van Doesburg's later architectural projects; and Dr W. Sandberg for his carefully reading the manuscript and bringing to my attention various details concerning Hans Richter's relationship with Van Doesburg as well as those of Naum Gabo and others.

The University Library in Amsterdam, the Royal Library in The Hague, and the Technical Department of the Public Library in Amsterdam were my principal sources of bibliographical material. Apart from the manuscripts at Meudon, almost every publication by Van Doesburg can be found in these institutions.

Finally, I would like to express my gratitude to the many private collectors and museums possessing works by Theo van Doesburg for their kind cooperation in providing photographs and other information.

It is my hope that the reader will find the present edition of this book, which is the final form of work started many years ago, surprisingly topical on the contemporary issues of the relationship of art, architecture and life as a whole.

joost baljeu 1973

Introduction

I imagined myself making a daring, spiritual crusade throughout artistic and intellectual Europe.
        Theo van Doesburg, 1914[1]

No attempt can be made to understand the history of the De Stijl movement without a knowledge of the works and writings of its founder, Theo van Doesburg.

While Piet Mondrian laid the basis for this movement with his abstract geometric painting, Van Doesburg's main concern was to develop it in all aspects of life through architecture. Whereas Mondrian could stay quietly in his studio, carefully selecting the exact position of each line, plane or colour in a painting to theorize about it afterwards, Van Doesburg travelled restlessly from one city to another, all over Europe, whenever he sensed that a new development was to be expected. On each such occasion he tested his work and ideas against those of other artists and movements in art. Many of the approaches he encountered this way reacted with his own, through either absorption or rejection, in the main with no other goal than synthesizing those elements which he considered could promote a new universal art.

Because he believed in the unity of art and life in a future plastic expression he often revolted against circumstances as they were. Van Doesburg was the prototype of the anti-bourgeois, the non-conformist. Thus Dada, the earliest 'action-group' of this century, to which he adhered under a pseudonym, I. K. Bonset, fitted him like a glove. It provided him with an excellent weapon to smash what was held sacred so as to prepare the grounds for a new art. Convention and dogma were further attacked under another pseudonym, as the anti-philosopher Aldo Camini.

He synthesized many characters in his own personality. Some of his work reveals him as a Surrealist as well as a Dadaist; he was Utopian and romantic, but preoccupied with the problems of translating his visions into reality. In art he was a painter, designer, typographer and architect; but he was also a prolific writer and included in his activities the roles of poet, novelist, art-historian and art-critic.

Many of the issues in the relationship between art and architecture upon which Van Doesburg focused his attention remain with us and are again under consideration today. Similarly, Van Doesburg provided much of contemporary Constructivism in the Western world with a basis for survival after the Second World War, when towards the end of his life he created his systematic Concrete Art.

When further comparing Van Doesburg to

Mondrian, an important difference in their contribution to modern art and architecture can be discerned. In spite of his contemplation on the significance of his Neo-plasticism for life as a whole, painting meant for Mondrian an end in itself. Thus his large oeuvre of excellent paintings represents itself the transition towards a new era, and at the same time marks the end of a period in art. In contrast, Van Doesburg's architectural models and theories opened up the road for the development of the future. Finally, if a lesson can be drawn from Van Doesburg's approach, it is that first and foremost the artist's life is a creative process rather than the production of many works of art. In this respect Theo van Doesburg can also be considered to represent an extremely modern man.

Part One

Life and Works

Some personal facts

Theo van Doesburg was born in Utrecht on 30 August 1883 and registered as Christiaan Emil Marie Küpper, son of Wilhelm Küpper and Henrietta Catherina Margadant. It has long been assumed that Theo van Doesburg was a pseudonym but the following facts, obtained from the civil registration offices of Utrecht, Rotterdam and Amsterdam, suggest that 'Theo van Doesburg' was not a pseudonym but his real name adopted from his so-called stepfather, Theodorus Doesburg.

In 1883, while his wife was expecting the birth of the future Theo van Doesburg, Wilhelm Küpper, a photographer born in Bonn, Germany, left her and returned to Germany. On 24 September 1884 Van Doesburg's mother was registered as having left Utrecht and settled with her children in Amsterdam. The previous day, Theodorus Doesburg, her future second husband who also lived in Utrecht, was registered as having moved to Amsterdam. On 7 March 1892 Wilhelm Küpper died at Lindenhöhe near Cologne, Germany. A year later, on 19 July 1893, Van Doesburg's mother married Theodorus Doesburg in Amsterdam. One explanation why Van Doesburg added 'van' (Dutch for 'of' or 'from') to his name might be that he wanted to show that, although registered as C. E. M. Küpper, he considered himself the son of Theodorus Doesburg. It is also important to note that Theo van Doesburg signed the works he produced before the age of twenty with this name long before he began to use it as a pseudonym for his writings or other public appearances. The matter is of importance because, if Theo van Doesburg knew or had good reason to believe that he was the son of Theodorus Doesburg and not of Wilhelm Küpper, the Dutch parentage of the artist is established.

Van Doesburg's adopted father owned a small factory in Amsterdam, and, since he had a choice between two stepsons to assist and succeed him, he agreed that Theo might take up another profession, an artistic one. The boy was sent to a school of acting, but after a short time he made up his mind to become a painter. Both parents disapproved; they did not believe he could earn enough to support himself. He stuck to his decision and ran away from home at the age of eighteen. To make a living he copied several paintings in the Rijksmuseum,

13

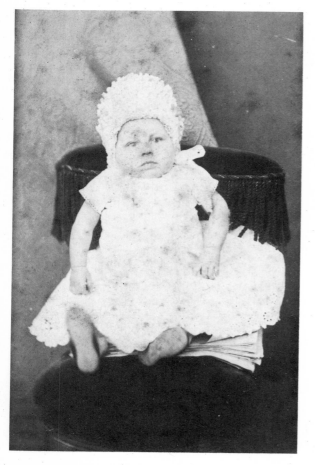

Amsterdam, and gave lessons to amateur painters. Later on his writing began to bring in some money, though very little. Indeed, his financial circumstances were to remain poor to the very end of his life.

Van Doesburg married three times. His first wife, Agnita Henrica Feis, was a poet who, like Van Doesburg, published regularly in the weekly *Eenheid (Unity)*. She wrote rhythmic poetry which was a mixture of Christian ethics and Eastern mysticism and published a small volume of poetry, *Verzen in Staccato (Poems in Staccato)* for which Van Doesburg designed an Expressionist cover.

After being divorced from his first wife, Van Doesburg married Helena Milius about the time of the founding of the De Stijl movement, of which his second wife was to remain an enthusiastic supporter.

Several years later Van Doesburg married Petronella van Moorsel, who became well known for her appearance as Petro van Doesburg in several Dada performances. Mrs Nelly van Doesburg now lives in the house Van Doesburg built in Meudon, France.

Theo van Doesburg as a baby

Theo van Doesburg around 1900

Opposite Facsimile of Theo van Doesburg's handwriting; fragment of a letter to J. J. P. Oud, architect, dated 11 November 1924
Collection of Mrs Nelly van Doesburg
Photo: P. Willi

The brown period   1902–9

Van Doesburg's earliest known painting dates from 1899. His first period, lasting from 1902–9, was of realistic paintings, chiefly portraits, some of which use a typical Rembrandtesque atmosphere of light-dark contrasts, thus revealing his activities as a copyist in the Rijksmuseum. Others employ an impressionistic or, subsequently, an expressionistic manner (from 1906 on). In *Some Biographical Notes on the Painter and Architect Theo van Doesburg,*[1] an unpublished manuscript written in 1928, he referred to these years as his 'brown period' and mentioned the artists who had influenced him as Rembrandt, Frans Hals, Vermeer, Fra Angelico, Michelangelo and Leonardo da Vinci. Around this time Van Doesburg also began to show an interest in writing. He kept a diary throughout this period, which is still in existence, but his short stories began around 1908.

In 1908 Van Doesburg's first public appearance, an exhibition of drawings and sketches at the Haagsche Kunstkring, an artists' society in The Hague, seems to bring to an end the uncertainty revealed by his early painting.

The blue period   1909–13

Impressionistic works again alternated with Fauve-like works. Colours are more vivid now than in the earlier period, and the brush-strokes are applied with firmness. Van Doesburg, who considered this period to have lasted from 1909–13, referred to it as his 'blue period'.

Around 1912 his first articles on art began to appear. Already Van Doesburg was prepared to be controversial; he had an article called 'Futurism' published in *Eenheid* which completely rejects that movement for being too 'superficial'. Here it is already posited that Futurism's 'superficial expression of velocity, the aeroplane, the racing-car and so on, is but a weak expression of the inner velocity of thought compared to which the velocity of radium represents nothing but inertia . . . The mimetic expression of velocity (whatever its form may be: the aroplane, the automobile, and so on) is diametrically opposed to the character of painting, the supreme origin of which is to be found in inner life.'[1] An article 'On Modern Art. Kandinsky',[2] published in 1913, rejected the art of Kandinsky because he thought it 'anti-nature' and 'selfish'.

The years 1909–14 represent a process of fermentation in Van Doesburg's development. He read the writings of artists such as Kandinsky, Berlage, Marinetti, Boccioni, and others. This exposed him to several influences, especially Kandinsky's, whose books *Concerning the Spiritual in Art* (1912) and *Backward Glances* (1913) can be seen reflected in Van Doesburg's article 'The Development of Modern Painting'.[3] This artist now seen as a founder of abstract art, especially attracted Van Doesburg, in spite of the negative criticisms which can often be found in the latter's early writings.

Self-portrait 1906
oil on canvas, $65 \cdot 5 \times 51$ cm. $(24 \times 20$ in.)
collection of Mrs Nelly van Doesburg.
Photo: L'Art en photographie

Beach 1912
oil on canvas, 29×33 cm. $(11 \times 13$ in.)
collection of Mrs Nelly van Doesburg.
Photo: L'Art en photographie

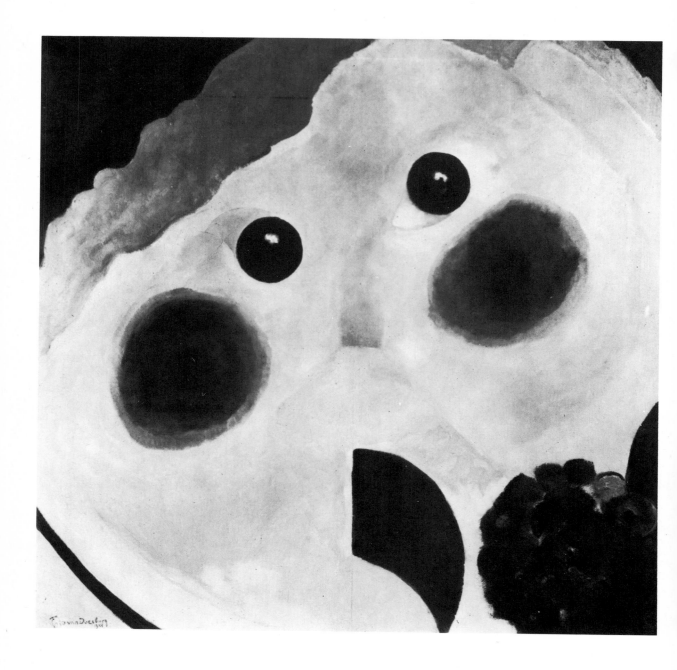

What especially attracted Van Doesburg was his description of a Russian peasant 'living within painting', the walls of his cabin being entirely covered with icons and other paintings – an interest which clearly anticipates the De Stijl interiors and especially Van Doesburg's interior designing in the Aubette.

Berlage's influence, mainly in his book *Studies on Architecture, Style and Community* (1910)[4] is evident in the series of articles 'Essay of a New Criticism of Art'[5] and 'Independent Reflections on Art' (1913–14). In the latter series, the first mention of an international art form to come can be found. Van Doesburg also puts forward for the first time the primacy of 'the straight line' as a future means of expression – an idea which is to be of great importance in his subsequent work. Van Doesburg wrote, 'For – to say a few words on technique – whereas the curved line was used predominantly for reasons of beauty (Phidias, Michelangelo, Raphael, Rubens) it has been used more and more economically for reasons of truth (Millet, Monet, Cézanne) until it will end as the straight line for reasons of Love. This will enable the art of the future to create an international form; a form understandable to all and vital enough to the expression of a general feeling of love in a monumental way. Such is the future.'[6] Whereas these ideas indicate that Van Doesburg had absorbed Boccioni's *Technical Manifesto of Futurist Sculpture*,[7] there is an important difference between their visions. Boccioni saw the straight line simply as a means towards 'a new architectural construction of sculptural masses and zones', but Van Doesburg, though not at this time using the straight line in his painting, singled it out as the sole means for all future art forms, in fact, for an international form of art to come, thus almost bestowing it with a spiritual significance. The weekly *Eenheid*, in which Van Doesburg published regularly, contained articles of various ethical and religious tendencies; Christian-scientist, Theosophist, Christosophic (M. H. J. Schoenmaekers), pacifist, utopian (E. Bellamy) as well as Eastern religious views were presented side by side. Van Doesburg's own interest in the East was reflected in his articles on Japanese and Asiatic art. It is interesting to see this concern culminate in the following statement from 1916, 'In fact, what happens is nothing but the shifting from an Eastern into a Western notion of art. Today this is possible, now that materialism has annulled itself.'[8] This belief in the end of materialism was one held by several idealistic intellectuals in Holland and was perhaps possible only in a country which at that time was passing neutrally and quietly through the devastation of the First World War.

There is an Eastern flavour, too, to some of his early stories, many of which contain a moral. Stress on the spiritual quality of art can be found again in his series 'Independent Reflections on Art'. Here man's inner life is seen to be chaotic. It is thus the task of the artist to create order in it, which is why art is described as 'an independent entity of our inner life', somewhat reminiscent of Kandinsky's point of view. This thought in its turn explains why 'religion and art can only be understood by the spirit'.

Girl with buttercups 1914
oil on canvas, 80 × 80 cm. (31 × 31 in.)
Yale University Art Gallery, on loan from
Mr and Mrs William N. Copley.
Photo: L'Art en photographie

On active duty   1914–15

In 1914 Van Doesburg was called up and sent to the Belgo-Dutch frontier. Since the Netherlands had mobilized her army as a security but stayed out of the First World War, this meant that her soldiers were privileged with lots of spare time. During these years Van Doesburg's writings were preoccupied with problems of warfare and the social aspects of life, revealing an anti-militarist temperament. He had a long series of articles called 'Meditations at the Frontier' published in *De Avondpost* (1915). In these he argued that war as a brutal destructive force with weapons would gradually disappear and change into a new form of struggle fought on spiritual grounds. In this latter realm art can help life in its search for perfection and absolute harmony. His belief that the world will become united, as the result of a socio-economic development, is related to the ideas of Bart de Ligt, at that time Holland's most influential pacifist, who was a close friend of Van Does-

burg's. Painting, on the other hand, almost stopped during these years. Instead, Van Doesburg produced numerous drawings of peasants, workers and soldiers.

In Tilburg he met Anthony Kok, a poet. Together they arranged soirées, with Van Doesburg giving his first lectures on modern art and Kok playing compositions by modern composers at the piano. It was Anthony Kok with whom Van Doesburg first discussed his plan for what later was to become the *De Stijl* magazine.

In connection with this, it is important to mention a lecture Van Doesburg gave in Utrecht, on 30 October 1915, under the title 'The development of modern painting'. This was also published in *Eenheid* and later appeared as the first of the *Three Lectures on the New Plastic Art*.[1] He made here another, important early statement: 'nature will become idea and idea is style'.

First contacts with Piet Mondrian and the architect J. J. P. Oud

Van Doesburg's earliest opinion of Mondrian's work can be found in his article 'Art criticism',[1] published on 6 November 1915 in *Eenheid* and presenting a review of the exhibition 'Moderne Kunst' in the Stedelijk Museum, Amsterdam, which contained works by Mondrian, Gestel, Sluiters, Schelfhout and Le Fauconnier (see p. 105). Van Doesburg's immediate enthusiasm

for what he called the spiritual and architectural quality of Mondrian's work quickly led him to seek a contact by letter, also in November 1915. Although it was to remain rather formal until they had met, this was the beginning of a long correspondence which lasted until 1923 when Van Doesburg also settled in Paris. Towards the end of 1915 Van Doesburg, again by letter, suggested founding a magazine with Mondrian, an idea rejected by the latter as premature.[2] In January 1916 they met for the first time, without, however, producing any change so far as the magazine was concerned.

Towards the end of February or the beginning of March 1916 Van Doesburg was demobilized and settled in Leyden. Shortly after his arrival he met the architect J. J. P. Oud with whom he was to have frequent discussions on the founding of his magazine. Again, Oud's response may explain why Van Doesburg turned to other organizational activities such as the founding of artists' associations. On 24 March he became co-founder of the artists' association De Anderen (The Others) in Amster-

dam. (The president was Erich Wichmann; vice-president, Joh. Tielens; secretary, Theo van Doesburg; executive members, Louis Saalborn and Phocas Fokkens.) Soon after, on 31 May, Van Doesburg helped to found a second artists' association, De Sphinx (The Sphinx), in Leyden. (Its president was J. J. P. Oud and the other officers were as follows: vice-president, D. Roggeveen; first secretary, E. G. Kessler; second secretary, Van Doesburg; treasurer, J. H. Kriest.)

Van Doesburg optimistically described The Others as a group of 'style-conscious' artists.[3] There were, however, as many styles as there were artists.

The transition to Neo-plasticism   1916

In 1913, a crucial year in the development of modern art in Holland, a group of abstract painters who were soon to become members of The Independents, had proclaimed 'Absolute Painting' as an ideal. The conflict this created with traditional and semi-modern groups resulted in the formation of two strongly opposed parties, known as 'the brown ones' (the traditional artists) and 'the blue ones' (the moderns). These terms were adopted by Van Doesburg to distinguish between the different styles in his early work.

It is interesting to see in *Some Biographical Notes*, written in 1928, that Van Doesburg also described 1913 as the year marking the end of the 'blue' and the beginning of the 'white' period. In actual fact, this does not correspond to the development of his painting which remained 'blue' until 1917 and produced

(abstract) 'white' works only thereafter.

Before this important choice was made Van Doesburg's Cubist period began, in 1916. The Cubist pictures, some of which are lost, largely represent landscapes and still-life subjects. From these paintings the process of translation from nature towards non-mimetic art developed via circular and triangular shapes, particularly in still-life works.

Though Neo-plasticism is a direct outcome of Cubism, there was at that time also another road leading to abstract art: the Kandinskian approach. Owing to their mutual interest in Kandinsky, who from 1912 on exerted a tremendous influence on modern Dutch painting, Van Doesburg dedicated a special brochure to Adrianus de Winter. The latter, only a year older than Van Doesburg, was one of Holland's earliest abstract painters and a member of the

Still life   1916
oil on canvas, 35 × 40 cm. (14 × 16 in.)
Collection of Mr and Mrs Harry Lewis Winston.
Photo: Lew Gilcrest Studios

(left) *Tree with houses*   1916
oil on panel, 70 × 56 cm. (28 × 24 in.)
Portland Art Museum, Portland, Oregon
Gift of Mr Jan de Graaf

artists' association De Onafhankelijken (The Independents). He exhibited together with artists such as J. Bendien, E. Wichmann and Vilmos Huszar. Van Doesburg wrote several reviews of exhibitions by The Independents, which were published in *Eenheid*. In spite of all these contacts Van Doesburg's paintings *Girl with Buttercups* (1914, p. 18) and *Heroic Movement* (1916) remain the two solitary examples of an abstract curvilinear trend in his œuvre. He did not develop these so as to diverge from his Cubist approach and his advance to Neo-plasticism. However, the extent to which the choice between these two roads to 'absolute painting' preoccupied his mind is revealed in a brochure *'The Painter De Winter and his Work'* and in a book, *The New Movement in Painting*, which was written this year and published in 1917. An early formulation about subjective individualism and the aim to replace it with 'individuality for the benefit of collectivity', anticipating his adherence to Neo-plasticism was presented in the following paragraph from his article 'The New Style in Painting':

Since all preceding schools of painting have

proved that the spirit of beauty does not lie in nature but in the 'I', now that painting in all its various expressions from Giotto to Cézanne has demonstrated that all beauty is in the 'I', that the 'I' is all emotion and that beyond the 'I' nothing can exist because all being exists only in relationship with the 'I', now the time has come to develop from this 'I' a new style. As soon as this 'I' becomes the general, universal 'I' instead of the individualistic or the rationalistic one, the new style will be a general style.[1]

Again, Neo-plasticism's expansion to 'De Stijl' can be found in the lecture 'The Aesthetic Principle of Modern Art' (1916), the second of the *Three Lectures on the New Plastic Art*. He states that this new style will be realized by a new form of collaboration between architecture and the arts, as well as that architecture will possess points related to universal space. The latter was Van Doesburg's first intuitive statement of his space in time approach in Neo-plastic architecture.

1917   Van Doesburg founds De Stijl

Van Doesburg continued to discuss the founding of the magazine *De Stijl*. One of the main problems was whether or not architects were to be included. Both Mondrian and Bart van der Leck, the latter in spite of his earlier collaboration with the architect Berlage, were not very willing to cooperate with architects. Van Doesburg had met the painter Van der Leck towards the end of 1916 on his visit to Laren, a well-

known artist's colony in Holland, where he went to see Mondrian.

On 16 May Mondrian agreed with Van Doesburg to call the magazine *De Stijl* (*The Style*). An earlier idea had been to call it *The Straight Line*, but probably because, following Marinetti's manifesto *The New Religion-morality of Velocity* (1916),[1] Boccioni stated that the straight line was most appropriate to the future, spiritual expression of creative man, Van Doesburg dropped his earlier idea and decided on the Berlagian *De Stijl*. Nevertheless, Marinetti's manifesto, as well as all 'technical' manifestos of Futurism, especially those by Boccioni, are of great relevance to Neo-plasticism, as is also revealed by Van Doesburg's lecture 'The style of the future'[2] which he gave this year. Both isms were very much concerned with the future, though from different starting points and with other aims, and there was to be a life-long dialogue between Neo-plasticism and Futurism.

On 17 May Van der Leck, in a letter to Van Doesburg, congratulated him on the founding of the magazine *De Stijl* and accepted an invitation to collaborate. He wrote, 'I think it is very good that you yourself have succeeded in founding a magazine . . . With all my heart I wish you success with this new enterprise.'[3]

On 21 May Mondrian suggested also inviting the philosopher-mathematician Schoenmaekers and the painters Severini and Picasso to join. He preferred Van Doesburg to remain sole editor since he and Bart van der Leck felt that with so few collaborators, their being mentioned as co-editors would strike the public as odd.

On 16 June Van Doesburg wrote the introduction to *De Stijl*. In October 1917 the first issue was published, containing this introduction, the introduction to his essay 'Neo-plasticism in Painting' by Mondrian, an article by Bart van der Leck 'Modern Painting and its Relationship to Architecture', one by Anthony Kok on 'The Modern Painting in the Interior', Oud's essay on 'The Monumental Town' and comments by Van Doesburg on a painting by Van der Leck dated 1917 and on Oud's 'Plan for a Block along the Seafront', which were both reproduced. The first issue clearly reflects the discussions on the relationship of art to architecture mentioned above.[4] (According to the list of contributors, presented in the Jubilee issue of *De Stijl* (1927), Kok, Mondrian, Oud and Huszar supported Van Doesburg in founding this magazine.)

The second issue, that of December 1917, contains the first part of a contribution called 'Avant-garde Painting' (La Peinture d'Avant-garde) by Severini, who was the first foreign artist to collaborate.

Van Doesburg's first Neo-plastic paintings using rectangles date from this year and some of them employ a black background, probably under the influence of Bart van der Leck (e.g. Van Doesburg's painting *The Three Graces*, later called *Composition VII*). A number of his early Neo-plastic paintings were destroyed during the bombing of The Hague in the Second World War. Van Doesburg's Neo-plastic paintings were produced at the same time as realistic paintings. These were the starting point for a series of pictures which show the translation from nature towards abstract, pure plastic expression. In *Some Biographical Notes* Van Doesburg referred to the works done from 1917 on as his 'elementary and architectural Stijl-period'.

From 1917 on Van Doesburg designed Neo-plastic stained-glass windows, tile floors (p. 27) and colour schemes for buildings by Jan Wils as well as for houses built by Oud. His first contacts with the architect Jan Wils, who was living in The Hague, and with Vilmos Huszar, painter and designer/typographer, then living at Voorburg, date from this year. Both places are very near to Leyden.

These projects, together with his writing in journals other than *De Stijl*, represented his main source of income. He made a mosaic in Villa Allegonda, built by Oud and Kamerlingh Onnes at Katwijk and he designed tiled floors in the holiday residence 'De Vonk' built by Oud at Noordwijkerhout in 1918. Both places are near The Hague. Some stained-glass windows

25

(left) *Composition IX, The Cardplayers* 1917
oil on canvas, 115·5 × 106·5 cm. (45 × 40 in.)
Gemeente Museum, The Hague

Tile floor in holiday residence, Noordwijkerhout,
Holland, 1917. In collaboration with J. J. P. Oud,
architect

were made in the houses mentioned above as
well as in the villa of Mr De Lange Woerden, at
Alkmaar, near Amsterdam.

In this year, Van Doesburg's book *The New
Movement in Painting*[5] was published. It had
appeared earlier, in 1916, as a series of five
articles under the same title in *De Beweging*
(*The Movement*), at that time a distinguished
Dutch periodical on literature, art, science and
politics. The book presents a survey of the
development of modern art, starting with
Impressionism and the other movements, such
as Expressionism, Cubism and Futurism, all
preparing for a new, geometric abstract monumental art, a style of the future.

The year 1917 brought the first mention of
two conceptions which were to be of major
importance in Van Doesburg's aesthetics:
'elementary plastic art' and 'the fourth dimension'. In a 'Public Letter', in *Eenheid* of 27
November 1915, he stated that 'the only elements' at the painter's disposal are line and
colour. In his review of Piet Mondrian's work,
also published in *Eenheid*, Van Doesburg wrote
that, in respect of its colours, this painting
provided him with 'an elementary pure impression of art'. The use of the word 'element'
is very probably based upon an important book
by the art historian, Heinrich Wölfflin which
also appeared in 1915, Kunstgeschichtliche
Grundbegriffe (*Principles of Art History*). In

this book, which discusses the period in art
from the early Renaissance to the Baroque,
Wölfflin promulgates concepts of the linear and
the pictorial, of closed and open form, of the
tectonic and the atectonic, in short the plastic
'elements' to describe the essence of art. Van
Doesburg, in a footnote to an article in his
series 'Great Masters of Art', (1917) already
presented this approach with a wider meaning.
He wrote, 'European art (however) has developed from mimeticism and only today is
arriving at an elementary plastic art.'[6]

The other concept, that of the fourth dimension, is also discussed in the series 'Great
Masters of Art', where the following paragraph
can be read:

However, Man as the appearance of utmost
internality, of spirit, does not possess any
point in front, at the side or the back, no
fixed point at all towards which he could
define a dimension. This explains why in
expressing the spiritual, in making spirit
an artefact, he will be forced to a
moto-stereometric form of expression. This
moto-stereometric form of expression
represents the appearance of a 4-n
dimensional world in a world of three
dimensions.[7]

Around the turn of the century, largely

27

owing to the theory of relativity, the static Euclidean view of nature was replaced by a dynamic, multi-dimensional concept which incorporated time – that is the element of change. In the above quotation it is typical of Van Doesburg's readiness for change that he strikes a parallel between this 'machinery' of nature and that of the mind. Furthermore, this passage anticipates the basic concept of Van Doesburg's important architectural programme of 1924 and his later theory of Elementarism by its use of the term 'moto-stereometric'. It means that Neo-plastic architecture, as well as a number of Elementarist paintings, possess a metrical screen of interrelated spatial points in their spatial layout, which not only connect

with the space of its environment (what Van Doesburg usually refers to as 'universal space') but make it expand into it.

The fourth dimension, moreover, was discussed with Mondrian. Though he sympathized with Van Doesburg's views on this matter and even stated that he too was then using that element in his art, Mondrian was to reveal shortly afterwards that in his opinion the fourth dimension was of no essential relevance to art. This is why he abstained from saying anything on the subject in his own Neo-plastic theory and left it to Van Doesburg to discuss. The latter's library contained many scientific publications on this subject.

Dr M. H. J. Schoenmaekers and Neo-plastic Theory

The first attack on the De Stijl artists came from the mathematician-philosopher, Dr M. H. J. Schoenmaekers in his lecture 'Art and Thought', published in the January 1918 issue of *Het Getij* (*The Tide*), an important art, literary and philosophy magazine. In addition to describing art as essentially 'capricious', Schoenmaekers remarks, 'Do not explain your works, you artists who want to be style-artists,'[1] which can be seen as addressed principally to Mondrian, whose art-philosophical ideas, as well as their formulation, are indebted to Schoenmaekers. Ironically, Schoenmaekers had written two years earlier, 'As long as the language of words has not explained clearly the new insight by direct, general forms from nature, plastic artists also will try to speak in words . . . They do not as yet consider their art to be sufficient.'[2] This was written at a time when Mondrian had

practically stopped painting, during the years 1915 and 1916. In these two years he produced only a few paintings in the proto Neo-plastic style he had ended with in 1914, and he was using this lapse of time to work on his large essay 'Neo-plasticism in Painting'. During these years Mondrian and Schoenmaekers, who both lived in Laren, frequently met. There is little doubt that Schoenmaekers saw in Mondrian's works of that period, which consisted of linear, horizontal-vertical constructive compositions and reduced colour to gradations of the three primaries, the visualization of his ideas as presented in his own books *Het nieuwe Wereldbeeld* (*The New Image of the World*) (1915) and *Beginselen der beeldende Wiskunde* (*Principles of Plastic Mathematics*) (1916). This is why he could include paragraphs on art which can be seen to fit this type of plastic expression. On

28

the other hand, Mondrian, who was sorting out his views and trying to determine his position in those years, considered that Schoenmaekers' ideas in general, in spite of their esoteric character, might provide his theory on Neo-plasticism with an objective, philosophical background. However, the process of inter-weaving several philosophical notions of Schoenmaekers with his own views posed so many problems that Mondrian invited Van Doesburg to go over his essay before publication. The latter collaborated on this theory by correcting several paragraphs and by occasionally re-writing larger fragments which were again considered by Mondrian before their final publication in *De Stijl* during 1917 and 1918.

Van Doesburg was searching for expressions of universal intelligibility in both the theory and practice of art, which explains why he, too, used some typical Schoenmaekers formulations in his articles of 1916 and 1917. However, Van Doesburg demonstrates much less affinity to Schoenmaekers than does Mondrian. On 30 January 1918 Mondrian drew Van Doesburg's attention to the lecture 'Art and Thought' and confirmed Van Doesburg's opinion that Schoenmaekers' view of their art was basically wrong. In spite of Mondrian's agreement with Van Doesburg shortly afterwards to withdraw an invitation to Schoenmaekers to contribute to

De Stijl, his own theory continued under the influence of *Principles of Plastic Mathematics*. This book in particular – the only one by Schoenmaekers in Van Doesburg's library – is a key document for the theoretical-philosophical background of Neo-plastic writing. In contrast to Mondrian, Van Doesburg was only more fully influenced by it much later, during the years when he introduced his Elementarism and his final approach, called Concrete Art. At this time, reacting to 'Art and Thought', Van Doesburg advised Mondrian to read Spinoza and furthermore revealed his difference of opinion with Schoenmaekers in a series of articles called 'The mysticism of Beauty and Love',[3] and in an article 'Thought-Vision-Creation' (p. 108).[4] Both articles demonstrate the difficulties involved in stating that Neo-plasticism represents in truth a predominantly conceptual art, since intuition, intellect, emotion and pure thought occur in an unsettled terminology. The entire matter – as will be discussed later – was to become more complicated by the fact that Schoenmaekers predicates art to be the final, concrete manifestation of universal thought, in contrast to Hegel, whose philosophy Van Doesburg was beginning to read and who expected a development leading from art towards religion and finally ending with philosophy.

The problem of four-dimensionality   1918–19

Through Gerrit Rietveld, whom he had met shortly before, Van Doesburg became acquainted with the architect Robert van 't Hoff. Both architects were soon to become members of De Stijl. Van 't Hoff executed two houses in 1916,

reproduced in *De Stijl*,[1] which manifested the influence of both Wright and Berlage. Van Doesburg introduced Van 't Hoff to J. J. P. Oud, and, as a result of Van 't Hoff's acquainting him with some new material on Wright,

(left) *Composition X* 1918
oil on canvas, 64×43 cm. $(25 \times 17$ in.)
Collection of Mrs A. Mueller-Widman.
Photo: D. Widmer

Theo van Doesburg and Lena Milius,
The Hague, 1918

Oud published the article 'Architectural Comment on Illustration 8. Groundplan of the Fred C. Robie house, Chicago' in *De Stijl*.[2] In his earlier *Souvenirs of an American Journey* (1913) Berlage had pointed out Wright's importance and provided illustrations of the Larkin building and Unity Church.[3] The marked influence of Wright can be met in nearly all of Oud's projects published during these years in *De Stijl*. The two dynamic projects by Van 't Hoff mentioned above with their fully equilibrated multi-sided plastic form, and the designs by Oud stand as precursors of the architectural models Van Doesburg was to produce with the assistance of the students of his De Stijl course at Weimar in 1922. These are the earliest examples of pure De Stijl architecture. Consequently, it was largely through Van 't Hoff that the mass and volume of Wright's dynamic architecture lies at the basis of Neo-plasticism's four-dimensional space-time architecture.

An example of Van Doesburg's debt to Van 't Hoff can be found in his prize-winning design of 1918 for a competition for a monument in Leeuwarden, the capital of Friesland, a province in the North of the Netherlands. The now-destroyed model for this monument showed great similarity with Van 't Hoff's *Plastic Stair-post* reproduced in *De Stijl*[4] and appeared striking due to the plastic character of its developing form.

The problem of movement proved to be the main issue in Neo-plastic painting in 1918. It is important to note that such Van Doesburg paintings as *Rhythms of a Russian Dance*, (p. 35) *Tarantella* and *Composition X* (left) differ fundamentally from Mondrian's by their greater dynamics. Van Doesburg was attempting to restore the element of the fourth dimension stemming from Analytical Cubism with its

31

overlapping of various points of view in space which then interpenetrate one another by using intersecting lines, thus suggesting the interpenetration of open plane areas, or 'open' planes. On the other hand, Mondrian's work of this time implied criticism of Cubism's sculptural use of overlapping planes creating the illusion of three-dimensionality; he placed the lines parallel to the horizontal and vertical sides of his canvas thereby producing 'closed' planes in juxtaposition which resulted in regaining the two-dimensional quality of the canvas-plane but also in the loss of this new dynamic element. Since Mondrian wanted to be an absolute, i.e. two-dimensional painter above all else, it is quite understandable that he told Van Doesburg that, in his view, 'the other dimensions', i.e. 'four- or n-dimensionality', will never make any essential difference.[5]

Around the same time a related problem, that of 'the diagonal', was discussed by Van Doesburg, Mondrian and Van der Leck. It was Van der Leck's view that the visual oblique in painting expressed the dynamics of the universe and therefore had to be used together with the static construction of the universe as expressed by orthogonal relationships.[6] Mondrian, who revealed his disagreement with Van der Leck some time before by criticizing him for using geometric patterns which remained too close to naturalistic form, disapproved of the visual oblique in combination with the orthogonal. Nevertheless, it was at this time that Mondrian began to use the lozenge canvas in an effort to mitigate the predominance of the horizontal-vertical relationships in nature and in architecture.

Van Doesburg this year added to his four-dimensional approach in painting another possibility by a novel use of kinetics in several designs for the tile-floor mosaics of a holiday-residence, 'De Vonk', at Noordwijkerhout. His design for the interior occupied by his friend, Bart de Ligt, represents still another example of incorporating dynamics. Here Van Doesburg employed red-green and black-white colour pairs, thereby clearly stressing the element of colour movement. His use of complementary colour pairs stems from Seurat, whose Neo-impressionist theory of 'simultaneous' colours was based on Delacroix's colour-circle.

As a consequence of his theory about the new expression of the element of time (i.e. movement) in art through 4-n dimensionality Van Doesburg, at this moment, could consider earlier expressions of dynamic movement in art by means of the visual oblique to be essentially 'baroque'. In June Van Doesburg stated in 'Notes on Illustration 12: The Saw and the Fishbowl, Painting by P. Alma', that the 'destruction' of the visual oblique, when used on a monumental scale with the horizontal-vertical character of architecture, though aesthetically satisfactory, was a remnant of the outmoded baroque style. In contrast, 'modern destruction begins where architectural structure is opened up and set into motion by colour relationships. The colour-planes, however, are always in orthogonal relationship.'[7] The last two sentences already present the earliest and shortest formulation of his later Neo-plastic architectural creed. Together with the statement from his article 'Great Masters of Art' (1917) quoted above, these sentences give full proof that at this time Van Doesburg already was the originator of a new architecture which (a) destroys mass and (b) consists of rectangular coloured planes in (c) a four-dimensional space-time relationship.

The discussions on the problem of 'the oblique' continued into the early months of 1919. Mondrian then presented as an explanation for his occasional use of a lozenge format that the diagonal boundaries of the canvas thus stress

32

Composition VIII. The Cow   1917
oil on canvas, $37 \cdot 5 \times 63 \cdot 5$ cm. (15×25 in.)
Collection of Museum of Modern Art, New York

Composition XI   1918
oil on canvas, $56 \cdot 5 \times 101 \cdot 5$ cm. (24×40 in.)
Collection of The Solomon R. Guggenheim
Museum, New York

(left) *Composition XIII.*
Variation 1918
oil on panel, 29·5 × 28·5 cm.
(12 × 11 in.)
The Contemporary Arts Center,
Cincinnati Art Museum, on loan
from Mrs Mary E. Johnston

(right) *Rhythms of a Russian*
Dance 1918
oil on canvas, 136 × 62 cm.
(54 × 25 in.)
Collection of The Museum of
Modern Art, New York

Left
Composition in discords   1918
oil on canvas, 63×58 cm. (25×23 in.)
Collection of Mrs M. Arp-Hagenbach

Counter-Composition XIII 1924
design for a stained-glass window,
commissioned by the Museum of
Hanover, not executed. Gouache on
paper, $98 \cdot 5 \times 35$ cm. (39×14 in.)
Collection of Mrs Nelly van Doesburg

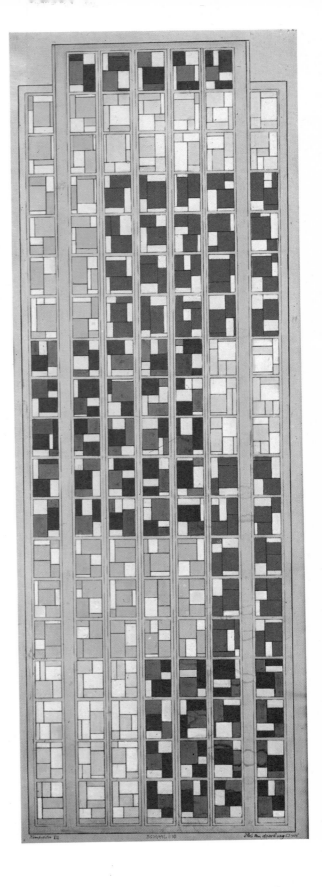

the orthogonality of the composition within. In an orthogonal composition within a rectangular format, when hung tectonically (that is to say parallel to the horizontal-vertical directions of its architectural environment), paradoxically composition suggests diagonality. The latter usage makes the diagonal in composition an implied rather than a visualized element as in the work of Bart van der Leck. However, Mondrian ultimately agreed with Van Doesburg that the diamond-shape canvas by its obliquity cannot go with architecture and defended himself by stating that his pictures still represented self-contained entities, without any relationship to the building they were in. The problem, in fact, implies a search for the combination of 'the static' and 'the dynamic' as approached from a dualist point of view typical of De Stijl and will recur in 1924 when Van Doesburg's concept of Elementarism, using the diagonal, comes to full development.

The problem of time, of movement in Neo-plastic art, is temporarily closed when, in April of the following year Van Doesburg and Mondrian discussed colour in relation to Vantongerloo's use of all the colours of the spectrum. It was Mondrian's view that this was precipitate. Though then using only the primary colours and black and white himself, he agreed with Van Doesburg that, from a theoretical point of view, the use of all colours of the spectrum was acceptable and perhaps better. In fact, Van Doesburg did not always restrict himself to the primary palette either. Around this time, a fragment of Ostwald's colour-theory was reprinted in *De Stijl*. Although differing from Seurat's theory by not being limited to the three primaries and to their complementaries, it continued research on the mutual distance between colours. It was the inclusion of black, grey and white as colours as well as the incorporation of the element of time in the (geometric) scientific approach of Ostwald, which aroused Van Doesburg's interest.

I. K. Bonset: Van Doesburg as a Dadaist and poet

In April 1920 De Stijl's second manifesto, called *Literature*, appeared, signed by Van Doesburg, Mondrian and Kok.[1] In May 1920 the first poem by I. K. Bonset, 'X-images', was published (see p. 112).[2] 'I. K. Bonset' was Van Doesburg's pseudonym as a poet and writer. This character seems to have come to life somewhat before the publication of 'X-images', for among his unprinted manuscripts there is a collection of poems entitled *New World-Images. Cubist and Expressionist Poems 1913–1920*, by I. K. Bonset.[3] Of the poems which were signed, only the early ones written before 1915 carry the name Van Doesburg. The first mention of I. K. Bonset is found in a letter from Van Doesburg to Tristan Tzara, written toward the end of 1918 and describing Bonset as a Dutch Dadaist.[4] Thus, the pseudonym seems to have been invented between 1916 and 1918. However, to follow the movements of Bonset seems always to have been a difficult job. Mondrian is known to have warned Van Doesburg against Bonset since he was under the impression that Bonset was using their ideas.

In addition to admiring Apollinaire, who also published 'Cubist' poems, Van Doesburg was strongly attracted by writers like Tristan Tzara and Hugo Ball. The influence of Ball's *Flight from Time*[5] which also featured the first sound-poems, can be found for example in 'The Other Face'[6], which consisted of a series of aphorisms, the first of which was a statement on Dada. (Later this work was turned into a novel.) There is little doubt that Van Doesburg saw Dada's revolutionary character and its engagement in the destruction of an old culture as a necessary preparation for the realization of De Stijl's utopian aims. He presented De Stijl's position on Dada in an article under the significant title 'Is a Universal Plastic Notion Possible Today?' In this he wrote, 'Only a radical cleansing of social and artistic life as, in the domain of art, is already done by Dada, which is anti-sentimental and healthy to the core since it is anti-art, only unscrupulously striking down any systematically bred amateurism in any field, can prepare civilization for the New

Vision's happiness which is greatly and purely alive in a few people.'[7] Consequently, Kok, Mondrian, Oud and Van Doesburg addressed their letters to one another or signed them with 'dada' added to the surname.

This relationship of Dada as a preparation for Neo-plasticism can again be met in 'The Task of the New Architecture'[8] which appeared in *Bouwkundig Weekblad* (Architectural Weekly). First, this contained an attack on Berlage, accusing him of rationalism and naturalism. This criticism was to meet with Mondrian's disapproval soon after. Secondly and consequent upon the Dada anti-philosophical attitude, the philosophies of Kant, Schopenhauer, Fichte and Hegel, in all of whom De Stijl showed interest, were criticized as obsolete systems. In this criticism, he presented views later to be developed in his own Dadaist anti-philosophy, 'Caminoscopy'.

The conflict with the Bauhaus

In the January 1919 *De Stijl* issue, Van Doesburg began a long series of critical articles called 'Modern Trends in Art Teaching', shortly before the Bauhaus was founded at Weimar on 1 April. In May of that same year, Walter Gropius appointed Leonard Feininger and Johannes Itten to its faculty and Van Doesburg began to correspond with Feininger. In July the first manifesto of the Bauhaus, illustrated by Feininger, was reprinted in *De Stijl* along with a critical note by Van Doesburg protesting against the Expressionist tendencies current there.[1]

In the September issue of *De Stijl*, Van Does-

burg published Feininger's painting *Vollersroda III, 1916* with a short but sympathetic comment,[2] expressing the hope that Feininger's work might soon develop towards purely geometric abstract art. The October issue of *De Stijl* carried his critical article 'Survey. On Expressionism'[3], which met with Mondrian's full approval.

In the first issue of the third volume of *De Stijl*, November 1919, Van Doesburg summarized his ideas on style as they stood at that moment in an editorial 'Survey at the Beginning of the Third Volume'.[4] In 1919 Van Doesburg's book *Three Lectures on the New Plastic Art*[5]

Counter-Composition V 1924
oil on canvas, 100×100 cm. (39×39 in.)
Collection of Stedelijk Museum, Amsterdam

appeared and he also published 'Principles of Neo-Plasic Art'[6] which was later to be published as a separate volume in the Bauhaus series.

Towards the end of December 1920 Van Doesburg travelled to Berlin, to meet Hans Richter and Viking Eggeling, who showed their abstract films to him. Van Doesburg also had a meeting with Bruno Taut who introduced him to Walter Gropius, Adolf Meyer and Fred Forbat. It was at this meeting that Gropius and Meyer expressed their interest in the works by De Stijl artists and remarked that they wished to include this direction in art in the Bauhaus at Weimar.

However, Van Doesburg did not become a member of the Bauhaus staff at Weimar but initiated a De Stijl course of his own instead. In the Jubilee issue of *De Stijl* (1927) Van Doesburg gave his account of his encounter with the Bauhaus artists in an article entitled 'Dates and facts (concerning the development of the influence of De Stijl) which speak for themselves':

At the house of the Expressionist architect Bruno Taut, the editor gets to know Walter Gropius, his assistants Meyer and Forbat, and several Bauhaus students. Here the editor shows an extensive collection of photographs of works by De Stijl group. While these photographs pass around, the wish is expressed to work in the Bauhaus in the way of De Stijl: 'We want something like this in the Bauhaus.' Invitation by Gropius to visit the Bauhaus. January 1921, visit to the Bauhaus, where, in addition to Expressionist degeneration, so-called 'root-compositions' in the manner of Vantongerloo, produced by Itten students, are found. There are also weak imitations of paintings by Mondrian.

Gropius puts at the disposal of the editor his complete press archive of the Bauhaus's struggle whilst defending itself against the government of Thüringen. In his turn the editor (in good faith) places all photographs, booklets, issues of *De Stijl*, and so forth at the disposal of the director of the Bauhaus and expresses the wish that the Bauhaus may develop in the same consistent way as De Stijl has done in Holland. He offers to support Gropius in his struggle. In the beginning of January, return to Holland. A correspondence between the editor of *De Stijl* and the Bauhaus develops. Gropius and Meyer express the wish to remain in contact with De Stijl. Proposals to come over. 17 March 1921, propaganda tour through Belgium, France, Italy and Germany. Lectures with the musical accompaniment of Petro van Doesburg. In April the editor of *De Stijl* is installed at Weimar by Meyer and De Stijl adherents.[7]

A contrasting version of these events as related by Van Doesburg in the Jubilee issue of *De Stijl*, is found in Bruno Zevi's *Poetica dell'architettura neo-plastica* (Poetics of Neo-plastic Architecture), published in 1953. There, a letter by Walter Gropius written to Zevi contains the following statement: '. . . I have never invited Van Doesburg to the Bauhaus. He came there of his own initiative because he was attracted by our courses. He hoped to become a professor at the Bauhaus, but I did not give him a position, since I judged him aggressive and fanatic and considered that he possessed such a narrow, theoretical view that he could not tolerate any diversity of opinion.' And a little farther on in the same letter, Gropius writes 'All who at that time participated in the Bauhaus, Josef Albers, Herbert Bayer and

Composition of three paintings, *XVIII* 1920
oil on canvas, 35×35 cm. each (14×14 in.)
Collection of Mrs Nelly van Doesburg

Marcel Breuer, are of the same opinion.'[8]

Lothar Schreyer, in his book *Erinnerung an Sturm und Bauhaus* (*Memories of Sturm and Bauhaus*), published in 1956, makes the following statement:

We were free to submit to the Ministry the appointment to the Bauhaus of another artist. Gropius rightly considered the Bauhaus to lack a representative of Constructivism. It was difficult to find the right man who had the inner understanding of architecture as it had been practised in Holland for several years. The obvious choice was Van Doesburg, who had stayed at Weimar several weeks and who was a very good representative of De Stijl. He had visited all of us several times, in order to establish personal contact with the Bauhaus, which he did mostly with Gropius himself. Subsequently Gropius also published a Bauhaus book by Van Doesburg. However, at that time he did not submit his name for appointment to the board of professors and thus Van Doesburg was not discussed.[9]

Several facts at least are clear. Van Doesburg visited the Bauhaus as early as January 1921 for a period of one or two weeks. His activities at that time were directed mainly against the ideas of Johannes Itten, one of the earliest and most influential members of the staff. In a draft of a letter written in 1924 to Moholy-Nagy, Van Doesburg says, '. . . I just ask, how does the Bauhaus expect to achieve its end and to put its programme into practice when it loses itself in Mazdaznan and the production of individualistic art. Thus it itself provokes criticism, etc. This was my point of view at Weimar.'[10] Mazdaznan was a practical, mystic way of life related to Eastern philosophy, which

Itten had introduced among staff and students of the Bauhaus to such an extent that these even appeared in monks' habits.

The manner in which this criticism was delivered is described in a letter written by Van Doesburg at Weimar on 7 January 1921 and addressed to Anthony Kok. He says 'At Weimar I have turned everything radically upside down. This is supposed to be the most famous Academy with the most modern teachers! Every evening I have talked to the students and spread the vermin of the new spirit. Within a short time De Stijl will reappear in a more radical way. I have tremendous energy and know now that our views will achieve victory over anyone and anything.'[11]

Before analysing the effect that these activities may have had on any potential professorship for Van Doesburg which could have been under discussion in December 1920 in Berlin, the following data could be relevant. It is apparent from the preface Gropius wrote for L. Moholy-Nagy's book *The New Vision*, that another professorship was offered by Gropius in Berlin, once again before this proposal was submitted for approval to the board of professors at Weimar. The first lines of this preface read as follows: 'It was in Berlin in 1922 that I first met Moholy-Nagy. Impressed by the character and direction of his work, I offered him a professorship at the Bauhaus, the school of modern design which I had founded and was then directing at Weimar.'[12] It seems likely that the same offer was made to Van Doesburg during his stay in Berlin in December 1920. Van Doesburg's attitude at Weimar during his first stay there in January 1921, however, made Gropius change his mind, which is why, according to Schreyer, this appointment was neither suggested by Gropius nor discussed by the board of professors when Van Doesburg arrived at

Weimar the second time, in April 1921. This interpretation could explain why Gropius wrote to Zevi that Van Doesburg came 'of his own initiative'.

However, Van Doesburg's first contact with the Bauhaus (between December 1920 and January 1921) apparently had earned him the support of several people. While Van Doesburg was journeying through Belgium, France and Italy, Adolf Meyer – the architect with whom Gropius was associated at that time – prepared and arranged a studio for the Dutchman at Weimar. In the list of constructivist members who, according to Gropius, shared his view on Van Doesburg at that time, Adolf Meyer is conspicuously omitted. Apart from the question of who took whose side, it is beyond doubt that the Bauhaus staff in its first period (1919–23) showed an open split between the Expressionistic and Constructivistic views it had always tried to combine. When Moholy-Nagy was appointed in 1923 – the year Itten took his leave – he met with the same hostility that had been demonstrated towards De Stijl, as is clearly proved in Schreyer's chapter 'The Machinery of the World' from *Erinnerung an Sturm und Bauhaus*.

Berlin and the rise of Functionalism

Van Doesburg became increasingly interested in technology and the machine, similar in this respect to Le Corbusier and the Berlin artists from whom the G-group, later developing into the 'Berlin Ring of Architects', was shortly to originate. He published a series of three articles called 'The Significance of Mechanical Aesthetics in Architecture and the Other Arts'.[1] These articles represent Van Doesburg's reaction to the Bauhaus, where, in the tradition of Morris and Ruskin, handicraft was still favoured over industrial production. The second article, criticizing handicraft methods was published in July 1921 when Van Doesburg had already been installed at Weimar for a few months. This same essay also includes, in the third and last article of the series, his reaction to Oud's lecture 'On Future Architecture and its Architectural Possibilities', delivered in February 1921 to the architects' association Opbouw in Rotterdam.[2] Oud disagreed with Van Doesburg and Mondrian over the use of colour in architecture – a disagreement that was to lead to his leaving De Stijl. In his lecture he considered that applying colour to architecture was impractical because paint is subject to weathering. Much of this was a direct criticism of Van Doesburg's activities in the preceding year, which were mainly dedicated to collaboration in architecture. At Drachten, a small town in the province of Friesland, the architect De Boer built workers' housing projects, shops and a school for which Van Doesburg designed the colour schemes. It was also at this time, just before he settled in Germany, that he executed stained glass windows for the School of Agriculture at Drachten, whereas the December 1920 issue of *De Stijl* carried Van Doesburg's second design for an interior, which had been executed in 1919 and incorporated furniture by Gerrit Rietveld.[3] Furthermore, Oud was

44

Poster for the international exhibition of
La Section d'Or, Cubists and Neo-Cubists, 1920
ink on paper, 69·9 × 67·8 cm. ($27\frac{1}{2} \times 26\frac{1}{2}$ in.)
Collection of Mrs. Nelly van Doesburg

looking for an immediate method of producing what he was aiming for and stressed the value of new construction methods and new materials – glass, iron, steel – in creating an architecture of a functional character.

Another major disagreement was about Cubism, which Oud saw as obsolete in architecture. The architect R. Van 't Hoff had already left De Stijl in 1919 since he believed the realization of its aims in any foreseeable future was an illusionary hope. At this time Oud's practical approach, regardless of whether his interpretation of Cubism was right or wrong, at any rate meant a direct attack against the eventual use of its multi-dimensional principle for architecture, via Neo-plasticism, as fostered by Van Doesburg. The disappointment it caused Van Doesburg, in addition to circumstances to be described further on, doubtless provided the impetus for him to already put into writing some of his ideas on the new architecture as a reaction for the above issues. The second article of his series 'The Significance of Mechanical Aesthetics in Architecture and the Other Arts' contains the earliest formulation of Points One, Five and

Nine of his architectural programme of 1924. He argues that the freedom of the new architecture replaces the system of preconceived schemes in building, such as the basic concept of a ground-plan consisting of one large rectangle to encompass all desired functions. The new architecture is to be related to environmental space, thus rejecting the use of monochrome, massive volumes. Of particular interest is a claim that the new architecture can be seen to develop from Neo-plastic painting. Whereas Oud's lecture places him in the ranks of those who initiated Functionalism, Van Doesburg's reply takes him close to his 1924 programme of an architecture of space-time, consisting of coloured planes. With a remark towards the end of his article Van Doesburg forecasts the direction his architecture will take with the Weimar models, built the following year and developing from Wright via the houses by Van 't Hoff. Here Van Doesburg quotes Van 't Hoff who used to refer to the roof as 'the fifth plane',[4] which can be seen as a further confirmation of their discussion of Wright's suggestion (of 1914) of building an architecture consisting of planes.

Aldo Camini: Van Doesburg as an anti-philosopher

In May 1921 Van Doesburg introduced the readers of *De Stijl* to his Dada anti-philosophy. This was in an article 'Caminoscopy' (p. 113), signed with the pseudonym Aldo Camini. It is very likely that this pseudonym came into existence as a result of Van Doesburg's reading Giovanni Papini's 'Roman Discourse', first published in *Lacerba* March 1913.[1] In this lecture Papini attacked Christianity, the Ger-

man philosophers Kant and Hegel and the Italian aesthetician and philosopher Benedetto Croce. In the first chapter of 'Caminoscopy', Camini writes that he pities Croce and refers to Papini. In the fourth chapter both Christianity and Hegel are rejected. Papini, in his 'Roman Discourse' proclaims that, instead of being tied to the apron strings of religion and philosophy, man must learn to stand on his own feet. His idea is *L'uomo che sa camminare da sé*, or, literally, 'the man who knows to go by himself'.[2] 'Camini' – Van Doesburg omits one 'm' – is the third person pronoun form of *camminare*, to go, to step out. Since 'Aldo' is a name of Gothic origin meaning 'the old', or, 'the eldest', the pseudonym 'Aldo Camini' means 'the old goes' or, as the Caminoscopy argues, 'the old must go'.

The introduction was written in Milan on 20 April 1921 and relates that, while in Milan visiting the studio of C.C. the metaphysician – initials that very probably stand for Carlo Carrà – Van Doesburg came upon a dusty manuscript by the late, totally unknown painter-author Aldo Camini. The full title of the manuscript was given as 'Caminoscopy, an anti-philosophical view of life without any thread or system'.[3] This anti-philosophical view was first apparent in Van Doesburg's article 'The Mysticism of Beauty and Love' (1918), in which he attacked the philosopher Schoenmaekers. There the following lines can be found: 'Everything consists of opposites. According to the anti-philosopher Giovanni Papini – the Futurist – this does indeed exclude any further philosophy.'[4] In 1918 the term anti-philosopher occurs elsewhere, namely in Tristan Tzara's *Manifesto of Mr Aa the Anti-philosopher* which is also influenced by Papini.[5] There is also some similarity of approach between Tzara's *Seven Manifestos* and Van

Doesburg's 'Caminoscopy'. The latter half of the subtitle of 'Caminoscopy', which reads 'without any thread or system', stems either from the Futurist manifesto *'Imagination without any Thread or System'*, published by Marinetti in 1913[6] or from Carlo Carrà's manifesto *Painting with Sounds, Noises and Odours.*[7]

Further, Van Doesburg's article 'Review of the Avant-garde'[8] reprints three Futurist manifestos and presents a comment on Futurism as a movement which attacks and renovates the old. Indeed, Van Doesburg was a subscriber to all Futurist manifestos, probably from as early as 1912, in which year the first exhibition of Futurist works was held in The Hague and Amsterdam. Moreover, Van Doesburg's article on Futurism was written in 1921, and such was his interest in Futurism that he followed a course in Italian with Professor Guarnieri in Leyden around 1916. A final influence of Futurism can be found in Bonset's 'Introduction to the new poetry'[9] which is especially indebted to Marinetti's *Technical Manifesto of Futurist Literature.*[10] The 'Caminoscopy' is another example of the dialogue Van Doesburg maintained between Neo-plasticism and Futurism. His ultimate rejection of this Italian movement is proved once more by taking as the basis for his 'Caminoscopy' the writings of Papini as although this writer had started as a Futurist, he soon made it known that he considered himself an anti-Futurist.

Constructivism in Western Europe

In August 1921, the De Stijl group published its third manifesto 'Towards a Newly Shaped World'.[1] It appeared in German, Dutch and

French and was signed 'De Stijl 1921'. It avoids all politico-economical questions and proclaims that a purely creative visual and mental attitude towards the future world is the artist's sole preoccupation. (See p. 113). This manifesto, written by Van Doesburg, was to exert great influence on artists such as Lissitzky, Moholy-Nagy and the architect Mies van der Rohe. The first issue of *Ves, Gegenstand* (Object) published in 1922 by Lissitzky and Ehrenburg carried an introduction, 'The Russian Blockade is going to meet its end', which betrays considerable similarity in approach as far as a creative attitude is concerned.[2] Still later, in 1927 at the occasion of the Weissenhofsiedlung, its stress on creation can again be found in an introduction by Mies van der Rohe.

In the October issue of *De Stijl* a manifesto appeared called 'Appeal for an Elementary Art' by R. Hausmann, Hans Arp, Iwan Puni and Moholy-Nagy.[3] This manifesto can be regarded as an early expression of ideas which can be retraced in the approach to architecture soon to be called Functionalism. It argues that art is elementary 'because it does not philosophize, because it is composed of its own characteristic elements' and calls for 'stylishness in order to arrive at style' – an idea consonant with De Stijl's rejection of conventional basic forms in architecture in favour of what Van Doesburg called 'formlessness'. The anti-philosophical attitude it proclaims probably derives from its two Dadaist signatories, Hausmann and Arp, whereas the term 'elementary art' probably stems either from Van Doesburg, who, as has been shown, began to use it as early as 1915, or from Wölfflin's *Principles of Art History* referred to above.

However, Van Doesburg added a sceptical note to this 'Appeal', which can be seen as an early indication of the controversies between De Stijl on the one hand and the incipient Constructivist and Functionalist trends – in art and architecture in Germany on the other. This notes reads 'We are pleased to comply with the request that we publish the following manifesto in *De Stijl*, whereas it will depend on the way this is "put into practice" whether we subscribe to or accept any responsibility for its content.'

The 1922 February and March issues of *De Stijl* printed Van Doesburg's lecture 'The Will to Style. A New Form of Expression of Life, Art and Technology'.[4] This lecture had been given in Jena, Weimar and Berlin. Seen in the context of the gradual development toward a functional style of architecture in Germany at this time, it was a rejection of individualism and materialism, of which handicraft was depicted as a remnant. Van Doesburg held that an 'art of the mind' goes along with the use of the machine. 'The Will to Style' is one of his most important documents and contains his entire artistic credo (see p. 115).

With his article 'Neo-plasticism in Practice in a Far Future and in Contemporary Architecture'[5] in the March and May issues of *De Stijl*, Mondrian was to add his reactions against the development towards Functionalism in general and Oud's above-mentioned lecture in particular. It was Mondrian's view that architects were afraid to put the new architecture into practice and that this explained why they turned to conventional building. He also assumed that Neo-plasticism would be developed first in works of art. Oud's argument that the weathering of colour disturbed the sought-for harmony of Neo-plasticism in architecture was answered by Mondrian with the suggestion that a laboratory for research on this subject be founded. Mondrian also attacked the concept of architecture as the form of masses and argued for an architecture of planes, possessing a multi-sided plasticity in accordance with the theory of relativity.

The latter view, of course, was based entirely upon Van Doesburg formulations described above. Their differing interpretations of Cubism produced another disagreement between Oud and Van Doesburg. Oud, in an article 'Architecture and Cubism'[6] in *De Bouwwereld* (*The Building World*) said Cubism represented 'a process of destruction and reconstruction' which explained why it was now obsolete. Van Doesburg's approach was called 'a permanent Cubism' and considered of 'provincial importance'. His answer, printed in abridged form in the same periodical,[7] was published in full in *De Stijl* under the title 'The consequence of Pen and T-square'.[8] His purpose was to rebut Oud's

statement in 'Architecture and Cubism', that it was his own ideas which had led to De Stijl's view of architecture. Instead, Van Doesburg stated that this new vision had developed from and been spread by the Neo-plastic painters only. In the meantime, in spite of his criticism of its use in architecture, Oud continued to apply colour, now without the collaboration of Van Doesburg, in several of his housing-projects.[9] Yet, the defence of Neo-plastic ideals made jointly by Mondrian and Van Doesburg could not prevent Oud from further promoting the Functionalist trend.

The International Congress of Progressive Artists, Düsseldorf 1922

Much of the turmoil in the artistic and social ideas current at that time were profiled at the occasion of the International Congress of Progressive Artists held in Düsseldorf from 29 to 31 May 1922. A report on this congress can be found in the issue of *De Stijl*, IV, 4, April 1922, which is entirely devoted to it. Van Doesburg quotes part of the invitation to attend the congress, in which it is posited that artists of all countries should unite, free from any political meddling or indivualist opportunism. The Düsseldorf Congress brought together delegations of artists of Expressionist and Constructivist tendencies. Since it did not succeed in formulating who was to be considered a 'progressive artist', it demonstrated the conflict between these two directions in art – a struggle also reflected clearly by the Bauhaus at this time. Van Doesburg representing De Stijl, read its first manifesto and listed its 'Creative

Demands'. (See p. 127.) However, he again found himself in opposition to the Expressionist trend when calling for a universal plastic expression in his point Three.[1] In a summarizing 'Proclamation' by the 'International Section of Constructivist Artists', signed by Van Doesburg, Lissitzky and Richter, the congress was declared a failure because its 'predominantly individualistic approach' hampered any 'international progressive solidarity'.[2]

This closing proclamation is of interest for several reasons. In the first place, it offers in a footnote by Van Doesburg an explanation for the use of the term 'Constructivist', which was chosen to distinguish it from the 'Impulsivist' (read, Expressionist) approach. Furthermore, it presents a definition of the progressive artist as one who rejects subjectivism and the work of art as a self-contained entity. Instead it declares 'art to represent a general and real expression of creative energy, organizing man's progress, that is to say, it is a means of the process of labour in general',[3] and thus calls for the unity of art and life. The 'Proclamation' represents a mixture of ideas presented at the congress by the Constructivist group Gegenstand (Ehrenburg and Lissitzky), which argues the unity of economic, scientific and technical life with art,[4] and those of De Stijl group, as set forth by Van Doesburg with his demands for pure creation, in his 'Creative Demands'.

The 'Proclamation' can also be considered one of the main documents concerning the birth of Constructivism in Western Europe. Two of its signatories, Lissitzky and Richter, will appear in 1923 as the editors of the Constructivist magazine 'G □, *material Towards Elementary Plastic Expression*'. This magazine served as a mouthpiece for the aims of the Constructivist group which were first made public at the congress. G □ then seems to replace, apparently in an attempt at political neutralism, the magazine *Ves*, *Gegenstand*, under the editorship of Ehrenburg and Lissitzky, of which only two issues had appeared in 1922. However, prior to the founding of G □, the first results of the activities of the congress at Düsseldorf were published in *De Stijl*, chiefly as result of a request forwarded at the congress by the Hungarian Ma-group (L. Kassak, Moholy-Nagy and others) which preferred publication in a periodical from a politically neutral country.

Much of the uncertainty at the congress resulted also from the confused situation in the contemporary art of Soviet Russia, where Constructivist, Expressionist, Realist and Folk-Art tendencies were all present. Following the publication in 1920 in Moscow of the *Manifesto on Proletarian Art*, the issue the same year of Gabo and Pevsner's Constructivist *Realistic Manifesto* and Lenin's speech on the New Economic Policy of 1921, the proletarian tendency, which later on produced Social Realism, began to predominate and, in fact, caused the permanent emigration of several Russian abstract artists to Western Europe.[5]

Much of the material discussed at the congress was elaborated upon in various subsequent issues of *De Stijl*. Werner Graeff published in the May 1922 issue of *De Stijl* his manifesto 'For the New'[6] which summarized once more the Constructivist point of view as presented in Düsseldorf and underlined the strength of the movement for machine art prevalent in Germany at this time, as well as the influence of De Stijl universalism.

In the June issue of *De Stijl* Lissitzky, a member of De Stijl in 1922, but also a close collaborator of Van Doesburg's in 1923, published his article 'Proun'[7] ('Proun' stands for PRO and abbreviations of U(twershdenije) NOW(ychform) IS(kusstwa): PROUNOWIS, meaning the founding of new forms in art) which shows great similarity with Van Doesburg's adherence to the scientific view of 'matter in space-time'. In the same issue, Hans Richter, a member of De Stijl from 1921 until 1925, published an article entitled 'Film'.[8] Van Doesburg again defended the new art in an article ' □ (meaning 'squarely') against Mimetic Artists'[9] which was another reaction to the Düsseldorf Congress. The July issue of *De Stijl* contained a contribution entitled 'Production and Reproduction'[10] by L. Moholy-Nagy, representing the Hungarian group Ma, and an article by the Futurist Enrico Prampolini, 'The Aesthetics of the Machine and Mechanical Introspection in Art'.[11] Both articles once again revealed the increased contemporary interest in the idea of machine art, which had been initiated on the Continent as early as 1909 by Futurism with its emphasis on cars, planes and electricity. It is interesting to watch Futurism, through the mouth of Prampolini, try to catch up with the rapid spread of the 'machine attitude' then current in Germany.

In his turn Van Doesburg was given space in the first issue of the magazine *Ves, Gegenstand* for his article 'Monumental Art',[12] while *Ma* published his article 'Architecture as the Synthesis of the Plastic Arts'[13] in its July issue. After having allowed a variety of opinions to be published in *De Stijl*, Van Doesburg, beginning in the same July issue, expounded the attitude of De Stijl towards all these phenomena in a series of articles called 'The Present State of Modern Art',[14] the first instalment of which had already been published in December 1921. In the July 1922 issue, which contained the Fragments *II*, *III* and *IV* of this series, he attacked the 'so-called modern magazines' in their negative reaction to Cubism and at the same time claimed that De Stijl was the outcome and culmination of Cubism. In Fragments *III* and *IV*, the need for an 'elementary plasticism' as expressed by the younger generation in Holland, Russia, Germany and Hungary, was discussed in terms of an aim typical of Van Doesburg, that is, to synthesize all constructive tendencies in an international and universal style. This objective seemed within reach when the August issue of *De Stijl* printed the manifesto 'K.I.: International Union of Creative Constructivists', signed by Van Doesburg, Richter, Lissitzky, Maes and Burchartz.[15] Although this manifesto was a collective effort, there is little doubt that Van Doesburg was its leading spirit since in the French translation the 'creative' constructivists are called 'neo-plastic constructivists.

Their manifesto further underlines the gap between those artists who favoured an impersonal mechanico-functional approach and those who considered art to represent exclusively a subjective, psychological manifestation of the individual. Its most important feature was a stress on collective creation that is to provide man's entire social environment with a new plastic quality, as opposed to the usual method of each artist's producing isolated works on his own. It is evident that with this new approach an attempt was being made to bring to art the approach of science and technology where teamwork was the established mode of working. Thus the single art product was stated to be of no concern except when through research or experiment it forwarded possibilities which so far had not been realized in life as a whole.

In continuing his series 'The Present State of Modern Art', Van Doesburg presented an article under the subtitle 'Plastic Art in Russia',[16] in which he went along with El Lissitzky's Constructivist views by criticizing Suprematism. He accused this movement of restricting the objective abstract means of expression, the geometric plane, for the purpose of demonstrating the end of painting with naturalistic form. In contrast to Suprematism's restriction, De Stijl, according to Van Doesburg, acquired a positive character by widening the use of pure plastic means for the expression of 'life as a whole in a precise and true way', without incorporating any additional symbolic or imaginary values as was the case with Suprematism. This concurs with the views Lissitzky put forward in the article 'Proun' where he describes how 'instead of remaining a mimeticist, the artist becomes the constructor of a new world of objects',[17] and ultimately takes this new world to represent man's entire built environment.

The Weimar models   1922

1922 was the year when Van Doesburg turned from producing paintings to architecture. Among the basic factors explaining Van Doesburg's awakened interest in architecture are, first, the abandonment by other architects of Neo-plasticism, which they considered an illusion or an impractical aesthetic for their medium (R. Van 't Hoff and J. J. P. Oud), second the experimentation with the three-dimensional art object by Constructivism, and, finally, the aim of fusing art with everyday life. This last factor was the most important and was repeatedly stressed in many art circles in Germany. It stimulated the movement to three-dimensional construction also by the way of architecture which then had to be considered as a form of fine art.

The Weimar models made that year can clearly be seen to possess Cubism's four-dimensional character by their multi-sided expansion into space. Two of them were reproduced in *Bouwkundig Weekblad* (*Architectural Weekly*), accompanying an article by Van Doesburg with the title 'The impact of the Stijl movement in Germany',[1] which was written in December 1922 and published early in 1923. The two models (see p. 116) were made respectively by B. Sturzkopf and by H. Vogel, students in Van Doesburg's De Stijl course. It is interesting to compare them with models made in approximately 1921 in the department of architecture of the Bauhaus, which reflect Gropius' experiments with standardization and automation in building.[2] In Gropius' models the groundplan continues to be based on a single rectangle comprising all functions. A certain degree of plasticity is achieved by the method of adding and taking

away repetitive standard volumes. In contrast to this construction method through juxtaposition, the models made under Van Doesburg's supervision exhibit a strikingly greater plastic movement in both groundplan and elevation, and, moreover, their effects are achieved in a more organic way. The dynamic unity of these models springs from the element of interpenetration incorporated in the groundplan. In particular, the groundplan of the model by Vogel consists of three interpenetrating squares and anticipates the four-dimensional architecture Van Doesburg was to produce in the Paris models designed in collaboration with C. van Eesteren the following year. As has been pointed out, the multi-sided plasticity of these models relates them via Van 't Hoff to the architecture of Frank Lloyd Wright.

The Weimar models must have been made before September 1922, since in this month *Bouwkundig Weekblad* carried an article by Van Doesburg entitled 'The New Aesthetics and its Realization'[3] in which it is apparent that Van Doesburg's ideas must have been realized in concrete form. This article would also be published in German in *De Stijl* the following year, and already contained Van Doesburg's entire architectural programme for 1924 (see p. 127). In reply to Wright's call for a Gothic-inspired architecture horizontal (that is classical) in appearance, he rejected an architecture based on either the Middle Ages or the Renaissance and expounded the modern space-time view instead. He wrote, 'Because of the advance in physics in our time, the concept of matter as solid substance was changed and, as in the field of art, came to be seen as an entity of energy.' Thus, this article gives clear proof that Van Doesburg knew he had taken architecture one step further by substituting a four-dimensional approach for a Wrightian method of extended three-dimensional architectural masses. Moreover, this development was largely the result of his experience in the art of painting, in particular of his own Neo-plastic paintings of 1918.

Van Eesteren, who was soon to become Van Doesburg's collaborator on the next set of models, was travelling in Germany this year. He had won the Prix de Rome with his design for a Royal Institute of Sciences, Literature and the Fine Arts, which was a rigidly symmetrical composition in the best academic tradition.[4] After Adolf Behne had drawn his attention to

Van Doesburg's presence there he paid a short visit to Weimar early in the spring. Although he attended some lectures Van Doesburg gave in his De Stijl course, he was at that time in no way involved in the architectural experiments which produced the Weimar models.[5] In the summer, Van Eesteren went to Berlin where he began to work on the design for the university hall to which Van Doesburg was to add colour in 1923. In October 1922 Van Eesteren returned to Weimar to attend the Constructivist Congress of which Van Doesburg was the host and at which Lissitzky, Richter, Moholy-Nagy, Kemeny and Schwitters, as well as many others, were present.

Mecano and other Dada activities

The Constructivist Congress turned into a Dadaist-Constructivist meeting because of the unexpected presence of Tristan Tzara and Hans Arp. They and Van Doesburg had belonged to the many signatories of a resolution which withdrew confidence in the committee of the Paris Congress that had been held a few months earlier.[1] This Paris Congress had split the Dadaists, mainly through an argument between Tristan Tzara and André Breton, in which the latter tried to take over the leadership of the movement from the former. The Paris Congress signified the end of Dada and the beginning of Surrealism in France.

The sudden arrival of Tzara and Arp at Weimar led to some difficulties since most of the Constructivists at that time considered Dada to be solely a destructive force in art. Because he was representing De Stijl, no one suspected him of being I. K. Bonset, the Dada poet, so

Van Doesburg was able to settle the controversies. However, according to Moholy-Nagy the congress ended as a Dada manifestation, since many of its Constructivist participants withdrew in disappointment.[2]

It was also in 1922 that Van Doesburg launched his second magazine *Mecano*, which had been planned for appearance as early as 1921. This magazine, entirely Dada in conception and largely intended to satirize the Bauhaus, was edited by I. K. Bonset, with the lay-out (rightly) attributed to Van Doesburg. Four issues appeared, each known by the colour of its cover. The order of the first two issues is uncertain, although according to an advertisement in the first issue of the magazine *G* □, July 1923, where, after the Paris Congress, it was described as 'the international magazine of mental hygiene and Neo-Dadaism', this order would be: yellow issue 1, blue issue 2, red issue

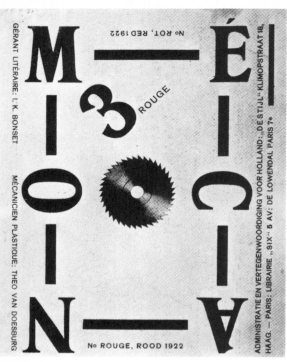

Mecano, Red issue, no. 3, 1922
$16 \cdot 3 \times 12 \cdot 9$ cm. ($6\frac{1}{2} \times 5$ in.)

The Congress of Constructivists and Dadaists,
Weimar, 1922.
Back row (from left to right): Max and Lotte
Burchartz, Peter Roehl, Hans Vogel, Lucia and
Laszlo Moholy-Nagy, Alfred Kemeny
Middle row: Alexa Roehl, El Lissitzky, Nelly and
Theo van Doesburg, Bernard Sturzkopf
Front row: Werner Graeff, Nini Smit, Harry
Scheibe, Cornelius van Eesteren, Hans Richter,
Tristan Tzara, Hans Arp

3, white issue 4/5 (this last issue appeared in 1923). The magazine contained contributions by Kurt Schwitters, Hans Arp, Francis Picabia and Georges Ribemont Dessaignes among others. The yellow issue contained I. K. Bonset's 'Anti-artandpurereason-manifesto'[3] which followed his attack on Hegel in 'Caminoscopy' with a further assault upon philosophy, particularly upon Hegelian notions expounded by Bolland, a professor in Hegelian philosophy at Leyden.

In the third, red issue, the 'ChRoNiClE-MeCaNo'[4] contained a Dada-report on the International Congress of Constructivists and Dada, Weimar 1922 as well as a description of the Dada tour made to Jena, Dresden and Hanover subsequently by Arp, Schwitters, Tzara, Hausmann, Van Doesburg and Petro van Doesburg (assisting on the piano). This chronicle also contained the first criticism of Moholy-Nagy's demand that actual motion should be included in art. This demand would be proclaimed in the manifesto 'The Dynamic-constructive System of Forces', which was soon to be published by Moholy-Nagy and Kemeny in the December issue of *Der Sturm*.[5]

The first three months of 1923 were taken up by a Dada tour through Holland, starting in The Hague, with Van Doesburg, Petro van Doesburg and Kurt Schwitters. Van Doesburg

appeared in a black dinner-jacket, wearing a monocle, and lectured on the meaning of Dada. At the end of each evening his pamphlet 'What is Dada?', published in The Hague under the De Stijl imprint, was on sale (see p. 132). Kurt Schwitters, by now a close friend of Van Doesburg's, followed his lecture by reciting 'Cause and Beginning of the Great and Glorious Revolution in Revon' ('Revon' represents the five last letters of Hanover when reversed.) He also recited sound-sonatas and from his collection of poems 'Anna Blume'. Van Doesburg again read poems by I. K. Bonset, and Petro van Doesburg played piano music by Vittorio Rieti. These evenings usually fell under the eye of the police and caused much uproar.

In close collaboration with Van Doesburg the first issue of Kurt Schwitters' Dada magazine *Merz* appeared in January 1923. The second issue of *Merz* contained a 'Manifesto on Proletarian Art',[6] signed by Van Doesburg, Kurt Schwitters, Hans Arp, Tristan Tzara and Chr. Spengemann, in The Hague, 6 March 1923. The same manifesto appeared in *De Stijl* as an article by Van Doesburg called 'Against Problem Art'.[7] This manifesto, of which Van Doesburg was the sole author, rejected all political meddling with art and can be seen as a reaction against the manifesto on proletarian culture, published in Moscow in 1920 (see p. 135).

De Stijl and Proun versus Functionalism   1923

The differences in approach among Constructivists became much more distinct in the course of this year. In his article 'The New Aesthetics and its Realization', (p. 127) now appearing in German in the March issue of *De Stijl*,[1]

Van Doesburg gave the first indication of a divergence of opinion with the significant sentence, 'The modern view (in contrast to the solely constructive view) conceives of plastic expression as *the organization of plastic means as an unmistakable unity.*' (Van Doesburg's italics.) Although the article accepted the idea of incorporating engineering in artistic creation, it expressly stated that painting is 'the most advanced form of art' and indicates the path leading towards modern architecture, in Holland through Neo-plasticism and in Russia through Suprematism and Proun. This stress on creative aesthetics makes it clear that Van Doesburg (de Stijl) and Lissitzky (Proun) had united against that third movement which was trying to absorb West European Constructivism into what later on was called Functionalism (i.e. function as the essence of everything constructed).

The key to the situation is to be found in the opening sentence of this article, where Van Doesburg wrote, 'Construction does not imply plastic architecture.' This criticism was addressed to Mies van der Rohe, a leading member of the G-group consisting of Richter, Lissitzky, Hilbersheimer and Graeff among others with whom Van Doesburg had had frequent discussions and had found himself in disagreement concerning matters of art. The fact that Van Doesburg published the article in German in the ordinarily Dutch *De Stijl* is significant. Mies van der Rohe, in a short article, 'Office building',[2] which was written in Berlin in May 1923 and published in *G* □, made the following statement: 'We reject any aesthetic speculation, any doctrine and any formalism.' The second issue of *G* □, published in September, carried a still shorter article from Mies' hand with two similar statements, 'We do not reckon with the problem of form but with the problem of building only' and 'The will to style also represents formalism. We have other worries.'[3]

The first two of these three statements, without doubt reflecting earlier pronouncements during discussions in the G group, comprise reactions to Van Doesburg's criticism 'Con-

struction does not imply plastic architecture'. The third statement was one Mies van der Rohe made in connection with Van Doesburg's important lecture 'The Will to Style', which was given in Jena, Weimar and Berlin in 1922 and published in *De Stijl* (see p. 115). Thus a gap between an utilitarian functional approach (the group of architects around Mies van der Rohe) and an aesthetic functional approach (the De Stijl group and Proun) among the Constructivists was made public.

Rather against the run of his previous writing Van Doesburg wrote a lead article in the first issue of *G* □ under the title 'Towards Elementary Plastic Expression'[4] in which he made a strong distinction between architecture, sculpture and painting as separate, independent forms of art. (See p. 127). In 'The New Aesthetics and its Realization', written the year before, he had stated them to be merged in an 'unmistakable unity'. The sole explanation for this seeming inconsistency lies in the fact that the utilitarian functional approach was to consider plastic art (aesthetics) as representing a speculation and thus a lesser thing. In sketching the importance of architecture, sculpture and painting separately Van Doesburg deals with this rationalist view by finding each of them to be of equal merit. This is reinforced by the publication, shortly after the appearance of the first issue of *G* □, of an article by Mondrian with the significant title 'Is Painting Necessarily Inferior to Architecture?'.[5] In this article Mondrian rejected the utilitarian functional approach in architecture considering plastic art an arbitrary thing, and proposed Neo-plasticism as the new aesthetics so as to produce a unity in which architecture and painting will completely fuse into one art form.

Amidst these opinions Hans Richter and Werner Graeff, also in the first issue of *G* □, attempted to keep things in balance by publishing a manifesto-like editorial which represented a mixture of Functionalist and De Stijl views. Lissitzky published an article called 'Space'[6] which similarly combined an aesthetical creative approach to the plastic expression of universal space with a functional-constructive approach to the expression of man's habitable space by means of Proun construction. There is also some similarity of approach between Lissitzky's article, which was written in The Hague in May 1923, and Van Doesburg's article, 'The Significance of Colour for Interior and Exterior Architecture'[7] published in the May 1923 issue of *Bouwkundig Weekblad*. (See p. 137). That time and place were the same indicates that these articles represent a cooperative effort. Both authors advocate a dynamic architecture consisting of planes and colour as the means to establish an aesthetic impression of spatial relationships. However, whereas Lissitzky limited himself to advocating that Constructivist architecture should embody aesthetic values, Van Doesburg attacked 'constructive and solely functional architecture'. This he felt, omitted any aesthetic notion and regarded architecture as the sum of stone, iron and glass, serving only 'the mechanistic function of life: living and working'. Apart from alluding to Le Corbusier and criticizing Oud's rejection of colour in architecture, this attack was again addressed to Mies van der Rohe, who in his article 'Office building' had said that architecture consisted of concrete, iron and glass which fulfil the demands of office-work, organization, clearness and economy. 'The Significance of Colour for Interior and Exterior Architecture', is also of importance in respect of Van Doesburg's architectural programme of 1924, since it comprises several notions on the use of colour in architecture.

With Van Doesburg's departure from Germany and Lissitzky's journey to Davos in Switzerland for the treatment of tuberculosis the two men who worked hardest to prevent universal Constructivism from turning into functional Constructivism had left the scene of battle. Some impatience with this development in architecture was expressed by Van Doesburg in 'Conditions for a New Architecture'.[8] This article was almost word for word the same as his essay 'Towards Elementary Plastic Expression' but elaborated upon it by criticizing Russian Constructivism for merely formulating the new constructive problems without managing to solve them.

Meanwhile, Gropius' Bauhaus, where Itten had been succeeded by Moholy-Nagy, was coming closer to the Functionalist approach as propagated by the group of architects around Mies van der Rohe. Mies' status can be seen from the second issue of *G* □, published in September 1923, of which he was co-editor, and which contained his attack on 'The Will to Style' and which included reproductions from W. Lindner's *Engineering in Building*.[9] This was significant in that it showed increased interest in the role of engineering in architecture, and the book was to exert considerable influence on Functionalist architecture in years to come. Van Doesburg contributed an article to this issue, called 'Parisian Novelties – Motive: if Only'[10], which was largely Dadaist in character. As such, it was irrelevant to the struggle between the aesthetic and the utilitarian approaches in architecture, which still continued but which had largely been won by Mies van der Rohe. Although his Functionalist theory remained uncommitted to any specific aesthetic approach, Mies van der Rohe made two designs in 1923 which reflected the influence of Van Doesburg's stay in Germany. For example, the groundplan of his design for a brick country-house derived from Van Doesburg's painting, *Rhythms of a Russian Dance* (1918) (p. 35). Moreover, his design for a concrete country-house, a model of which was reproduced in the September issue of *G* □, extends the component architectural volumes in all directions in space in the same manner found in the brick country-house. However, it also reveals a similarity of approach with Gropius's pre-fabricated housing projects, which were equally based on spatial extension, be it through the addition or subtraction of architectural parts. The results of Mies van der Rohe's direct application of Van Doesburg's *Rhythms of a Russian Dance* are mannered owing to his combining the method of extending by juxtaposition with the method of the original in which the planar areas seem not only to expand but also to interlock in mutual interpenetration. This mannerism can be seen in Mies' brick country-house with its severe separation of the living and the other functional areas and its long walls extending into the environmental space for no specific reason. Mies van der Rohe's closeness to Gropius was once again revealed when shortly afterwards Mies' spatial lay-out recurs in the Gropius' Bauhaus building in Dessau.

Thus, after Van Doesburg and Lissitzky had left Germany, the road toward an additive, Functionalist architecture lay open. This is why, in fact, 1923 should be considered the year in which Functionalism, later called the International Style, was born. In the hands of Gropius' and Mies van der Rohe's followers this was to lead architecture toward an impasse as Van Doesburg predicted this same year in 'The Significance of Colour for Interior and Exterior Architecture'. This approach, he wrote, could only turn architecture into 'an anatomical, constructive sterility'.

The Paris models,   1923

However, in this same year the Functionalist challenge was met by Van Doesburg and Van Eesteren with their Paris models exhibited from 15 October until 15 November 1923 in the De Stijl architecture exhibition at Rosenberg's art gallery in Paris. There were three models executed in the following order: the Rosenberg house; the private house; the studio house. This sequence follows the development of the architectural problems involved in the models.

Van Doesburg's new insight regarding architecture, acquired during the work on the Weimar models, came under discussion among Oud, Wils, Rietveld and Van Eesteren by early 1923. According to Van Eesteren, it was during these meetings that Van Doesburg discussed with them a proposition by the Parisian art dealer, Leonce Rosenberg to design a private house containing an art gallery and suggested that each of them submit such a plan.[1] Of those present, Van Eesteren alone subsequently presented a design, which he took to Paris to discuss with Van Doesburg, who, in the meantime, had settled there.

Apart from its highly plastic appearance, the Rosenberg house did not possess the characteristics of Van Doesburg's Weimar models, most notably the interpenetrating spaces in the groundplan. The various architectural spaces were juxtaposed, and although the Rosenberg house represented a much richer example of architecture than, for instance, Oud's design

58

Theo van Doesburg (right) and Cornelius van
Eesteren working on the model for the private
house, Paris, 1923
Photo: Gemeente Musea van Amsterdam

of 1919 for a factory, it nevertheless possesses a baroque quality. The enveloping, continuous wall is felt to be in motion rather than to express the space-time relationships of planes circumscribing interpenetrating spaces. Neither does the Rosenberg house possess any colour, another of Van Doesburg's prerequisites for a new architecture. The drawings of the Rosenberg design were sent to Rietveld who built a model for the De Stijl exhibition from them.

Immediately afterwards Van Doesburg and Van Eesteren began working together on the second model, the private house (far right) which possessed the same great number of functional demands as the Rosenberg house. The ground-plan (right) clearly derives from Van Doesburg's hand since the interpenetration of architectural spaces is an enriched elaboration upon the Weimar models. Another Van Doesburg characteristic is the coordination of various spatial points (the beginning and ending of walls and partitions) joining at an implied forty-five degree angle, which will recur later on in his second and third designs for the Meudon house. Moreover, the element of colour was restricted no longer to such architectural parts as window frames, doors and so forth. This had been Van Doesburg's method in his colour schemes for Oud's housing projects, but colour now became a concern of the architecture as a whole. The axonometric drawings which accompanied the elevations show a construction of planes suspended in space. These drawings by Van Doesburg demonstrate his ultimate conception of architecture, which is no longer based upon an arrangement of masses, but rather upon the expression of space-time relationships in terms of freely related planes.

The third model, the studio house (p. 146), marks another step forward in the development of a new four-dimensional architecture by combining the element of space-time realized in the

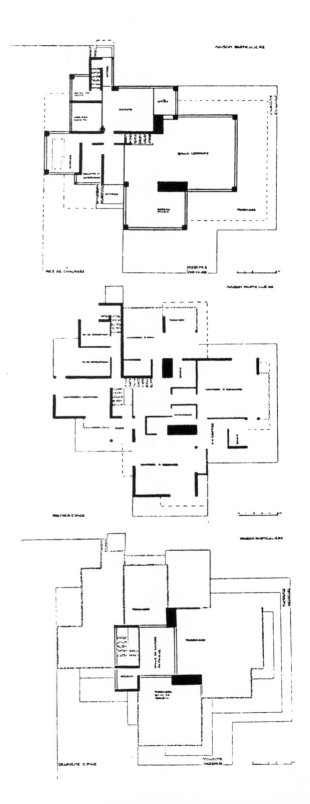

60

(left) Drawings of the groundfloor, first and second floor of the private house. Theo van Doesburg and C. van Eesteren, 1923

Two views of the model (destroyed) of the private house. Theo van Doesburg and C. van Eesteren, 1923

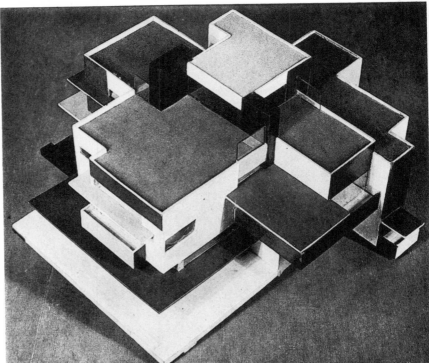

groundplan with its vertical appearance in the elevation. According to Van Eesteren, the third model was mainly by Van Doesburg. The latter's idea for making a piece of architecture which would demonstrate its plasticity on all sides explains why the cantilevered parts were not sustained by columns. However, this model represents an intrinsic attempt to annul the force of gravity, and thereby anticipates Elementarism, although by the time this latter conception had been evolved the problem of gravity had been visualized in an entirely different way.

All three Paris models were executed in 1923. Thus, the 1922 date attributed to them in the special issue of *L'Architecture Vivante* dedicated to De Stijl is incorrect. Similarly, even in Bruno Zevi's authoritative book *Poetica dell'Architettura Neoplastica*,[2] the second model, the private house, is erroneously given the date 1920. Van Doesburg himself, in *Principles of Neo-plastic Art* (1924), correctly dates the private house and the studio house to 1923. It is also significant that Van Doesburg reproduced his models for these works, but did not include a reproduction of Van Eesteren's Rosenberg house.[3]

The De Stijl exhibition of architecture at the Rosenberg Gallery also included the design for an octagon-shaped university hall by Van Doesburg and Van Eesteren. The ceiling of this hall consisted of a large stained-glass composition. At this exhibition the manifesto 'Towards Collective Construction' signed by Van Doesburg, Van Eesteren and Rietveld was distributed. Later on it was published in several magazines including *De Stijl*,[4] albeit signed there only by Van Doesburg and Van Eesteren. The name of Rietveld was added to the exhibition manifesto offered at the gallery and appeared with the models reproduced in the De Stijl issue of *L'Architecture Vivante* as a result of the De Stijl desire to be seen as a collective creative force (it has been shown that Rietveld's only contribution consisted of the maquette of the Rosenberg house). This attitude also explains why Oud and Wils participated in the exhibition, although by this time neither was any longer actively involved with De Stijl. Other participants were the architect W. van Leusden, who worked in the De Stijl manner for a short time, and Vilmos Huszar, the designer of the original *De Stijl* cover.

Le Corbusier's criticism of De Stijl

The De Stijl exhibition attracted much interest and was discussed in *L'Esprit Nouveau*, in an article by Ozenfant and Jeanneret (Le Corbusier) called 'The Straight Angle'.[1] They described it as a 'negative demonstration' of a movement in art which, by restricting itself to the rectangle, could merely 'stammer'. Criticism continued in the next issue of the same periodical, in a review of the publication

Staatliches Bauhaus – Weimar, with the title 'Pedagogics'.[2] Ozenfant and Jeanneret in this article stated that Gropius had associated with 'the idea of the De Stijl group from Amsterdam, also represented by the painter Theo van Doesburg – painter, but also theoretician of a young architecture, the aesthetics of which are based on principles that are rudely simple (though very interesting since, at any rate, they demon-

62

strate the strength of any system whatsoever)'. In the same issue Le Corbusier commented upon the architecture in the Rosenberg Gallery exhibition in an article called 'Le Salon d'automne'.[3] In a dialogue between a certain Mr X and Fernand Léger, under the heading 'Confusing Derivations That Had to Follow', Mr X considered the use of colour on the exterior a form of camouflage destroying architecture, whereas the colour designs of the interiors chauvinistically were said to stem from Léger, who was described as having 'made school' with them. This criticism stems from the fact that the Purism of Le Corbusier and Ozenfant was the outcome of Synthetic Cubism with its return to representational form, via a novel use of 'standard objects'. Conversely De Stijl represented the logical continuation of Analytical Cubism towards an art of pure plastic means. In an article with the significant title 'No Axiom but a Plastic Principle'[4] Mondrian came to the defence of this fundamental Neoplastic norm on ideal development. His short essay served as a reply to the criticism of De Stijl architecture published in both issues of *L'Esprit Nouveau*.

Early this year Van Doesburg gave a series of lectures in Germany. A lecture on De Stijl and its consequences in painting, sculpture and architecture, alternated on successive evenings with a lecture under the title 'Art as an Obstacle to Progress',[5] which was directed against the many imitations of De Stijl, especially those to be found in industrial design.

There followed an exhibition of Van Doesburg's work at Weimar, which also included his architectural designs, although without the models. In the spring the De Stijl architecture exhibition moved from the Rosenberg Gallery to the Ecole Spéciale d'Architecture in Paris, as part of the larger exhibition, 'Architecture and the Arts Attached to it'.

In the May issue of *L'Esprit Nouveau* Le Corbusier produced another review with the title 'The Exhibition at the Ecole Spéciale d'Architecture'.[6] He used theory derived from his interpretation of Wright to criticize the Van Doesburg and Van Eesteren models. This use of Wrightian comment can be interpreted as an effort to defeat De Stijl on its own grounds. Le Corbusier wrote:

After the initial revival facing us here, with its multiple forms leaning against one another and arbitrary and tormented silhouettes that create at first an architectural sensation, the time will come when it is realized that light is much more generous with a simple prism. Then this complexity, this abusive richness and these exuberant forms will become disciplined under the shield of pure form. One will know that the whole possesses a greater value than five or ten parts. This tendency towards a pure whole, covering abundance with a mask of simplicity, can be the only outcome. We have time to wait.

Le Corbusier, confronted here with a dynamic four-dimensional architecture, explains why he did not envisage from his more classical point of view its organic unity in spite of the many parts.

In 'An Answer to Our Enquiry: Where is Modern Painting Going?',[7] a series of articles published in *Bulletin de l'Effort Moderne*, Van Doesburg in turn presented the following answers to all previous criticisms: 'The future will be against any illusion that painting and sculpture are separated from life, in short, any subjective expression of life by means of illusion will disappear', and 'The constructive painter has already understood that colour is a creative element in architecture.' His most important point – one derived from Kandinsky – is that instead of 'form', which refers to Le Corbusier's 'single prism', there will be a coloured construction in three dimensions. 'In this construction the onlooker will find himself right in the middle of painting.' These statements were addressed to the Purist artists who assumed Synthetic Cubism, with its return to the recognizable object, to be the logical outcome of abstract Analytical Cubism and continued this development by employing naturalistic objects which were reduced to their basic or pure form and which were accordingly called 'standard' objects. At the same time these criticisms were addressed to the Functionalists who considered the fine arts a lesser thing and discarded any aesthetic approach in their architecture.

Another attack on *L'Esprit Nouveau* and defence of De Stijl came from Hans Richter, who, in an article in $G \square$ using the same title as that of the French magazine, accused its editors of holding patriarchal, sentimental and academic views in spite of their boast to foster the new.[8] This criticism was preceded by an appreciative article, also by Richter, dedicated to De Stijl and to Van Doesburg,[9] and mentioned at the same time the latter's influence at the Bauhaus. In addition, the same issue of $G \square$ carried a short contribution by Van Doesburg entitled 'The Spiritual . . .'[10] It accompanied a reproduction of one of Van Doesburg's paintings from 1918 and expressed some thoughts on the human character of 'completely abstract art' addressed to the 'confused sentimentalism' and 'acclaimed' humanism of Purism. Interestingly, the painting reproduced closely resembled *Rhythms of a Russian Dance*. At a time when criticism was being directed against his architectural models, the choice of this painting indicates that Van Doesburg realized that his use of the four-dimensional principle in architecture was closely related to that visualized in his early Neo-plastic paintings.

Van Doesburg's architectural programme, 1924

At the occasion of the second exhibition of De Stijl architecture in Paris Van Doesburg published a sixteen-point programme, called 'Towards Plastic Architecture' (p. 142).[1] Points Three and Four summarize the notions of an architecture which is both economical and functional. The third paragraph of Point Five is strikingly similar to a remark by Lissitzky in 'Proun' on the construction of space. Van Doesburg's description of architectural construction as 'a coordinated system in which all points correspond to an equal number of points in universal, unlimited open space', can be compared to Lissitzky's comments on space: 'The void, chaos, the anti-natural becomes space, that is to say order, definition and plastic form, if, in a certain way, we define the marking-points through co- and inter-relationships. The construction and the measure of the manifold marking points bestow a certain tension to space. When we change the marking-points, we change the tension of the space that has been created from one and the same void.'[2] Both formulations, though differently worded, represent one and the same Einstein-like approach, which Van Doesburg had presented for the first

64

time in 1916. This similarity largely stems from the fact that both Proun and De Stijl descended from Analytical Cubism with its interest in 'plural dimensionality'. It reveals once more the closeness between the artistic viewpoints of Lissitzky and Van Doesburg at this time. Both men would walk and talk together for hours at Weimar and in Berlin, and Lissitzky confided to Van Doesburg in a letter from Ambri-Sotto (in Tessin, Switzerland), 'I am always interested in what you write to me about your theoretical work, both in those cases where our visions are very similar and, in particular, when we possess a different opinion.'[3]

There is no doubt that several aspects of Van Doesburg's architectural programme represent reactions to Wright's theories. Specifically four of the points – One, Seven, Twelve and Fifteen – which reject former style-types and openings (windows, doors and so forth) as passive moments, as well as symmetry and decoration, correspond to notions in Wright's *In the Cause of Architecture*.[4] Van Doesburg's programme as a whole constituted an exchange of thought with, and a further development of, both *Ausgeführte Bauten und Entwürfe*,[5] the book by Wright which most influenced European architecture, and Le Corbusier's *Vers Une Architecture*.[6] Van Doesburg's Points Eight and Nine, rejecting an architecture of load-support and advocating mobile interior screens, were influenced by Le Corbusier, whereas his rejection in Point Twelve of standardization of housing was again opposed to views of both Le Corbusier and the Bauhaus.

In an article published in the same week as the programme Van Doesburg illuminated the paradoxical claim that De Stijl architecture was 'formless yet defined': 'Indeed with a view to elemenary architecture we should rather speak of an a-style since this architecture goes beyond style. This is precisely what constitutes its style. In this new notion of an a-style, the two extremes formlessness and style are unified.'[7] This statement in turn is a development of Wright's thoughts on style in *Ausgeführte Bauten und Entwürfe*.

It must be pointed out that the De Stijl movement had never repudiated its debt to Wright nor its relationship to Cubism, and had in the meantime introduced a new phase of development in architecture by way of the models designed by Van Doesburg in collaboration with Van Eesteren (see p. 61). As with these models, Van Doesburg's architectural programme posits a fundamentally new approach in so far as it deals with a four-dimensional architecture of a space-time quality. The relationship of this programme to his article 'The New Aesthetics and its Realization', which was written in 1922 and already substituted the space-time view for Wright's approach, has been pointed out above (see p. 56).

The impact of the Paris models was varied. The Schröder house built in Utrecht in 1924 by Rietveld,[8] owes little to them, but their new use of colour, employing larger areas and thereby dealing with architecture as a whole, had a direct effect on J. J. P. Oud's café De Unie (1924/25) in Rotterdam.[9] It is possible that through Lissitzky, the new De Stijl architecture exerted some influence on Kasimir Malevich. His isometric drawings produced around 1924[10] attempt to accentuate planar relationships, but nevertheless remain visualizations of an architecture of extended mass. While resembling Proun constructions, their treatment of space is superficial when compared to the Paris models. Later, when reproducing one of Malevich's models among the examples in architecture he considered to be influenced by De Stijl, Van Doesburg referred to them as pieces of 'fancy-architecture'.[11]

65

The appearance of his architectural programme was immediately succeeded by two related publications, 'Towards Collective Construction'[12] (p. 147), and '$-\square + = R_4$'[13] (p. 148). Both were written by Van Doesburg but published with Van Eesteren listed as co-author. 'Towards Collective Construction' (published in the magazines *Bulletin de l'effort moderne, Pasmo* and *Stavba* as well as *De Stijl*) contained a further attack on Purism's return to illusionism and the remarkable statement that the machine in art is another illusion. This statement was made in reaction to views adhered to by Moholy-Nagy, Gropius, Mies van der Rohe and Le Corbusier. Lissitzky also repudiated the machine in art in 'Nasci'.[14] These articles furnish further examples that Van Doesburg and Lissitzky were united against Functionalism; they both critized it for its extravagant admiration for the machine and its belief that in the machine could be found the solution for architectural problems. The other article, '$-\square + = R_4$', comprises a description of the architectural studies by Van Doesburg and Van Eesteren placed under the 'sign' of the fourth dimension.

In the autumn Van Doesburg received an invitation from the City of Vienna to give a lecture, which he presented under the title 'The Development of Modern Architecture in Holland'.[15] This lecture had been given earlier in Prague and Brno, as well as in Berlin at the beginning of the year. In Vienna he met the architects P. Behrens and J. Hoffmann (incredibly enough, neither had he any acquaintance with Adolf Loos nor could any publication by the latter be found in Van Doesburg's library) and also became acquainted with F. Kiesler and his designs for the Vienna theatre and exhibition hall. Soon afterwards, Kiesler became a writer for *De Stijl* and published on methods for display as well as on architecture.

In this year he had a book, *Principles of Neo-plastic Art*[16] published at the Bauhaus. The text, in an excellent translation by Max Burchartz, was almost identical with the article of the same name which had been written between 1915 and 1918 and was first published in Dutch in 1919.[17]

Elementarism: another search for dynamics in painting

Towards the end of 1924 or the beginning of 1925, Van Doesburg began to develop a new approach in painting which he called Elementarism. He was looking for a new form of artistic expression appropriate to the scientific concepts of matter in motion and the law of gravity in painting, and at the same time reconsidering the philosophical principles of Hegel and Schoenmaekers that he had earlier rejected.

The feature that distinguishes Elementarism from Van Doesburg's earlier work is that the compositions are turned at a forty-five degree angle. Accordingly they make a contrast with (that is, an oblique counter-movement against) the horizontal-vertical structure found in nature as well as in architecture. The term he uses to describe this method, 'counter-construction', first appeared in Point Seven of his architectural programme, in which it is said that the new architecture determines everything by means of contrast. This attribute can be discovered in the 'counter-constructions', which prove to be the axonometrics drawings of the Paris models reproduced in *De Stijl*. These axonometric (i.e. spatial projections under a forty-five degree angle), though using this oblique angle in drawing, nevertheless present an architecture of strictly orthogonal relationships. This apparent paradox is an essential feature of the transition from Neo-plasticism to Elementarism, since both techniques, orthogonality and obliquity, are now referred to by one and the same term, 'counter-construction'. Van Doesburg always considered his axonometrics drawings as a highly important way of visualizing architecture and claimed them as a presentation typical of De Stijl. Apparently he was attracted by the dynamics of these drawings to such a degree that with Elementarism he substituted their function (to replace perspective by means of spatial projections drawn at a forty-five degree angle) for their aim (the visualization of orthogonal architectural relationships). Later Van Doesburg was to call the Elementarist paintings 'counter-compositions' instead of 'counter-constructions', in an effort to distinguish again between the two disciplines painting and architecture. In the early nineteen-twenties 'composition' was seen as a characteristic of painting, whereas the term 'construction' was applied to works using three-dimensional space.

Elementarism derives in part from the discussions with Mondrian on 'the oblique', held between 1917 and 1920. Having developed Neo-plasticism into a spatial, four-dimensional conception of architecture, Van Doesburg again became concerned with the earlier phase, the two-dimensional art of painting, at this stage because his architectural research had come to a temporary halt. Elementarism was also meant to excel Futurism by substituting the Elementarist oblique for the Italian movement's mimetic suggestion of motion by means of succession. The use of the oblique in painting, although already touched upon in the years 1917 and 1918, was only developed after the Paris models. Van Doesburg considered that Mondrian's Neo-plastic paintings lacked the dynamism achieved in his own architecture through interpenetration. It was this very result of Mondrian's painting purely two-dimensionally, which had led to a juxtaposition of the pictorial elements placed parallel to the horizontal-vertical structure and, consequently, to the loss of the dynamic fourth dimension in Neo-plastic painting. This aspect of Neo-plasticism, now referred to as a static, classical approach, in 1918, had provoked the four-dimensional linear Neo-plastic paintings by Van Doesburg as well as the discussion on the use of the oblique, which latter means was then rejected. It is important to observe how, from this moment on, the new application of the element of time by means of the oblique, representing an approach very different from the expansion of space-time in Van Doesburg's architectural models, was to remain restricted to two-dimensional painting only.

There is little doubt that Georges Antheil's 'Manifesto of Mechanico-Music'[1] written in Berlin in 1922 and published in *De Stijl*, also played a role here. Antheil, who had been a member of De Stijl since 1923, drew many parallels between music and contemporary plastic art. He argued that the sole solution to the creation of a new musical dimension was to be found in the oblique. Another article published in *De Stijl* by this American composer, 'My Ballet Mecanique',[2] identifies the 'oblique' with the 'fourth' dimension and describes music composed by its rules to be of a scientific, mathematical character in contra-distinction

67

to the superficial approach in Futurist 'noise-music'.

A reflection of this 'two-sided' approach can be found in 'Surrealism. Realistic Dialogue',[3] in spite of the fact that this article was mainly intended as a parody of a movement which had come into being under André Breton's leader-

ship, following the failure of the Paris Dada Congress. Realizing that he was at the same time a promoter of a new architecture in which all arts will fuse and a painter with the classical view of painting to present an end by itself, Van Doesburg dissected himself into 'my past I' and 'my future I', both of whom delivered com-

(left) *Counter-Composition VIII* 1924
oil on canvas, 100×100 cm. (39×39 in.)
Collection of the Art Institute of Chicago,
gift of Mrs Peggy Guggenheim

Counter-composition XII 1924
oil on canvas, $52 \times 21 \cdot 5$ cm. (21×8 in.)
Collection of Mr O. Reutersvaerd

ments on Cubism. He also made clear his dissatisfaction with an intuitive approach in art, which he wanted to see replaced with a scientific (mathematical) determination.

In this article Van Doesburg answered Kemeny's and Moholy-Nagy's manifesto 'The Dynamic-Constructive System of Forces'[4] and Kemeny's 'The Dynamic Principle'.[5] Both manifestos, in their turn, are reactions against Cubism, Suprematism, Constructivism and De Stijl, declaring these 'isms' important but obsolete, because they maintain 'statico-classical' approaches. Such approaches, they argue, should be replaced by one leading to moving art objects. These views were typical of the technico-functionalist attitude in their elaboration upon the element of motion initially, if 'primitively', expressed by Futurism. To Van Doesburg such a view was closely related to so-called Vitalism in Western philosophy and was far too materialistic with its stress on the chemistry of the universe to be acceptable. His visual diagonal with Elementarism, which according to Kemeny and Moholy-Nagy was as static and classical a means of expression as the horizontal and vertical in Neo-plasticism, and therefore considered equally obsolete, was actually intended as an illustration of an inner, dynamic dimension, namely that of the spirit, in contrast to the static, horizontal-vertical structure of external (physical) nature.

A similar debate on the element of motion in art is found in an important book, which appeared that year. *Painting and its Laws. The Outcome of Cubism*,[6] was written by Albert Gleizes, whom Van Doesburg knew very well, and had been first published as an essay in *La Vie des Lettres et des Arts* the year before. Gleizes' book was inspired by his reaction to several technical manifestos of Futurism as well as to those of Kemeny and Moholy-Nagy. It rejected a purely mechanical reproduction of motion in art, and substituted a psychological and scientific approach towards this same problem without stressing mathematics and arithmetic to the degree of Gino Severini's 'Avant-garde Painting',[7] published in *De Stijl* in the years 1917 and 1918. There is little doubt that Severini's essay was being reconsidered by Van Doesburg at the same period and with equal care.

From the above, it is evident that the element of motion, as differently conceived by Cubism and Futurism, was being reconsidered simultaneously by a number of important artists representing the various 'isms' of the nineteen-twenties. As stated above, Elementarism was also intended as an improvement on Futurism to which Neo-plasticism had been opposed from the beginning. Seen in this light, Van Doesburg's unfinished article, 'The end of modernisms: An analysis of Futurism, Cubism, Expressionism, Purism, Dadaism, Constructivism and so forth',[8] which was directed primarily against Futurism, was an almost inevitable occurrence.

Towards the end of 1924 Van Doesburg made an interior design for the 'flower-room' of the Count de Noailles, who commissioned his house at Hyères, in the Department of Var, France, to be decorated by several artists, among them Fernand Léger. The design (1924–5) for a small room with a high ceiling, in the colours black, white, grey, and red, blue, yellow, was the earliest Elementarist interior to be produced (p. 150), since it preceded construction of Van Doesburg's interior design in the Aubette. Just as the relief in fine art represents a typical no-mans-land between the border limits of painting and sculpture, so interior design may have appeared to Van Doesburg as a realm to experiment with the fusion of art and architecture without the strict application of any premeditated principle.

Mondrian leaves De Stijl

Abstract art, including Neo-plasticism, was viewed as being an extreme refinement of the Renaissance in an article by Van Doesburg which appeared with the Hegelian title, 'The End of Art'[1] and contained a further attack on the 'classical' in art. This article represented a continuation of thoughts expressed in 'Answer to Our Enquiry: Where is Modern Painting Going?'[2] and, in fact, is the outcome of Van Doesburg's final point of his architectural programme called 'Architecture as the Synthesis of Neo-plasticism' (see p. 149). However, this time it states the common De Stijl aim to fuse art with life in quite different, in fact almost Functionalist, terms, which is why it results in the proclamation of an anti-art attitude. As such this article is the clearest demonstration possible that Van Doesburg had arrived at an impasse. His synthetic activities in architecture had come to a temporary halt, whereas the end of all modernisms was not to be expected except in the future. Apparently he had not quite reconciled himself to the idea of returning to brush and canvas. Lingering doubts regarding what path to pursue may partly explain why he wrote, 'For the sake of progress we must suppress any notion of "art" as an aesthetic speculation.' One can almost hear reflected in these words Mies van der Rohe's 1923 argument against De Stijl. (It was in this year, 1925, that the Deutsche Werkbund charged Mies with the organization and planning of the Weissenhofsiedlung, to which, however, neither Van Doesburg nor Van Eesteren, nor Rietveld were invited to contribute.) At the same time Van Doesburg's statement shows his dissatisfaction with the role of intuition in Neo-

plasticism, which was to be replaced by a more scientific approach. Whatever the reason for his uncertainty, the article shows Van Doesburg to be far from having found a balanced attitude towards his new Elementarism.

Van Doesburg's Elementarism, his changing theories, and particularly his view on the 'classical' in abstract art, produced differences of opinion with Mondrian which led to the latter's leaving De Stijl as a protest. In spite of the split, Mondrian was to subject his painting to a renewed investigation of the problem of the oblique. During 1925, 1926 and 1927, he again produced several canvases at a forty-five degree angle, thus returning to the early diamond-shaped painting of the years 1918 and 1919.

Another indication of the temporary split between Van Doesburg and Mondrian can be found in the latter's attitude towards the Dutch Wendingen group, which advocated an Expressionist type of architecture to which De Stijl had always been opposed. This issue came into the open with the 'Exposition des Arts Décoratifs' in Paris, where the Dutch pavilion did not contain any De Stijl exhibits but consisted largely of Wendingen architecture. Van Doesburg wrote a protest of which a copy was deposited in the Austrian pavilion for the collection of signatures. On this occasion Mondrian did not express any antipathy to the Wendingen type of architecture, and, thus, a relatively unimportant affair demonstrated the widening gap between both artists. The exhibition was reviewed in *De Stijl* by Van Doesburg, in an article entitled, 'The Dutch Failure in the Paris Exhibition in 1925'.[3]

Counter-composition XV 1925
oil on canvas, 50 × 50 cm. (20 × 20 in.)
Collection of Museum Sztuki u. Lodzi, Lodz

72

Van Doesburg's isolation in France

Van Doesburg's articles 'The End of Art' and 'The End of Modernisms', discussed previously are strongly connected by a common tenet. Although 'The End of Modernism' restricted itself to Futurism, since it was to be continued at a later date, Van Doesburg peremptorily advocates the end of all art-isms and the fusion of art with life in 'The End of Art'. However, the subtitle of 'The end of Modernisms' also mentions Constructivism, touching upon divergence of opinion which arose between Lissitzky and Van Doesburg this year and which would end their artistic relationship. Its immediate cause was the book *The Isms of Art 1914–1924*[1] published by El Lissitzky and Hans Arp. Van Doesburg's objections were directed chiefly against the incorrect dates Lissitzky gave in his book and in particular against the statement that Suprematism had begun in 1913. Lissitzky extended the conflict in his article 'A. and Pangeometry'[2] ('A' was an abbreviation for art) by stating once more that Malevich began the use of the square in 1913 and, in a footnote, that 'the artists of De Stijl, when using Mondrian's principle in three-dimensional space, will turn into decorators'. This last remark, together with a statement in *The Art Isms 1914–1924* that 'Proun is the station for change from painting to architecture', clearly reveals the competition between Lissitzky and Van Doesburg that developed after the latter had more fully realized the principles of his Neo-plastic painting in the Paris architectural models. Moreover, Van Doesburg's new architecture represented a visualization of the four-dimensional concept, opening up mass and leading to an architecture of space-time, much more than did either Malevich's archi-

tectural designs or Lissitzky's project for a skyscraper, both of which date from 1924 and maintained an architecture of mass.

According to a note in Van Doesburg's handwriting in the margin of Lissitzky's article in the *Europa-Almanach*, Malevich started to use the Suprematist square only in 1918. He was correct in this assumption as far as Malevich's painting *White on white* was concerned, as is confirmed by Ludvig Hilberseimer in his introduction to Malevich's *The Nonobjective World*,[3] a translation of *Die Gegenstandslose Welt*, published in 1927 at the Bauhaus. However, in this book Malevich himself presented several drawings using the Suprematist square in various compositional ways and carrying the date 1913. But Constantin Umansky in *Neue Kunst in Russland 1914–1919*,[4] states that Suprematism came into being in Russia only in 1915 and that the immediately preceding years were devoted to a Cubist-Futurist phase.[5] As he was the friend of many Russian artists and apparently, since he described himself as having also represented many of their administrative interests, some art officials feel he is the more reliable source.

Apart from this disputed matter,[6] the article 'A. and Pangeometry' shares the demand for a switch from the intuitive to a scientific approach in art. Although he did not mention his name, Lissitzky made clear reference[7] to his discussions with Van Doesburg on the fourth dimension in art, but criticized his use of it in his architectural models as 'superficial'.

In the same *Europa-Almanach* Van Doesburg's architecture was also attacked by Le Corbusier in 'The Change-over in Architecture'.[8] While admitting that he had 'breathed in the aesthetic directives for a contemporary architecture', Le Corbusier again rejected them in Functionalist terms with his remark that 'a house is like a chest with many drawers', and argued that the main architectural problems were not to be solved by the aesthetician who was 'lost in fantasy and arbitrariness'.

Finally, another criticism of Van Doesburg appeared in the *Europa-Almanach*, which, in fact, contained contributions from nearly all leading artists of the time except Van Doesburg. Oud contributed 'Yes and No',[9] as a third attack upon the editor of *De Stijl* in that single publication, mainly with respect to his points on mannerism and propaganda.

Meanwhile, Van Doesburg commenced a long series of articles on the renovation of architecture in various European countries. These articles, in *Bouwbedrijf*, possessed a neutral informative character, despite several paragraphs of a typically Van Doesburg tendentious flavour. His unpublished and incomplete manuscript *European Architecture*[10] represents a condensed extract of the most significant statements from these articles and was intended as a short history of modern architecture.

Writing apparently represented to Van Doesburg a means to compensate for the temporary lapse in his other activities. In the summer, during a stay at Belle-Ile-en-Mer (Morbihan), a bare and rocky island to which from this time on Van Doesburg regularly retreated because of increasing trouble with his hay fever, he completed *The Other Face: An Abstract Surhumanistic Novel*[11] which had been published earlier as a series of aphorisms. This novel differs from his 'Caminoscopy' in being less philosophical and more literary in intention and for reminding one of Dadaist as well as of Surrealist literature. According to Van Doesburg, it presents 'a world of plastic form, of pure creation, in which the impossible becomes possible, a world without gravitation or space-temporal coordination'.[12] Its content is related to Elementarism and to Surrealism, which share a common need to turn everything into spirituality.

In *De Stijl* Van Doesburg published his last project in collaboration with Van Eesteren, which was the 'Design for a Shopping Centre'.[13] Van Doesburg's role in this project was limited to the application of colour, and the architecture itself was entirely by Van Eesteren. The younger artist used this opportunity to show his preference for the general trend in modern architecture in abandoning the space-time innovations of Van Doesburg. Van Eesteren's prize-winning project for the renovation of Unter den Linden in Berlin also dates from this year and equally demonstrates his return to an architecture of mass. From this point on Van Eesteren was to dedicate himself exclusively to town-planning, the first results of which were published in *De Stijl*.

In August, under Jean Badovici's editorship, the Editions Albert Morancé in its series *L'Architecture Vivante* published a special issue dedicated to *De Stijl*. It was prefaced by a general introduction by Jean Badovici which was in actual fact an article by Van Doesburg rewritten and signed by Badovici, and the issue also contained articles by Mondrian and Van Doesburg on more specific topics. Mondrian's contribution had been written the year before under the title 'Future Neo-plastic Architecture'[14] and restated views expressed in his article 'Neo-plasticism in Practice in a Far Future and in Contemporary Architecture', published in *De Stijl* in 1922. Mondrian thus continued to stress his view that architecture consists of a plurality of planes rather than of the prisms found in 'massive building' concepts like those of Le Corbusier. Van Doesburg's 'The Evolution of Modern Architecture in

Holland'[15] rejected Berlage's architecture for having the same mixture of gothic and classical elements he had criticized in Wright. Since De Stijl had always felt its indebtedness to Berlage, Van Doesburg's comment indicates that he considered his own architecture a definite progressive step.

His architectural programme was also included in this issue of *L'Architecture Vivante* and had been expanded to seventeen points instead of the earlier sixteen published in *De Stijl*; the second half of Point Ten became Point Eleven, and stated that 'The plastic aspect is obtained by the fourth dimension of space-time.' The fact that Van Doesburg isolated the aspect of space-time in architecture with his new Point Eleven, apart from explaining his comments on Berlage and Wright, makes it clear once more that he was fully conscious of his own contribution in bestowing architecture with a space-time quality. The expanded programme also included for the first time two drawings of three-dimensional crosses called *Tesseracts* and intended as basic plastic forms, the one indicating a centripetal, the other a centrifugal movement. These illustrations are consequently of great import-

ance in connection with the four-dimensional aspect of Van Doesburg's architecture. (See ill. on p. 145). The drawings are also of interest in reference to Kemeny's manifesto 'The Dynamic Principle'. This manifesto portrayed the space-time continuum of the universe as its aboriginal function and viewed this mechanism as based on centrifugally and centripetally directed forces, which should be expressed by a mobile art. Van Doesburg's centrifugal and centripetal cross-like, basic plastic forms, in their statico-dynamic existence, are intended as a reply to this purely physical view. In conformity with the new *De Stijl* architecture, they were meant to embody the ideal that man, in his art, expresses the dynamic vision of the universe without the physicality of actual motion.

1925 also saw the publication of the book *Die Scheuche* (*The Scarecrow*),[16] a children's tale written by Kurt Schwitters, enriched by a typographical layout by Van Doesburg, and executed under the care of Käte Steinitz. In his typography Van Doesburg made playful use of typical Morris plant motives by rotating them forty-five degrees according to Element-arist principles, whereas the figures remind one of Lissitzky's collages built of matches.

De Stijl's dualism of mind and matter

In the early spring of 1926, the De Stijl exhibition held in Rosenberg's Gallery went on to Nancy on the initiative of the architect, André Lurcat. This time the exhibition did not include the architectural models which the year before had been ruined by humidity when stored in the cellars of Albert Morancé's publishing house. Around this time Van Doesburg became

acquainted with A. F. del Marle, the editor of *Vouloir. Organe Constructif de Littérature et d'Art Moderne* and a former Futurist, who was soon to become a follower of Neo-plasticism.

In March *Vouloir* published Mondrian's article 'Art, purity + abstraction',[1] written that same month, and Van Doesburg's 'Towards Elementary Art',[2] written the month before.

Curiously, Van Doesburg's contribution, though possessing many characteristics of a manifesto, failed to become one. Instead, it presented a summary of all earlier achievements in the manner of his 'Towards Elementary Plastic Expression' published in 1923. It describes the earlier achievements as also being 'elementaristic' but does not say what Elementarism has come to represent, nor mention the visual oblique. The only indication of Van Doesburg's new thinking on the expression of movement was to be found towards the end in the sentence, 'Due to the confidence we can have in our spiritual Power, we have renovated the Plastic domain.'

The explanation for Van Doesburg's restraint can be found in Mondrian's article 'Art, purity + abstraction'. This key document in the controversy between Neo-plasticism and Elementarism puts forward an unusually sharp critique for Mondrian. At the same time, Mondrian used this opportunity to outline his position on several phenomena in the art of his time. *L'Esprit Nouveau* is attacked by a formulation of what truly represents the new spirit, namely, the union of matter and spirit in pure abstraction rather than through the return to a naturalistic art (i.e. Purism). Functionalism is seen as substituting utility for art. There is, in the criticism of Functionalism an undertone of disagreement with Van Doesburg's 'The End of Art' which, in Functionalist terms, rejected 'aesthetic speculation'. In contrast to Van Doesburg Mondrian believed that art should be based on 'pure intuition' instead of 'cerebrality'. He answered Van Doesburg's rejection of Neo-plasticism's 'classical statics' by stating that Neo-plasticism was also an expression of vitality, capable of evoking the force of life or life's joy. He defended himself against Van Doesburg's opinion that abstract Neo-plastic art was an extreme refine-

ment of Renaissance traditions of naturalistic art by stating that abstract art, although derived from the abstraction of nature and manifesting itself in the geometric appearance of horizontal-vertical polarity, cannot be called abstract art for this reason alone. To this end 'creativity' is an indissoluble ingredient, which is why the work of art is a human counter-construction to nature's construction, 'whether in architecture or in painting', Mondrian added significantly.

These notions were soon to be elaborated upon in Van Doesburg's manifestos on Elementarism and on Concrete Art. They clearly reveal the passionate character of the debate between both artists on an issue which concerned the very nature of the duality of matter and mind. From this point on, each artist was to solve this problem in a different way. Mondrian would continue to secure the annulment of conflict between the two poles through the equilibrium of horizontal and vertical elements, whereas Van Doesburg would try to achieve the same end through the combination of the spiritual (the oblique) with the physical or natural (the horizontal-vertical) element by means of contrast. For Mondrian, the spiritual was expressed in the work of art which used the horizontal-vertical right-angle relationship in its composition, which is why in his view Van Doesburg's use of the forty-five degree angle introduced a superfluous cerebral, visual element. This projected schism between man and nature and the resulting disagreement about the nature of the concrete, the real in abstract art, is the cause of their conflict. It explains why Van Doesburg temporarily hesitated to say in 'Towards Elementary Art' that the dynamic 'spiritual force' is literally and tangibly expressed by the visual oblique.

However, shortly after Mondrian had stated his point of view, *De Stijl* published Van

Doesburg's 'Painting: From Composition Towards Counter-Composition' (p. 151).[3] Here the Elementarist oblique was described as being in opposition to the horizontal-vertical structure in nature and architecture, 'although no duality is created', and as the result of providing 'a new dimension again to our imagination'. In this article, Van Doesburg's unsettled attitude towards ideas borrowed from Hegel and Schoenmaekers becomes very clear. Elementarism, as an effort to introduce greater spirituality in art, arose precisely at a time when his architectural activity had temporarily halted. Van Doesburg's persistent search for the material expression of his artistic ideas, now that it appeared his new concept of life could not be immediately realized through architecture (Neo-plasticism), generated the urge to embody philosophical concepts in painting by means of Elementarism.

In large part Elementarism is, of course, a remnant of the Rationalist view held in the last phase of the mimetic period in art, which saw art as being in competition with nature. This explains why the ideas arose of philosophy beginning when art ends (Hegel) and of philosophy finding its deepest, ultimate manifestation in plastic visualization (Schoenmaekers). Although Van Doesburg was gradually to decide in favour of Schoenmaekers' view, he differed even from him in letting the spiritual prevail over the material element. With Hegel, spirit itself is all reality, thus representing an opposition to the physical. For Schoenmaekers, however, spiritual and material reality exist as a unity of counterparts (the horizontal-vertical) in equilibrium. It is on this latter view that Mondrian based his criticism of Van Doesburg's visual oblique as a superfluous cerebral element. It remains to be said that the terms 'counterpart' and 'opposite' are of extreme importance in both Neo-plastic and

Elementarist theory. From their use one can often detect whether Van Doesburg was inclining towards the ideas of Schoenmaekers or of Hegel, although in several instances he tried to evade all difficulty by fusing both terms with his use of the relatively neutral term 'contrast'.

Furthermore, it was not by accident that Van Doesburg referred to articles written in 1914, since Elementarism was also the outcome of ideas originating at that time. The article, 'Painting: From Composition Towards Counter-Composition' and the fragmentary manifesto that was to follow, 'Painting and Plastic Art' (p. 156)[4] also were a reaction to the manifestos of Kemeny and Moholy-Nagy. Both articles state their opposition to Futurism and Gleizes' 'Painting and Its Laws' by advocating instead of the mimetic suggestion of motion and the shift of rotation of planes, the use of the oblique as the unique way to visualize movement. In part, Elementarism went along with the ideas on culture found in an article on abstract film, 'Principles of Motion Art' by Hans Richter,[5] which advocated the cinema as the ideal form of kinetic art, but it tried also to demonstrate that the element of motion need not imply the replacement of painting, since painting can realize sensations of motion with the dynamics of the visual oblique.

Some roots of Elementarism can also be seen in 'Modern Painting and its Relationship to Architecture' by Bart van der Leck, published in *De Stijl* in 1917.[6] There Van der Leck stated, 'Modern painting is the destruction of plastic natural form in contrast to plastic natural constructive form in architecture' (Point One), and, 'modern painting represents painting in spatial two-dimensionality, that is extension in contrast to the space-limiting two-dimensionality of architecture' (Point Four). Moreover, in 1918 Van der Leck wrote to Van Doesburg,

'Not only the construction of the universe, that is stability, but also universal movement must be taken into account in the plastic expression of painting. In painting this can be achieved by the free and the oblique.'[7]

Van Doesburg's visual oblique came ultimately to represent for him the (fourth) dimension of the (human) spirit in contrast to the three dimensions of nature-reality, visualized in a concrete way. To achieve this view he had reasoned as follows: naturalistic art, the Renaissance, had reached its perfection in abstract art, Neo-plasticism, where natural reality turned into abstract reality. Now that art had become abstract reality it must become 'real' art which, in the Hegelian sense, was to say purely 'spiritual'. Thus, the following paradox came into being, that is to say, the spiritual element was materialized in a concrete, that is to say, a realistic (naturalistic) way, by means of the Elementarist visual oblique. This was one reason why subsequently mathematics and arithmetic, representing pure activities of the mind and products of reason, would come into the picture. The same paradox indicates that Elementarism was a reaction to Mondrian's essay 'Natural Reality and Abstract Reality', which will be discussed at a later point.

The fragmentary manifesto 'Painting and Plastic Art' was written in Rome, where Van Doesburg discussed Elementarism with the Futurists Marinetti, Prampolini and Balla, among others. The manifesto revealed Marinetti's suggestion that the term 'counter-composition' be replaced by 'anti-static' painting. Apparently, after having been confronted with Mondrian's opinion, Van Doesburg wanted to hear the views of the Futurists, apart from or perhaps just because of the fact that, in his own painting, he had worked out the visualization of dynamics in a non-Futurist manner. The tone of these discussions can be seen in the Elementarist manifesto in the occasional use of the typically heroic tone of Futurism. In particular, Marinetti's manifesto 'The New Religion Morality of Velocity' (1916) again influenced Van Doesburg's artistic theories. Marinetti's view that the spirit of contradiction represents the expression of life and that creative genius expresses velocity are of special relevance here. Marinetti's thought, in its turn, was related to that of Bergson (especially *Spiritual Energy*, 1911), the philosopher par excellence for Futurism, according to August Joly.[8] It remains to be added that, in discussing artistic theory with the Futurists, Van Doesburg came into contact with their new political views as well. In an unprinted article 'The Situation of Modern Art in Italy'[9] written in Rome in August, he came out strongly opposed to Fascism. (An earlier rejection can be found in the 'The End of Modernisms'.)

At this time in Rome Van Doesburg completed his colour theory which was intended as the first part of 'The Theory of Plastic Construction' (in four parts).[10] The other three parts were never written, and the first remained unprinted. Two points are of especial importance in this theory. First, Van Doesburg expressed his dissatisfaction with the current situation in architecture which he divorced from the other arts and considered a science instead. Second, he stated that the end and the means represent one and the same thing – a view new to him whose ramifications made matter and mind not equivalent but equal.

As I. K. Bonset, Van Doesburg wrote in 'To be', from *The other face*, the lines 'not to be consistent (to be oneself) is not being inconsistent but never being true' (p. 161).[11] This might have been intended as a paradoxical rejoinder to Mondrian who reproached Van Doesburg for being inconsistent as far as his 'additional' oblique was concerned.

Nowhere was the schism between Neo-plasticism and Elementarism drawn more sharply than in another fragmentary manifesto dating from April 1927, 'Painting and Plastic Art: Elementarism' (p. 163).[12] In the opening lines Van Doesburg related Elementarism to Neo-plasticism by describing the former as having come into existence 'partly as its (Neo-plasticism's) consequence but ultimately from what is primarily a radical correction of Neo-plastic ideas'.

Apart from representing a correction of Van Doesburg's own ideas, the article was again intended as a criticism of Mondrian. Thus, Mondrian's horizontal-vertical composition, because it was 'homogeneous' with natural construction, was condemned as 'an accentuation of our *physique*, of the natural structure and functions of the organism'. (Van Doesburg's italics.) This approach must now be replaced by a 'heterogeneous, contrasting, unstable manner of plastic expression based upon planes which are oblique in relation to the static, perpendicular axis of gravitation'. As early as 1925, some Elementarist compositions appear to extend endlessly beyond their canvas limits without depending upon a stabilizing gravitational centre. Van Doesburg in this respect was approaching, although from a reverse direction, the concept of the absolute as expressed in the dynamic manifestos of Kemeny and Moholy-Nagy. Although they had opposing views on the relative primacy of the spiritual or the material Van Doesburg and Kemeny and Moholy-Nagy shared common ground in believing that energy, either spiritual or material universal, is an irreducible substance. With Van Doesburg 'human spirit' was to become identified more and more with 'absolute spirit', in accordance with Hegel's philosophy. In Hegel's view, the mind realizes that whatever is opposed to it as an object, as matter, the entire physical and non-physical universe, is nothing other than spirit itself. It can thus grasp that it is itself all being and all reality, which is to say, in fact, the Absolute.[13] (To what degree the divergence of opinion on the relationship of matter and mind between the various isms of the 1920s was also closely related to political preferences, goes beyond the scope of the present survey.)

Between these two positions, the predominance of either the spiritual or the material, can be found a third approach, which posits matter and mind to be equal. This is, in fact, the attitude Van Doesburg was injecting into Mondrian's Neo-plasticism which, paradoxically enough, the former artist now came to see as abstract naturalism or even abstract mimeticism. As such, Elementarism developed as a reaction to one of Mondrian's most important essays, written in 1919–20, 'Natural Reality and Abstract Reality'. However, in the third scene of the dialogue, Mondrian's principle of 'equivalence' of the 'spiritual' and the 'physical' expressed in equilibrium, is explicitly stated not to represent any 'equality' of or any 'similarity' between these two.[14]

Having established his theories, Van Doesburg now said that Neo-plastic composition was 'homogeneous' with nature, while Elementarist composition was 'heterogeneous' or opposite to nature. If, through positing mind and matter as equal, Mondrian's orthogonal composition became homogenous with the horizontal-vertical construction in nature, then the next step one might expect, would be that mind is substituted for matter. This is what happens when Van Doesburg's oblique (spiritual) composition replaces orthogonal (naturalistic) composition. This development suggests that Van Doesburg himself first went through a phase in which matter and mind were posited as equal (e.g. as in his 'Theory of Plastic Construction').

Mondrian's view does, in fact, correspond to Hegel's fundamental ideal of classical composition. It is also related to Schoenmaekers' philosophy as expressed in his *Principles of Plastic Mathematics*, in that it argues the perfect balance and union of spirit and matter – a notion which is equally based on the Hegelian 'the something being determined by the other'. Thus, for Mondrian, 'the something' cannot go without 'the other'. In Van Doesburg's interpretation, however – and here we touch upon the core of the matter – this is, ultimately, changed into the substitution of 'the something' for 'the other'. As Hegel does in *Philosophy of Spirit*, he singles out one extreme of a polarity (in this case the spiritual) and turns it into an absolute. Yet Van Doesburg did not follow Hegel to his definition of the fundamental type of romantic art in which the spirit predominates over matter, but tried instead to surpass it by substituting spirit entirely for matter. In so doing he was breaking with Hegel's idea that the three fundamental types of art, the symbolic, the classical and the romantic, in this order describe the evolution of art, and that, through its increasing spirituality, ultimately art would cease to exist and turn into religion, before culminating in philosophy. Thus, Van Doesburg argued in 'Painting and Plastic Art' that religion and philosophy represent obsolete forms that now had been replaced by the art of Elementarism. In fact, by fusing the abstract (spirit) with the visual (painting as a sense-object) in a kind of 'visual philosophy', he was moving away from Hegel and coming closer to Schoenmaekers' *Principles of Plastic Mathematics*. Schoenmaekers held the anti-Hegelian view that thought (the spiritual) would find its deepest and most meaningful manifestation by visualization.

'Painting and Plastic Art' is also the best example of the unsettled mixture of notions derived from Hegel and Schoenmaekers to be found in Van Doesburg's writing. In attempting to evade the implied difficulties, Van Doesburg substituted the word 'contrast' for 'opposition' and for 'counterpart' in almost all cases, and furthermore demonstrated his annoyance with the problem of terminology by calling the dualities nothing but formulae.

In summary, Van Doesburg followed Hegel's philosophy in its striving for absolute spirituality but – as an artist – turned against it when it demanded that he move towards religion or philosophy. Schoenmaekers, on the other hand, was much more sympathetic, describing art as the most meaningful presentation of philosophy. It is this hesitation between two opinions, both closely connected with a philosophical definition of as well as his direct, sensuous approach to reality, which explains several discrepancies in his theory.

The Weissenhofsiedlung

The above considerations on the duality of matter and mind leave untouched Van Doesburg's achievements in four-dimensional architecture. A need for further theoretical clarification on the relationship between his Neoplastic architecture and his Elementarist painting did not escape Van Doesburg either, for in the manifesto 'Painting and Plastic Art' he wrote, 'Elementarism entirely rules out architecture as an art. Experience and research over the years have shown art and architecture to represent two completely different and incompatible entities.' This statement almost amounts to a denial of Van Doesburg's greatest achievement. His attitude was, however, to prove a temporary one, pointing towards other related circumstances.

First, Van Doesburg's position as an artist in France as has been shown, was more or less isolated when compared to the active role he had played in Germany between 1921 and 1923. Moreover, the Weissenhofsiedlung in Stuttgart, a plan for a modern town-quarter which was submitted and accepted in the summer of 1925, and realized in 1927, caused the Dutch artist considerable uneasiness. Apart from the influence of Hoffmann and Loos and the Futurist architecture of terraces, the Weissenhof architecture also reveals a debt to De Stijl. In spite of his criticism, Le Corbusier produced a cantilevered architecture which was strongly reminiscent of the Van Doesburg and Van Eesteren model for a studio house. Further indebtedness to De Stijl can be noted in the following quotation from Mies van der Rohe, from his introduction to a special issue of *Die Form* dedicated to this Werkbund exhibition, called 'Die Wohnung' (The House). He wrote, 'The battle-cry "rationalization and standardization", as well as the cry for building houses economically, deals only with fragmentary problems which are certainly important but which possess true significance only when related to an appropriate degree. Besides, or rather above this, there is the problem of space, the creation of a new house. This is a problem of the mind which can only be solved by creative force and not by calculation and organization. Therefore I have abstained from presenting any directives and have

restricted myself to choosing collaborators from whose work one might expect interesting contributions toward (solving) the problem of the new house.'[1] The Weissenhofsiedlung was the earliest and perhaps the finest achievement of Functionalist architecture (since 1930 called the International Style because the multi-national architects showed a profound similarity in their form-expression).

As a former leader of the Berlin G-group and having again become the main figure in the Berlin 'Ring' of architects, probably because he professed not to be interested in any style, Mies van der Rohe visibly focused attention upon the International Style. Both the statement quoted above and his reference to the Weissenhofsiedlung as an 'experiment' in the same article, contradict the views he expressed in 1923. Then architecture was seen as the sum of concrete, iron and glass, answering the rational demands of organization, clearness and economy and rejecting any 'speculation' (the experiment) or the 'formalism' of a will to style. Actually, Mies van der Rohe had always been attracted to ideas first presented by Van Doesburg in the architectural models of De Stijl, in his lectures and writings, and in the influential third De Stijl manifesto 'Towards a Newly Shaped World' (1921), which stressed the creative aspect of artistic activity. From its earliest formulation De Stijl architecture had rejected completely the characteristic Functionalist feature of demonstrating visibly the structure of the building, called a bare, anatomical approach by Van Doesburg in 'The New Aesthetics and its Realization' in 1922. The passage quoted above by Mies van der Rohe may be compared with profit to an introductory paragraph of the Van Doesburg article which states, 'Neither does the placing side by side or on top of each other of boxes or cells of a predetermined standard type connote plastic

81

architecture . . .' and 'the (seemingly) economic organization of space found in standardized town-planning actually stands in the way of the progress of plastic architecture'.[2]

In the following year, 1928, *De Stijl* carried some reproductions of works by Mies van der Rohe.[3] Their presence in *De Stijl* indicates that Van Doesburg realized the change which had taken place in Mies van der Rohe's aesthetic ideas. Yet, as a consequence of his reaction to the upsurge of Functionalism at this time Van Doesburg emphasized the importance of painting in an article published in September, 'On the Relationship of Plastic Form in Painting and Architecture'.[4] Nevertheless, his remarks on the Weissenhofsiedlung in an article of his series 'The Renovation of Architecture in Other Countries', published in *Bouwbedrijf*, leave no

doubt about how Van Doesburg truly felt about the current situation in architecture. The December issue of this periodical carried a Van Doesburg contribution specially dedicated to the exhibition, 'The House' (the Weissenhofsiedlung) in Stuttgart. He observed that, 'Due to the initiative of the architect, Mies van der Rohe, by far the strongest personality of the German Constructivist group and the core of the group around *G* (a magazine which published only five issues), the collective ideal of a demonstrative exhibition of architecture was almost completely realized', and that 'There are no buildings which reveal so much of the painter and so little of the constructor as those by Le Corbusier.'[5] This sentence was, of course, a reference to the fact that, like Van Doesburg, this architect was originally a painter.

De Stijl's jubilee issue, 1917–27

In the Jubilee issue of *De Stijl*: 1917–27, prepared in 1927 and published early in 1928, Van Doesburg presented a mixture of feelings. On the one hand, he had every reason to be satisfied, since, despite many misinterpretations, much of what he stood for, in practice as well as in theory, was already exerting its influence. On the other hand, he realized that his enthusiasm for a De Stijl culture of a new plastic expression had led him to neglect his personal interests. It was his conviction – and this is essential for the understanding of his personality and of the collective idea of De Stijl – that there could be neither cultural nor personal achievement without self-denial. In his view De Stijl represented a supra-individual conception of plastic art to be realized collectively by men who have divested themselves of their individualism, but

not their individuality. However, it proved difficult to bring principle and practice into harmony. The article in this Jubilee issue, 'Dates and Facts (Concerning the Development of De Stijl's Influence Abroad) which Speak for Themselves',[1] must be read with care regarding several dates. Presenting a survey of De Stijl, Van Doesburg himself acknowledged that these dates needed to be checked, since he wrote the article in the Vosges, without having at his disposal all the documents in his studio in Paris.

The Jubilee issue contains contributions by Van 't Hoff, Huszar, Kok, Mondrian, Oud, Van Leusden, Rietveld, Vantongerloo, Wils, Arp, Ball, Brancusi, Burchartz, Domela, Van Eesteren, Graeff, Kiesler, Röhl and Vordemberge Gildewart. All were represented either with photographs or with texts, the latter in most cases especially written for the occasion. Van Doesburg, however, did not obtain a recently written contribution from Mondrian. Instead Mondrian wrote the following note, dated 4 December 1927: 'Dear Van Doesburg, After your authoritative improvement (?) of Neo-plasticism any collaboration has become impossible. I regret being unable to prevent any reproduction of my articles and photos in the present *De Stijl*. For the rest, I do not feel any rancour either, Piet Mondrian.'[2] In view of the differences, this reaction need cause no surprise.

The Jubilee issue included a Neo-plastic design for a house interior by Del Marle, made at Wimereux in 1927, and a theatre design by Kiesler from 1925. Theories related to Van Doesburg's were condensed in a series of maxims by Kiesler who called for 'A system of tension in free space. The change of space in urbanism. No foundations, no walls. The detachment from the earth, the suppression of the static axis. By creating new possibilities for life, a new society will develop.'[3] A concern with the law of gravity was fundamental to the thinking of both Kiesler and Van Doesburg. Kiesler's Elementarist construction, which was to become an important model for much modern design, especially in relation to methods of public display, was directed towards creating an architecture which seemed to hover in space. Like Van Doesburg's model for a studio house, Kiesler's design was equally indebted to Cubism. For both men the static (Newtonian) world order based on the law of gravity was superseded by the concept of matter in motion.

However, their struggle against the law of gravity and static forms did not necessarily imply that the two men sought to produce dynamic works in which the gravitational centre had been lost. Although Kiesler had suppressed the static axis in his constructions, he did not precipitously eliminate all sense of a gravitational centre. Only in some of Van Doesburg's Elementarist paintings did this happen, and not in his four-dimensional Neo-plastic architecture, which always maintained its sense of gravitational centre. Where he did 'abandon' gravitation in his Elementarist painting, this was because Van Doesburg believed life was a 'perpetual transformation', accepting its 'chaos' and rejecting its 'intervals'. In some Elementarist paintings (e.g. *Counter-composition XVI*, 1925, p. 152) the space-time continuum can become the visual expression of a continuous flow, of an endless infinite.

A series of photographs (pp. 65–8) in the Jubileee issue was intended to demonstrate the influence of De Stijl on architecture by Mallet-Stevens, Malevich, Le Corbusier and Gropius.

The Aubette, Strasbourg, 1926–8

The redesigning of the interior of the Aubette which Van Doesburg began in 1926 was completed early in 1928. The Aubette was a large restaurant and, in fact, an historic monument, built by Francis Blondel in Strasbourg in 1764–7. Van Doesburg had obtained this commission through Hans Arp, who was also to participate in the project, together with his wife, Sophie Tauber-Arp. It was a gigantic task which was to involve Van Doesburg in making

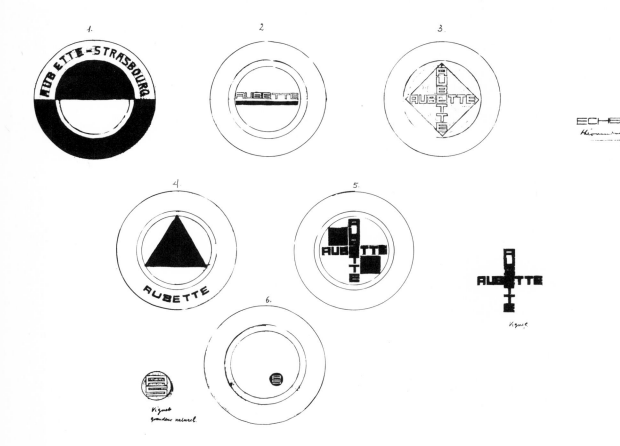

Design for text on ashtrays and vignette for the
Aubette, Strasbourg, undated, around 1927
ink on paper, 42×64 cm. (17×25 in.)
Collection of Mrs Nelly van Doesburg
Photo: P. Willi

199 drawings during the two-year period. The
drawings range in function from designs for the
large cinema and dance hall (pp. 172, 173, 176)
to sketches for a new type of ashtray (above).

A special issue of *De Stijl* was devoted to the
Aubette. A description of Van Doesburg's
method of working can be found in it, and in
the last issue of the magazine. He applied large
coloured rectangles, separated by contour strips
(see p. 176). This produced the effect of low
relief when the strips were mounted, as in the
decoration of the Festivity Hall, and of high

relief when the planes were mounted, as in the Cinema and Dance Hall. Van Doesburg explained this attempt at colour-construction by writing that the, 'Painting of the ceiling and the walls in the Festivity Hall and in the Cinema and Dance Hall was executed in relief for two reasons; first, because in this way I obtained a better defined surface avoiding the predominance of any colour, second, because the fusion of two colours became an absolute impossibility'.[1] No doubt, apart from the two-dimensional aspect (i.e. those of height and width which lead the eye from top to bottom and from left to right along the wall surface), another spatial direction, that of depth, played a role in transforming painting into relief. Van Doesburg explored both possibilities: in one case he mounted thirty-centimetre-wide and three-centimetre-thick strips on the wall surface, which produced planes separated in low relief; in the other he raised the planar surfaces four centimetres above the wall surface, with thirty-five-centimetre-wide strips lying in between, which produced high relief. Thus Van Doesburg came very close to that phase of spatial development which would evolve from Neo-plasticism and Constructivism, and in which painting evolved into relief and subsequently into the construction of coloured planes in actual space. His earlier experience with the architectural models notwithstanding, actual working in the architectural space of the Aubette doubtless provided the necessary opportunity suited to such an approach. The Neo-plastic design of the festivity hall employing strictly orthogonal elements, and the Elementarist oblique composition of the Cinema and Dance Hall showed respectively how 'static' Neo-plasticism was presented in (passive) low relief, whereas 'dynamic' Elementarism employed (active) high relief.

The compositions for these walls, consisting of planes predominantly coloured with several shades of grey, were based on the multiplication of a standard measure of 120 by 120 centimetres. Apart from presenting painting as the destruction of architecture, they embody a concept of architecture as an expansive entity, especially in the design for the Cinema and Dance Hall.

Another interesting feature was the staircase (p. 168), designed by Van Doesburg and painted by Hans Arp, the form of which was reminiscent of Oud's Wrightian staircase in the holiday resort at Noordwijkerhout.

Van Doesburg also designed an alphabet especially for the Aubette, which was used for the neon façade and for several other signs.

Although he had put into practice in the Aubette an ideal similar to Kandinsky's idea of man standing within painting, Van Doesburg, in his diary, expressed doubts about his achievement by weighing the design of this interior against the argument for a neutral, that is to say, white architecture.[2]

Shortly after the Second World War, the owners of the Aubette decided to have the interior design changed. It was replaced with decorations consisting of palm trees and nude figures.

In Strasbourg Van Doesburg simultaneously had executed another commission, the redesigning of the front and the interior of a shop, Maison Meyer (Rue du Vieux Marché aux Poissons).

The Aubette issue of *De Stijl* contained another important article, 'Elementarism and its Origins' (p. 166)[3] which was a kind of summary of earlier fragmentary manifestos. Now reminiscent of Futurism, there was more stress on the heroic character of Elementarism. Once more Van Doesburg posited a scientific basis for Elementarism. However, in spite of the 'rapports' (i.e. intervals) in Elementarist painting, this was still experienced as an infinite

Two views of the cinema and dance hall in the
Aubette, Strasbourg, France, 1928 (destroyed)

extension, and did not as yet include, as it was to later, arithmetic and mathematics as the basis of art.[4]

A much clearer statement in the same issue is contained in the article 'Space-time and Colour' (p. 175).[5] In connection with the use of relief in the two main halls in the Aubette, Van Doesburg described earlier 'monumental wall-painting' as a 'linear termination of the picturesque in space' (possessing two dimensions) in contrast to the interiors in the Aubette where man is placed within painting, architecture and painting having become 'the plastic expression of a tangible object' (in three dimensions). Not surprisingly, he referred again to his collaboration with Van Eesteren in 1923 and explained his use of colour in the architectural models as serving to stress the dimensions of height, width and depth.[6]

The Meudon house

The fact that much of the earlier theoretical ambiguity has been eliminated may have resulted from Van Doesburg's return to pre-1924, to Neo-plastic principles, with the designing of his private studio house in Meudon (pp. 170, 171 and 174). In 1927 he drew his first design for this house, which it was intended was to be shared with Hans Arp's family. The strip-like size of the lot, which was bought in 1926, ensured that the design would have a rectangular character. This produced a rather formal design, in which an interior wall, centrally placed, separated the apartments. In 1928, the first site had come to be considered unsuitable due to its rectangular character, and both the Arp and the Van Doesburg families had their eye on another, better proportioned piece of land. The second design was thus still intended for both families (in contrast to the third). Its groundplan is very interesting as it shows a new preoccupation of Van Doesburg's: the element of number. It consists of four interpenetrating squares of approximately six metres to a side. With the addition of two interpenetrating squares of the plan for the top floor (the second apartment), this amounts to six squares of six metres to a side.

Like his earlier visualization of the fourth dimension in the second and third of the Paris models, this design employs interpenetration, with the implied forty-five degree angle again present. In these two designs nearly all spatial points which determine the length of the walls, the position of the separating walls and even those of beds and cupboards are once more co-ordinated along this one basic angle. But since the oblique is implied rather than visible, the designs belong to Neo-plasticism rather than to Elementarism. Significantly, in one example of Elementarist architecture – Elementarist in Van Doesburg's sense – Le Corbusier, in one of his designs for the Citrohan series in 1924, constructed a mezzanine along the diagonal of the groundfloor, thus visibly and tangibly establishing the forty-five degree angle.

The third design (p. 171), which was made after each family had decided to build a separate house, was nonetheless intended for the same site, since it retained approximately the same width. This later groundplan employed three interpenetrating squares of approximately six metres to a side, in addition to a terrace which is only sketchily indicated and loosely related to the building. Again an implied forty-five degree angle serves to coordinate several points in space. Both the second and third designs possess an identifiable centre.

The third design was never produced either, because the site Van Doesburg was ultimately able to buy possessed only half the width required for that plan, consequently a fourth design became necessary.

Nevertheless, the second and third designs, crudely drawn by Van Doesburg, are very important. They reveal his instinctive intention to build the Meudon house according to his stated artistic principles, which only adverse financial circumstances forced him to abandon in his fourth and final design.

The final plan for the Meudon house came under construction in 1929. The narrow limits of the new site forced Van Doesburg to use a groundplan consisting of one rectangle. In other respects, too, the design was not very different from the then modern, so-called studio-type of architecture based on Le Corbusier's

Theo van Doesburg, Nelly van Doesburg and
Antony Kok, The Hague, 1926

'Maison Citrohan', which in its turn was a development from that tradition in architecture which via Loos leads back to Tony Garnier. In his Meudon house Van Doesburg employed movable screens to limit or extend space; some tables were built in and he designed several chairs as well for its furniture. Because of his sudden death, little was realized of the original colour-scheme for the house, and as a result its over-all impression is white. The drawings for the final Meudon house were made by A. Elzas, an architect who came to study with Van Doesburg in 1929.[1]

Simultaneously with the design for the Meudon house Van Doesburg produced a plan for a city without streets, published under the title, 'The Traffic Town'.[2] Here Van Doesburg was both influenced by and synthesizing ideas presented by Sant'Elia (traffic on different levels above the earth; the 'passerelles') and Le Corbusier (the design for a town quarter standing on columns of 1915 and the ground-

89

plan for a quarter of a 'sky-scraper town' of 1920). Possibly Sant'Elia and Le Corbusier as well as Van Doesburg, who was a great admirer of Da Vinci, were elaborating upon ideas for an ideal town which this Italian master had con-

ceived towards the end of the fifteenth century. Da Vinci's town was meant to consist of two levels; the one below facilitating all commercial and industrial demands, the one above serving the enjoyment of living and recreation.

Two chairs, 1929.
Metal frame, leather upholstery.
Photo: L'Art en photographie

In contrast to Le Corbusier's Weissenhof architecture, where several parts were cantilevered as the result of the columns having been placed within the periphery of the design, Van Doesburg's town plan pushes the columns outward so that the architecture is hung between four poles. Each pole contains a lift for access to the different floors which can be reached through suspended corridors ('*passerelles*').

An unpublished drawing by Van Doesburg closely connected with the plan for a traffic town is more interesting than the actual design. This drawing was based on the final design for the Meudon house, where the extending studio part above the terrace is supported by columns placed at the outer edge of the building. As such the Meudon house is in accordance with the design for a studio house of 1923, where cantilevered parts were also intended to rest upon columns that remained visible. They were not built into the model, since Van Doesburg wished to produce a purely demonstrative piece of new plastic expression in architecture, and the problem of construction thereby remained unsettled.

The 1929 drawing, also made by A. Elzas, presents three Meudon houses placed one above the other with the spatial position of each building respectively showing a rotation of ninety degrees on the previous one. In order to remove the impression of kinetics, this rotation takes place both clockwise and anti-clockwise in reference to the first house which is placed as if on ground level. Moreover, the three houses are not exactly on top of one another but partly overlap in an effort to suggest the notion of vertical interpenetration. Though far from presenting a solution, this drawing makes an interesting contribution towards the most difficult technical problem in Neo-plastic architecture; how to realize the four-dimensional aspect *simultaneously* in the groundplan and in the elevation, so that this plural-dimensional architecture would not remain restricted permanently to the bungalow type of building. Thus the drawing makes clear that Van Doesburg was well aware of the intricate problems of construction involved in his vision of a new architecture. This is why he began to use a method common in the architecture of his day – construction with columns.

Years of reflection

The many articles as well as the books Van Doesburg had in preparation between 1928–30, make it clear that he hoped to make art-historical writing and art-criticism a future source of income. At the same time, he was trying to bring some system into his views as a theoretician. He began to write an auto-biographical sketch, which he called, *Some Biographical Notes on the Painter and Architect Theo van Doesburg*,[1] and in the January 1929 issue of the *Neue Schweizer Rundschau*, he published the first of five articles entitled 'The Struggle for the New Style',[2] dealing with the aims and achievements of De Stijl.

These five articles represent in their entirety the first two parts of a book which he intended to publish under the same title and as the fourteenth volume to appear in the Bauhaus series.

The book was to consist of three parts: an introduction, a brief summary of the principles, and a discussion of architecture as the synthesis of a new plastic expression. The introduction is an historical survey not very different from the article 'Dates and Facts, etc.' in the Jubilee issue of *De Stijl*. The 'Brief Summary of the Principles' is identical with the manuscript 'The Importance of the Fourth Dimension in the New Plastic Art and Architecture',[3] announced as in preparation in the last issue of *De Stijl* (the Van Doesburg issue), but which appeared in the *Neue Schweizer Rundschau*, no. 8, August 1929. The third part, 'Architecture as the Synthesis of a New Plastic Expression' remained an incomplete, unprinted manuscript. Van Doesburg designated it Part Two (a); the only sections complete in themselves are, 'Aims', 'Systematics' and 'Graph of the Development from Perspective Illusionism, Towards the Plane (F) and Onwards to the Creation of New Realms' (see p. 188).

In the third point of 'Brief Summary of the Principles' Van Doesburg discusses the square. This is of particular interest in reference to his second and third design for the Meudon house and to his later arithmetical compositions. The square, despite its symmetry, is posited as 'the basic form of modern times'. In his fifth point he discusses the expression of space-time and makes important statements on the plurality of axis in architecture, and on the plane of the canvas as a limited medium. He sees this limitation as the reason why the contemporary painter was forced to acknowledge architectural, functional space as the sole meaningful plastic realm. In this connection 'Graph of the Development from Perspective Illusion Towards the Plane (F) and Onwards to the Creation of New Realms', is a revealing document. Apart from presenting the theoretical basis for the development from painting towards constructing in

actual space, it shows that the Aubette reliefs represent an integral part of Van Doesburg's research in these years. Thus, in his 1929 'Simultaneous Composition' we find painting closely connected with the approach of two- or three-dimensionality, when horizontal-vertical lines are superimposed upon horizontal-vertical planes.[4] On the other hand, in the section 'Systematics' the Elementarist forty-five degree angle, until this moment posited as the expression of contrast to the horizontal-vertical, is now said, surprisingly, to express 'the oppositionless' as distinct from 'the strongest opposition' which is expressed by the horizontal-vertical. Hegel's *Philosophy of Spirit* again plays a role here, since the spirit which knows itself as all reality, which has no opposite, which sees in itself the whole of being, is said to be entirely free.[5]

The 'Systematics' was written approximately around the same time as the 'Brief Summary of the Principles', which was published in August 1929. There is no doubt that the notion of 'the oppositionless' also derived from the friendship between Van Doesburg and Mondrian which had been restored a few months earlier in that same year. The horizontal-vertical again is viewed as the expression of the strongest opposition, through which circumstance the plastic visualization of the oblique, which expresses 'the oppositionless', is almost denied. This would involve a return to the implied oblique of Neo-plasticism.

Instead Van Doesburg tried to synthesize a new 'polarity', that of the oppositionless and the oppositional in *Simultaneous Counter-composition XXI* of 1929 (p. 94) a painting in which the diagonal planes are combined with horizontal-vertical planes and lines. This painting resulted from his almost desperate effort to bestow again upon Neo-plasticism a dynamic quality. In his *Simultaneous Counter-composi-*

Simultaneous Counter-composition XXI 1929
oil on canvas, 50×50 cm. (20×20 in.)
Collection of Mrs A. Mueller-Widman

tion of 1929, which is in the collection of the Sidney Janis Gallery, New York, the forty-five degree angle is replaced by an obliquity of both lines and planes set at various 'free' angles, which illustrates the Hegelian concept of entirely free spirit (see p. 98).

The extent of Van Doesburg's influence had spread, as became apparent from Moholy-Nagy's Bauhaus book *From the Material Towards Architecture*,[6] later called *The New Vision*.[7] Section Four especially, which deals with architectural space, is indebted to ideas Van Doesburg spread during his stays in Weimar and Berlin between 1921 and 1923. Illustration thirty-six, showing the scattered side walls of a volume, thereby originating planar spatial relationships, described by Moholy-Nagy as containing the conception of a new architecture, is a reproduction of Van Doesburg's drawing of architectural planes suspended in space, made in 1923 on the occasion of the Paris models and published by 1924 in his Bauhaus book *The Principles of Neo-plastic Art* as illustration three. Moreover, since Van Doesburg's Bauhaus book consisted of a translation of a text written as early as 1918, it does not present as clear a description of his notion of mass as does his architectural programme of 1924. In the Bauhaus book it is said that, 'The pure means of expression in architecture are the plane, mass (positive) and space (negative). The architect expresses his aesthetic experience by means of the relationships of planes and masses to inner and outer space.' Van Doesburg's programme of 1924, however, makes clear that not architectural 'mass' but 'form' is built of space-cells (Point Eleven), which consist of separating and protecting planes (Point Nine) possessing a direct relationship of tension with open, exterior space (Point Five). Thus it is clear that for Van Doesburg, architectural 'mass' must be understood as the plastic articu-

lation of space-plane relationships, which create space cells of non-massive architectural 'form'.

One section of Moholy-Nagy's book, which appears under the heading 'Instead of Static: Kinetic', argues that 'real spatial experience rests on simultaneous interpenetration of inside and outside, above and beneath, on the communication of the in and the out, on the invisible play of forces present in the materials and their relationships in space'. This 'spatial experience' also rests on 'space-creation' conceived as 'an interweaving of the parts of space, which are anchored, for the most part, in clearly traceable relations extending in all directions as a fluctuating play of forces'.[8]

This discussion in fact summarizes concepts presented by Van Doesburg in 'The New Aesthetics and its Realization', and 'Towards a Plastic Architecture'. Moholy-Nagy's Points Six and Seven, which are found under the heading 'The Historical Sequence', respectively refer to Wright's architecture, illustrated by the Robie house, as being on 'every side perforated, fluctuating horizontally', and to Gropius' architecture, illustrated with a fragment of the fenestration of the Bauhaus building, as representing 'the same, opened in the vertical direction; the interpenetration takes place not only sideways, but also up and down, as, for example, a ship's bridge, the work of Gropius, Corbusier, Oud, Mies van der Rohe, and the young architects'. The latter statement, however, is an incorrect interpretation of the facts. The elevations of the Bauhaus building and of the other examples of modern architecture to which Moholy-Nagy refers in his Point Seven do not show vertical interpenetration. Only Van Doesburg's Paris model for a studio house of 1923 attempted to achieve as much vertical plasticity as was demonstrated horizontally in its groundplan. The technical problems of constructing this vertical plasticity have proved so great that the whole of modern architecture, with the chance exception of Le Corbusier's cantilevered buildings in the Weissenhofsiedlung, has left them unresolved to the present day. As was demonstrated above, Van Doesburg was quite aware of this problem. It is very likely that he drew the three Meudon houses vertically interpenetrating in reaction to Moholy-Nagy's Point Seven. Another proof that this drawing is a reaction to Moholy-Nagy is that in contrast to his 'Instead of Static: Kinetic' Van Doesburg wanted to avoid kinetics by projecting the Meudon house in both a clockwise and anti-clockwise direction. By so doing he was rejecting the suggestion (or incorporation) of physical motion as posited by Kemeny and Moholy-Nagy in their manifestos.

Another influence of Van Doesburg's can be found in Mies van der Rohe's German Pavilion at the International Exhibition in Barcelona, which was built in 1929. Its elevation is a clear demonstration of Van Doesburg's Point Seven, since it displays a strong contrast between 'openness' in the glass-partitions and a 'closed' quality in the wall surfaces. The groundplan only partially realizes Van Doesburg's concepts by maintaining a U-shaped enclosure at each end. Mies van der Rohe's Tugendhat house in Brno, Czechoslovakia, which followed in the next year, was to show that the new architecture posed much more complicated constructional problems when dealing with a building consisting of two floors than for a bungalow type of building.

To what extent Van Doesburg, in spite of his return to painting and his building a house not entirely expressing his architectural aims, remained attached to his theory of architecture, is also proven by his article on 'The Renovation of Art and Architecture in Italy'[9] in reaction to an article by Fillia, called 'Futurism and Fascism'[10] and published in the first issue of

La città futurista of April 1929. Fillia's piece was extremely chauvinistic in describing Sant-'Elia as the father of all modern architecture. Van Doesburg, by way of reply, discussed the eight points of Sant'Elia's architectural programme of 1914. He criticized specifically Sant-'Elia's concept of architecture as a synthesis of pure plastic expression instead of as a combination of utilitarian demands (Point Two), his notion that a dynamic architecture cannot exist without oblique and elliptic lines (Point Three), and his belief that future architecture would provide the architect with a maximum of freedom and audacity so that the material world would be the immediate projection of the spiritual world (Point Seven). Van Doesburg's criticism illustrates again his life-long discussion with Futurism and explains why Neo-plasticism soon shunned the curve. Neo-plasticism is now seen as combining the economy which is an essential characteristic of all (classical) composition in art with the economy which results from practical demands:

> From points Two, Three and Seven the essential difference between the new international and Italian Futurist architecture becomes sufficiently apparent. These points cannot serve as the basis of a rigidly constructive, elementary-plastic architecture, but, on the contrary, produce rather an arbitrary-aesthetic architecture mainly dependent upon personal fantasy and superficiality. The worship of elliptical and oblique lines in architecture is incompatible, not only with the most economical methods of construction, but also with the principle of velocity which was always favoured by the Futurists. Velocity, the outcome of a new pragmatic vision of life, is the basic cause of mechanical perfection and modern

intelligence as expressed by the image of the straight line. This new manifestation of velocity, on which the straight line is based, thus necessarily became the characteristic fundamental of a new style. The viability and durability of this orthogonal style is dependent on the mastering not only of form but also of the architectural means.

This quotation further shows that Van Doesburg kept his orthogonal architecture separate from the visual oblique of Elementarism, since here the oblique in architecture is rejected. It also indicates the increasing need by Van Doesburg to realize his new architecture in actual practice, which is implied by the last sentence in the quotation.

Art Concret

Although in 1929 the friendship with Mondrian was restored, Van Doesburg continued to further explore his Elementarist direction. References Van Doesburg wrote in his diary, 'The renewed friendship with Mondrian provides both of us with the pleasant experience of mutual support. In spite of the differences, a more profound friendship has now become possible . . .' (May 1929).[1]

These artistic differences would further crystallize in the following year, when because of his need for absolute objectivity, Van Doesburg was to introduce arithmetics, despite its 'classical' character, as the basis of his Concrete Art. This scientific attitude shows Van Doesburg still at odds with Mondrian's intuitive approach.

In April, the first and last issue of Van Doesburg's third magazine *Art Concret* appeared, containing a new manifesto 'The Basis of Concrete Painting',[2] which was signed by Carlsund, Van Doesburg, Helion, Tutundjian and Wantz (p. 180). The second point of this document reads as follows:

> The work of art should be fully conceived and spiritually shaped before it is produced. It should not contain any natural form,

sensuality or sentimentality.

We wish to exclude lyricism, dramaticism, symbolism, and so forth.

In 'Comments on the Basis of Concrete Painting', he calls for:

> *Concrete* and not *abstract painting*, because we have finished with the period of research and speculative experience.
>
> In their search for purity artists were obliged to abstract from *natural forms* in which the plastic elements were hidden, in order to eliminate natural forms and to replace them with *artistic forms*.
>
> Today the idea of *artistic form* is as obsolete as the idea of *natural form*. We establish the period of pure painting by constructing *spiritual form*. Creative spirit becomes concrete.[3]
>
> (Van Doesburg's italics)

Creative spirit is then further defined as follows: 'Only thought (intellect) which doubtless possesses a speed superior to that of light is *creative*.'[4] Van Doesburg shortly thereafter states that anything not created by thought is

an expression of the baroque. He was repudi-
ating Hegel's fundamental type of romantic
art, and also reacting against Hegel's idea that
religion or philosophy were eventual substitutes
for art. In so doing he came very close to
Schoenmaekers' *Principles of Plastic Mathematics*, as pointed out earlier, and doubtless his
term 'concrete' derived from this same mystic

philosophy. It is possible that Mondrian, who
always remained much closer to Schoenmaekers'
ideas, again drew Van Doesburg's attention to
the Dutch philosopher's criticism of Hegel.
Schoenmaekers defined Hegel's 'pantheism' as
a characteristic example of 'contemplative-
concrete pantheism' in contrast to his own
'visual-concrete pantheism'. He wrote, 'Visual-

concrete pantheism also acknowledges, consistently, the relationship of counterparts of Creation and Nature, but, in its elaboration, does not commit the error of substituting opposites for counterparts. It visualizes externality in nature as a plastic union of counterparts.'[5] Thus it was Schoenmaekers' view that one thing can be another's counterpart without

(left) *Simultaneous Counter-composition*   1929
oil on canvas, 50×50 cm. (20×20 in.)
Collection of Sidney Janis Gallery, New York

Arithmetic composition   1930
oil on canvas, 101×101 cm. (40×40 in.)
Collection of Mr F. Witzinger

being its opposite. Art and nature are thus considered as counterparts, without necessarily being taken as opposites. This is in fact a criticism of what, in his view, comprised Hegel's categorical use of opposites, which leads to the isolation of one of the components of a polarity (i.e. the spirit). This component is then turned into an absolute entity 'by and for itself', as a substitute for the real unity of related counterparts. Schoenmaekers' criticism of Hegel could equally be applied to Van Doesburg's Elementarist art in that it isolates the spiritual.

The quotation above is taken from Schoenmaekers' eighth chapter: 'The Three Spheres', in which he also says that, 'Arithmetics provides plastic mathematics with the material for plastic thought'.[6] However, it must be added that Hegel's philosophy, too, accepts the notion of number, and another article (or manifesto) by Van Doesburg, written this same year, but posthumously published in 1947 and called 'From Intuition Towards Certitude',[7] describes arithmetical control as the sole means to achieve cultural value. Thus the intuitive approach was finally replaced by a scientific one, which is also illustrated by the arithmetical painting of this year.

Significantly, the first title Van Doesburg had in mind for his magazine *Art Concret* was *Nouveau Plan* (New Plan(e)), which possessed the same initials as Neo-plasticism and doubtless was intended to indicate that intuitive Neo-plasticism survived on a new scientific or arithmetical level. In a fragment from his 'Journal of Ideas',[8] dated 20 August 1930, he admitted that the arithmetical approach may be basically a classical principle, but added that it is universal as well, and the argument was completed by the remark that music and architecture also possess number as their basis. This remark also reflects Van Doesburg's

interest in J. H. de Groot, an Amsterdam architect who published a booklet on arithmetic under the title *Form-composition and Centrality*. While having certain ideas in common with Van Doesburg, De Groot conceived his architectural method as an effort towards the realization of Semper's idea of style as a 'general style',[9] which further relates to the Hegelian views in Kandinsky's *Concerning the Spiritual in Art* that 'the final expression of every art is number'.

Van Doesburg's concept of concrete art also relates to the last chapter in Schoenmaekers' *Principles of Plastic Mathematics*, which follows the chapter 'The Three Spheres' and is called 'The Essence of Catholic Thought'. Schoenmaekers maintained that his mystic philosophy is essentially catholic in the sense that it represents a general (universal) philosophy, in contrast to Roman Catholicism and Protestantism which are based on dogmatism. As he claimed that 'internality' and 'externality' were 'counterparts in unity', Schoenmaekers believed that sensory perception is part of true thought.[10] He described his catholicism as a New Catholicism because it is fully humanistic, adding that a new 'constructive symbolism' would be needed to visualize the essence of the cosmos in terms of an art of relationships or plastic mathematics. Van Doesburg showed a revived interest in religion at this time, almost certainly prompted by this chapter. In 'Towards White Painting', (p. 183) which was written in December 1929, and published in *Art Concert*, he claimed that white was the highest phase of spiritual development in man, an idea which must also be seen in the light of Schoenmaekers' thought. Only after the Second World War, in particular via Swiss Konkrete Kunst (Max Bill, Richard P. Lohse etc.) were Van Doesburg's ideas on concrete art to have a wide impact on Constructivist art circles.

100

Last activities

At approximately the same time that his magazine *Art Concert* appeared, Van Doesburg was involved in designing a studio house for the Hungarian painter, B. Por (p. 193). The groundplan was designed around the interpenetration of three squares, although less clearly than in earlier designs, and several points in space again were determined with an implied forty-five degree angle in mind. In contrast to that of the Meudon house, the terrace is not underneath but above the studio. Regrettably, the building was never made.

In May 1930, Van Doesburg went to Spain to lecture in Madrid and Barcelona. He gave an address on 'The Fundamental Spirit of Contemporary Architecture', which again contained the architectural programme of 1924, albeit in a completely altered version owing to the introduction of new ideas on construction with a system of columns in its Points Eight, Ten, Eleven and Twelve (the latter three, however, were compressed into one point). It is not clear how Van Doesburg intended to combine the linear quality of a construction with columns and an architecture of planes. Remarkably, the last point of the programme of 1924 and 1925, which treats architecture as the synthesis of the arts, has been suppressed, perhaps because, in the meantime, Elementarism and Concrete Art had been born. In this last programme Van Doesburg was aiming at synthesizing his space-time architecture with Functionalism, which was spreading rapidly at this time. There is little doubt that standing criticism of the constructive problems his architecture posed had disturbed Van Doesburg to such a degree that he sought its realization with the con-

struction methods prevalent at the time.

Shortly after his return from Spain in July, Van Doesburg wrote the last fragment of a manifesto on Elementarism, called 'Elementarism: the Elements of the New Painting'.[1] Number and measure are posited as the objective means to complete subjective composition and to elevate it to a general, universal level.

His last remarks in the manifesto, are that the artist's studio must resemble a medical laboratory possessing the atmosphere of high mountains where the cold kills the microbes. Perhaps this statement springs from Van Doesburg's increasing illness at this time. Following his return from Spain, his hay-fever developed into a severe asthma, which caused high fevers and long periods during which he was unable to work. Nevertheless, he went out to supervise the construction of his house at Meudon, and bad weather made him even more ill. Towards the end of the year, the Arp family invited Van Doesburg to come and stay in their house at Meudon, which was quite near the building-site. However, Van Doesburg was not sufficiently well to undertake moving from Paris.

Van Doesburg's Elementarism did not leave Mondrian unaffected. As has been demonstrated above, under this influence, a definite increase in rhythm can be observed in Mondrian's work beginning in 1925, although his compositions remained strictly orthogonal. He also reacted in his written theory. 'Art and Life',[2] contains his reply to Van Doesburg's manifestos on Elementarism. The first section of this essay, called 'New Art – New Life' and written in 1931, contains many paragraphs which can be seen as rejecting ideas presented in the

Theo and Nelly van Doesburg, Davos, 1931

Elementarist manifestos,[3] whereas the second section, 'The True Value of the Oppositions', written in 1934, already reveals by its title the underlying problem facing De Stijl of its dualistic attitude towards matter and mind, nature and art.

The difference between Mondrian's essays 'Natural Reality and Abstract Reality' (1919/20) and 'Art and Life', is that the earlier one demonstrates the relationship of the new art with natural phenomena, whereas the later essay, under the influence of Elementarism, stresses the inventive, creative approach of the artist, thus fully placing art within the domain of man.[4] Although Mondrian realized that 'non-equivalent oppositions'[5] represent a working method for gathering knowledge and insight, his essay 'Art and Life', in which he attempts to verbalize the predominantly conceptual approach as distinct from the purely conceptual approach of the new art of Van Doesburg, does not succeed in establishing theoretically the true equivalence of the material and the spiritual. This conflict between matter and mind increased in all Mondrian's writing which followed. Accordingly, while drawing closer and closer to Van Doesburg's 'prevalence of the spiritual', the difference between Mondrian's orthogonal and Van Doesburg's oblique composition was maintained. One explanation for this fact certainly lies in the different temperaments of the two men. Mondrian, who apparently chose a position of artistic isolation, took as his starting point the new art work which, by its equivalence of pure, orthogonal relationships resulting from inner life, demonstrated the more spiritual 'culture of pure relationships' that would follow in the course of time. Van Doesburg, who considered himself as more or less forced into artistic isolation, assumed the position that life is hostile to the proposed elevation of it by the new art (by means of Neo-plastic architecture). Consequently, he began to isolate the spiritual, demonstratively and with illustrative directness, by giving it form in the visual oblique in painting. Paradoxically, it is from this point of view that Van Doesburg's statement that the spiritual in life is always dynamic when contrasted with life in general, represents, in effect, a renewed effort to reconcile art with life.

Van Doesburg intended the Meudon studio house to become a new centre for De Stijl activities. He hoped to attract there a number of young artists and architects and to start another De Stijl course. At the same time, he occupied himself with the founding of the Abstraction-Creation group, which was to embrace various trends in abstract art. Accordingly Van Doesburg wrote to Kupka:

As it is absolutely impossible to arrange interesting exhibitions or publications by limiting the participants too strictly, we are obliged to unite ourselves on a larger basis. The best artists of Paris and abroad should participate, even when their tendency is not ours.[6]

On 12 February a first meeting was held in Van Doesburg's studio where it was agreed that the group should comprise of the following artists: Albers, Arp, Brancusi, Boothy, Buchheister, Carlsund, Dexel, Van Doesburg, Fernandez, Foltyn, Freundlich, Gabo, Giacometti, Grabowska, Helion, Herbin, Kandinsky, Kiesler, Kupera, Kupka, Lissitzky, Malevich, Man Ray, Miró, Mondrian, Neugeboren (Henri Nouveau), Pevsner, Sartoris, Schwab, Schwitters, Stazewski, Striminski, Taüber-Arp and Tutundjian. This group was to come into existence only shortly after Van Doesburg's death, although in a different combination of artists.

Towards the end of February the increasing gravity of Van Doesburg's asthma forced him to go to Davos, Switzerland, to recuperate. There he painted what were to be his final three canvases. He suddenly died from a heart attack on 7 March 1931, at forty-seven years of age. In January 1932, the last issue of *De Stijl*, the 'Van Doesburg issue', appeared under the editorship of Nelly van Doesburg. In it were printed several of his articles and reproductions including some of his most recent paintings and the groundplans, elevations and cross-sections of the studio house in Meudon. A personal touch was added by printing some fragments from his diary as well as from his 'Journal of Ideas'. Several contributors to *De Stijl*, old and new, wrote on their personal contact with Van Doesburg. Collectively they picture a man with an indestructible belief in a new world which was to appear in a new plastic form. And all acknowledge Van Doesburg's sudden death as a severe loss to the most powerful means of forwarding this aim: De Stijl – the magazine, the idea, the movement.

Part Two

Writings

Articles

Art criticism, modern art in the Stedelijk Museum, Amsterdam, Exhibition Mondrian, Leo Gestel, Sluiters, Schelfhout, Le Fauconnier

(Fragments concerning Mondrian)

Mondrian. The works of this painter above all produce a most spiritual impression. They achieve this all the more because they are hung opposite the prismatic colour-compositions of Leo Gestel in the same room. The problem which Mondrian undertook to solve in nr. 116 was handled very successfully. This work spiritually dominates all others. It gives the impression of Repose; the repose of the soul. Its pre-determined structure embodies 'becoming' rather than 'being'. This represents a true element in art, for art is not 'being' but 'becoming'. The idea of 'becoming' has been expressed in black and white; it derives from the theories of Picasso and Uexkuell. The first of these artists arrived at a metaphysical palette which reduced Luminist prismatic colour to white, black, grey and sepia.

Through years of hard work my own experiences have led me, before I came to know the theories of Uexkuell or Picasso, to prefer the use of the white-black-grey palette in works of a purely spiritual content. The feeling I obtained from painting 116 was of a purely spiritual, almost religious character, which, however, possessed no zeal. . . .

To reduce the artist's means to such a minimum and to produce an impression of pure art using only black paint on a white canvas and horizontal and vertical lines is most extraordinary. This work, however, should be hung separately.

(above) *Composition XIII, Still life* 1918
oil on panel, 29·5 × 29·5 cm.
(12 × 12 in.)
Collection of Mrs J. J. P. Oud.
Photo: L'Art en photographie

(left) *Composition XII, Composition in black
and white* 1918
oil on canvas, 75 × 54·5 cm. (29 × 21 in.)
Collection of Kunstmuseum, Basle,
on loan from E. Hoffmann Foundation

I would like to draw attention to this kind of work. . . .

The other works by Mondrian could be described as coloured architecture. Here too one colour emanates from another. The colours mutually influence each other. In some works the motives which inspired them can still be discerned, without, however, these becoming aesthetically disturbing ('aesthetic' here is not used in its traditional meaning but in the sense of a 'feeling for art'). These works, which produce an extraordinarily elementary or pure impression of art, remain reposeful and dignified in spite of the scornful laughter of the public who always seek the familiar. Mondrian realizes the importance of line. The line has almost become a work of art in itself; one cannot play with it as when the representation of objects perceived was all-important. The white canvas is almost solemn. Each superfluous line, each wrongly placed line, any colour placed without veneration or care, can spoil every-thing – that is, the spiritual.

Eenheid no. 283, 6 November 1915

Thought – Vision – Creation

The development of plastic art is determined by the will to visualize. Art of the past represented the subjective vision of *naturalistic relationships*. Neo-plasticism embodies a subjective vision of *plastic relationships*.

It is wrong to identify the essence of thought with vision, just as it is wrong to identify vision with the sensuous expression of naturalistic form. The latter concept derives from Classical and Roman-Catholic origins and was opposed by Protestantism (iconoclasm).

The nature of thought can be subdivided into three classes: first, pure abstract thought or thought for thought's sake, second, concrete thought or thought for the sake of vision and third, the intermediate class of deformed thought. In pure abstract thought no sensuous associations in perception (of nature) are incorporated. Instead, we find a relationship of concepts. This relationship can be visualized in a precise (mathematical) figure and is also contained in numbers. In this case, expressing the content of pure conceptual thought, one can already speak of plastic vision.

I call concrete that thought which demands the visualization of sensuous associations in perception, for instance of an

Alphabet, 1919

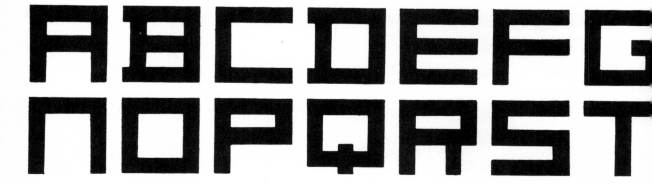

image of memory, which lacks and therefore does not produce any concept.

I call deformed that thought which demands the visualization as an image of memory wherein, however, this image is affected or deformed by the concept. Such images do possess associations with concrete phenomena, but are in an amorphous condition.

Although one has always to operate more or less speculatively in the domain of abstraction, there is good reason to accept this latter manner of visionary thinking about plastic art as true. It displays a similarity with phantasm, and the amorphous character of these mental images or concepts is caused by the predominant influence of feeling (emotion) on thought. We therefore could speak in this case of emotional thought.

The best reason for accepting these three classes of thought as basic to plastic art is the fact that these three classes of thought are expressed in plastic art, or rather in the arts. Secondly, my own development in plastic art during a period of twenty years actually embodied these three classes in successive phases. Anyone who has searched for truth in the plastic domain will have met the expression of this development of thought individually in his life's work – a development which is similar to that experienced by art in general. In the history of art this development is irregular and this is probably also the case with the individual; however, this does not

imply any denial of the distinction of three classes or phases of thought in plastic art.

The normal concrete or realistic type of thought revealed itself in representational art, for example, in the art of Van der Helst (the question of whether or not representation alone is art transcends this argument). This phase in human thought is reflected in physico-plastic art from the paleolithic times until the present day.

Deformed thought, which involves both the concept and sensuous associations in visualization, although neither is manifested definitely, is revealed in the many varieties within the main bulk of ideoplastic works or art from neolithic culture until Van Gogh and others. This class of thought seems to be particularly suited for the production of art, and implies at the same time that in art the concept is predominant.

Pure thought, which does not signify a concept derived from natural phenomena but which is contained in numbers, measures, relationships and abstract lines, is revealed conceptually (as Reason) by Chinese, Greek and German philosophy and aesthetically by contemporary Neo-plasticism.

The artist visualizes plastic relationships. The painter visualizes colour, the sculptor form and the architect spatial relationships. It may be that these relationships are associated with naturalistic or representational form. Then, however, the class of thought containing the will to visualize and the influence

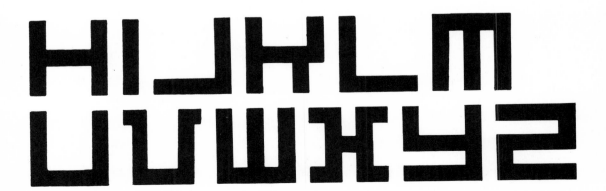

thereof on quality is indicated.

All people are subject to a different class or phase of thought and, as far as the development of thought as mirrored in art reflects this in our times (and probably in all times), it follows that works of art can be distinguished for reflecting one of these three phases of thought.

Deciding which one is the truest phase of thought constitutes the kernel of the debate. This debate can end only when one of the classes or phases is fully dominant, which is to say, when a new manner of thought guides life as a whole and our attitude towards it.

All appreciation or criticism of the plastic expression of a cultivated manner of thought can be seen as valueless, because the truth (philosophical, aesthetic, religious, political or scientific) externalizes itself as real life, as matter, within time.

October 1918
De Stijl vol. II, 2, December 1918, pp. 23–4

Design for a monument in concrete for the city of Leeuwarden, Holland, 1918 (destroyed).
Photo of the model in the collection of
Mrs Nelly van Doesburg

Manifesto II from De Stijl   1920; Literature

LITERATURE
the bulk of contemporary literature is still fed by the sentimentality of a
weakened generation

THE WORD IS DEAD
the naturalistic clichés and the dramatic films of words with which
　　　　　　　　the manufacturers of books supply
　　　　　　　　us
　　　　　　　　by the yard or pound
contain nothing of the new courageous flash of contemporary life

THE POWERLESS WORD
the asthmatic and sentimental
'me' and 'he' poetry

110

which is practised everywhere
and chiefly in Holland
is influenced by an individualism which shuns space,
is the fermented residue of earlier times
and fills us with disgust
the psychology in our novels
is based only upon subjective imagination
psycho-analysis
and encumbering rhetorics
have KILLED THE SIGNIFICANCE OF THE WORD
these sentences put carefully behind and underneath one another
this cold and **FRONTAL** phraseology
in which the earlier realists presented their own narrow
experiences to themselves
are entirely powerless and unable to express the collective notions of our times.

just like the old conception of life
literature is based upon
LONGUEUR and DURATION
it is
VOLUMINOUS
conception of life rests on
PROFUNDITY and INTENSITY
and hence it is this which we wish poetry to encompass

in order to construct verbally the multiplicity of events
around and within us
it is necessary to reestablish the word
according to both its SOUND and its MEANING
since in previous poetry
by means of the predominance of associative and
subjective sentiments
the intrinsic significance of the word was destroyed
we wish to grant with all the means at our disposal
syntax
prosody
typography
arithmetic
orthography
a new significance to the word and new power to the expression
the dualism between prose and poetry cannot survive
the dualism between content and form cannot survive

for the modern writer form will therefore possess an immediate
spiritual significance
he will not describe an event
he will not DEscribe at all
instead he will WRITE
through the word he will re-create events in their interrelation
a constructive unity of content and form

we count upon the moral and aesthetic support of all those who collaborate
towards the spiritual renovation of the world

Leyden, Holland april 1920   theo van doesburg/piet mondrian/anthony kok

De Stijl vol. III, 6, April 1920, pp. 52–4

X-Images (I. K. Bonset)

I am penetrated by the room where
        the streetcar slides through
        I am wearing a cap

the sounds of an organ
are-within-me and-outside-me
fall and break behind me
        small fragments
        TIN TIN TIN
        and glass
little black cyclists
glide and vanish in my image
           + LIGHT
the like-mad rustling top of the tree
        splits up my environment
        into multicoloured dust
        the black and white water piles
                4 × HORIZONTAL

        countless vertical piles
        and also the high
        curved blue
           SPACE
           AM I

De Stijl vol. III, 7, May 1920, p. 54

Caminoscopy (Aldo Camini)

An anti-philosophical view of life without any thread or system

1   A chapter without a head

Electricity is my line. I despise Pascoli (Giovanni Pascoli, famous Italian poet of the old school). I pity Croce (Benedetto Croce, the famous Italian philosopher and aesthetician). In my belief, art, religion, philosophy, science and alcohol are all consequences of doubt. However, as soon as we face and conquer through conviction the errors upon which we have founded our lives we shall arrive at a new stage of life which will lead us towards the supremacy of being. I enjoy observing the automatic and careful movements of the somnambulist. These movements are visibly more assured than the consciously executed tick-tack of telegraph instruments, although the latter may succeed admirably in answering our need for the conquest of space and time. Those who think I am writing an apology for Futurism are wrong. I see life as conceived and described through me, and it impresses me as utterly astonishing that no straight line exists in the spaces of our realistic, anti-abstract thinking capacity. This shows me that no definite content exists for the basis of life. Consequently, a philosophy or a science which follows a systematic hypothesis is impractical. I therefore consider philosophy either absolute charlatanism or childishness. For fear of wandering from the only truth that interests me (i.e. life), I must let this train of thought slip into limbo. . . . Truth is not the whole of life, which is why all intellectual activities are fictitious. Thought never touches life, and everything described as 'the purpose of life' changes *neither* life nor ourselves. The mistake is obvious; professional thinkers and scientists always considered 'life' and 'ourselves' as two different things, with our mind being considered a kind of trap and a hypothesis viewed as the bait with which life could be caught. However, we belong to life and each acknowledgement is 'caught' by its negation. If we once study the amalgamations of metal which (by the contrast between dynamic and static) motorially exercise a power definable in numbers and acknowledge them as totally equivalent to our flesh and the wounds in our flesh, we shall no longer be able to differentiate between the functioning of our brains and that of a drilling machine. I never wondered about this like Papini, nor did I consider the mind a pit containing everyone and everything as does Gentile.

De Stijl vol. IV, 5, June 1921, pp. 66–7

Manifesto III   Towards a newly shaped world

The creation of a new world has commenced. Capitalists are deceivers and so are the Socialists. The former want to possess, and so do the latter. The former seek to swallow large amounts of money, large numbers of human beings and many steaks; the latter

wish to swallow the former. Which is worse?
Will either succeed?

We do not care in the least.

We know just one thing; only the
exponents of the new spirit are sincere.
Their wish is solely to give. Gratuitously.
They arise among all nations, among all
countries. They do not boast in deceiving
phrases. They do not call each other 'brother',
'maestro' or 'partisan'. Theirs is the language
of the mind, and in this manner they
understand each other.

The creators of a new mentality for our
time do not found sects, churches or schools.

In the old world spiritual concentration
(Christ) and material concentration
(Capitalism), *property*, represented the axes
around which everyone rotated. *Today,
however, the spiritual concentration has been
dispersed.* Yet exponents of the new creative
mind are linked together through a common
inner life.

There is no escape for Europe. Spiritual
concentration and property, intellectual and
material individualism, were the basis of
the old Europe. It has imprisoned itself
within those ideas, and it cannot liberate
itself. The situation is fatal. We are watching
this situation quietly; even if it were in our
power to intervene, we would not. We do
not desire to prolong the life of this old
prostitute.

A new Europe already is arising thanks to
us. The first, second and third Socialist
Internationals constituted ridiculous
nonsense; they were merely words. The
International of the Mind is an inner
experience which cannot be translated into
words. It does not consist of a torrent of
vocables but of plastic creative acts and inner
or intellectual force, which thus creates a
newly shaped world.

We do not summon the various nations to
'unite' or to 'join us'. *We do not incite nations
to anything. We know that everybody who joins
us belongs to the new. The spiritual substance
of the new world will be modelled by them alone.
Create!*

De Stijl vol. IV, 8, August 1921, pp. 125–6

X-Images (1920) (I. K. Bonset)

hey   hey   hey
did you experience it physically
did you experience it p h y s i c a l l y
did you exPERience it ph y s i c a l l y
0ⁿ
    — space and
    — time
    past present future
    the behindhereandthere
    the mix-up of the nought and the phenomenon
            a small crumpled almanac

114

which is read upside down

MY CLOCK HAS STOPPED
zig-zag   a chewed cigarette butt on the
              WHITE NAPKIN
moist brown
decay
SPIRIT
346 MO TOR TRUCK
diagonal   trembling sterile centre
caricature of heaviness
uomo electrico
pink and grey and dark wine—red
the splinters of the cosmos are in my cup of tea

Note: '0^n' should be read as zero^n; '$-$space' and '$-$time' should be read as minus space and minus time.

De Stijl vol. IV, 11, November 1921, p. 161

The will to style

The new form expression of life, art and technology (Lecture held in Jena, Weimar, and Berlin)

In addition to commercial and economic problems of renovation in Europe, the position of art is a matter for great concern. Apart from the extent to which these problems are intrinsically related, we know only that the solution for both economic and artistic problems transcends an individual approach, and this we consider an advantage. It means that the predominance of the individual (the Renaissance attitude towards life) has been supplanted.

Only collective solutions can be decisive in the realms both of politics and art.

If we study the full picture of contemporary life through the medium of our *eyes*, we must conclude that this picture is chaotic in character. It should therefore not surprise us that those who feel uneasy amidst this seeming chaos either withdraw from this world or lose themselves in spiritual abstractions. However, it must be clear to us that this escape from reality is as much an error as the acceptance of pure materialism. Neither the transcendentalism of the Middle Ages, nor the reconstruction of Olympus as advertised by several art historians can provide us with a solution. Our period has a mission to fulfil other than that of studying the Middle Ages or Hellenism. In order to grasp the correct task of our times, it is

115

 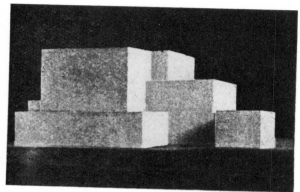

Study of a purely architectonic sculpture, based
on its groundplan. Model at Weimar by Bernard
Sturzkopf, student of architecture in
Van Doesburg's De Stijl course at Weimar, 1922

Study of a purely architectonic sculpture, based on
a groundplan. Weimar model by Hans Vogel,
student of architecture in Van Doesburg's
De Stijl course at Weimar, 1922

 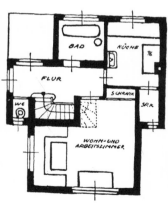 

necessary to understand the structure of life, although not so much merely with our eyes as with our *inner vision*. Once we have achieved a synthesis of life by utilizing our most profound inner being and acknowledging this life to represent the content of culture and art, it will be easier for us to arrive at a solution to the problem of art by using the means of the documents handed on by Tradition. We are not the only ones who strive for a solution to the problem of art; many generations have attempted this before us. This is illustrated in all important works of art from the past. Despite the variety of forms which these expressions of art present to our visual experience, such human creations appear to our inner vision only as the surface image of a struggle taking place within our inner being.

Of what character, then, is this struggle which takes place not only in art, science, philosophy and religion but in our daily life as shown in the struggle for a spiritual-materialistic existence?

Every work of art, past or present, provides an answer. This struggle is based on the structure of life and comprises a battle between two opposite forces.

Whether we call these forces nature and spirit, the feminine and masculine principle, the negative and the positive, the static and the dynamic or the horizontal and the vertical, they represent the *constant elements* upon which the paradox of our life is based and which manifests itself in variation. The cessation of this struggle, the equilibrium of these extremes or the annulment of duality, represents the content of life and the elementary subject of art. This equilibrium is expressed in art by harmony or vital rest and represents the criterion for judging the essential significance of any work of art.

This is the case not only with the work of art, as an individual expression, but also with art as the collective expression of a nation, of a style. Each national culture has been confronted with these basic truths which far transcend the limits of individualism. The outlook of any period of art clearly demonstrates to what extent man has succeeded in creating the expression or style which balances the dualities mentioned above. If the element of nature is predominant in *one* nation, spontaneity predominates in *another* due to the spiritual element or contemplation; the use of this polarity rarely produces an equilibrium.

In order to explain this further, I have made use of a simple, schematic drawing. In this drawing I have presented in a synthetic manner the various periods of art since that of the Egyptians until the present.

As I have explained in minute detail in my lecture, *Classic, Baroque, Modern*, I replace the scheme birth, flourishing and decay with a continuous evolution. This continuous evolution in life and art is a spiritual one, which, however, is manifested in space and time as the old concept of birth, flourishing and decay.

Hence, one may conclude that each new development contains the germ of decay, and moreover that all decay also contains the possibility of a new beginning.

Nowhere and never do we find an end.

Everything is in a state of continuous development.

The entire system of evolution is based upon an increasingly spiritual profundity which causes the revaluation of all values.

In this short explanation I have summarized the basics of my approach to art. I shall now turn to the schematic diagram, which follows:

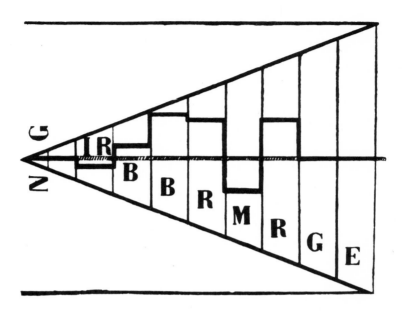

The two horizontal lines represent the polarity nature (on top) and spirit (below), the 'one extreme' and 'the other extreme'. From the gradual equilibrium of these two forces emanates the triangle which comprises the types of cultural development found from the Egyptians until the present day. The meaning of the capital letters is reading from right to left: E = Egyptians, G = Greeks, R = Romans, M = Middle Ages, R = Renaissance, B = Baroque, B = Biedermeier, IR = Idealism-Reformation, NG = Neo-Plastic Expression, the era which has now begun. The shaded line in the middle represents the median, the absolute unity of the 'duality' nature-spirit. (Continuous evolution.)

The strongly variable trend within the triangle is meant to express the relationship within this polarity through which the artistic-cultural life of each epoch was established.

With the Egyptians unity was achieved; within the cultural and artistic expressions the absolute median level was maintained. The same was true for the Greeks.

With the Romans we notice a strong tendency towards the natural, whereas in the Middle Ages which followed we find exactly the opposite, a tendency towards the spiritual.

With the Renaissance we observe again a tendency towards the natural which was reinforced during the Baroque. In the Reformation period art again manifests a strong equilibrium. At the time of Idealism we meet another tendency towards the spiritual, whereas, in the period of Neo-Plastic Expression, the road towards the unity of matter and mind is regained. (The annulment of duality.)

We need only to look into the essence of philosophies and religions which differ merely in form in order to see recurring this idea of polarity as the meaning of life. This polarity represents the symbolic form of a truth which it is our task *to establish*; and perhaps never before has the struggle between nature and spirit been expressed so clearly as in our time. We are not dealing here with nature and spirit as they are seen from a philosophical point of view. It is sufficient to observe that in the reality of our own existence the content of all our activities is based upon two principles which complement one another.

In earlier art these principles remained veiled, as they do in nature where they are disguised by various outer appearances. It was the task not only of *the artist* but also of the philosopher and the scientist to discover the essence of Being behind these forms and to mould them into a different, new expression. This explains why the mimeticism of outer form has nothing in common with art. Each artist – whether belonging to the past or present – attempts to use his own means of expression to establish the balance of all those opposites which lie beyond natural form or outer appearances. All great art, whether produced as a style, individually or collectively, presents this balance as an harmony or rest (example: Egyptian sculpture). This rest or harmony cannot be obtained without struggle. Struggle, which reveals itself in creativeness, is proof that spirituality experiences nature as its counterpart, as its contrast. Thus *the relationship* of the artist towards his inner and his environmental world is one *of contrast*.

I considered it indispensable to begin my lecture with this short metaphysical introduction in order to make clear the true relationship of the artist towards nature. The great difference between the artists of earlier times and those of today can be pinned down to the fact that the latter have understood this relationship quite clearly. They approach reality as consciously creative men, whereas earlier artists, admirers of the unconscious, were obliged to rely upon an intuitive, raw spontaneity. In their works emotion usually predominates by means of *tragic form* (example: Sassetta's *St John the Baptist*, Sienese School). The tragic reveals best the experience of struggle; that is to say, the will towards the annulment of nature. The tragic in art represents the psychological expression of imperfect, unbalanced man who believed in the great dualisms, which he primitively conceived as those of the here and the hereafter, of heaven and earth, and of good and bad, and which never were achieved in complete harmony.

Whereas imperfect man attempted to express the one extreme in terms of the tragic, the troubles of this world, so he would express the other extreme in terms of the liberating angelic, the joys of heaven (example: Fra Angelico's *Ascension of the Angels*). The balance of these two extremes could only be expressed by a symbol, such as Christ's Ascension (Grünewald's *Ascension of Christ*). This also explains why Christian tragedy remained a subject for art until far into the Renaissance, although scientific and philosophical clarity had created doubts about a predominantly emotional and symbolic approach towards life. We must realize that in all works of art from the past the synthesis of life is presented in terms of *representation* and never through an *image*.

Representation constitutes an indirect *symbol* realized in terms of analogy.

The image represents a direct *expression* through the means characteristic of art (example: Piet Mondrian's *Composition 1921*). The difference between the indirect or secondary and the direct or primary expression of the content of life, between representation and image, explains clearly the strong contrast between the old and the new. Everything which occurred in between these two historical approaches in art, such as Romanticism, Impressionism, Cubism, Futurism, Expressionism, Purism and so forth, may be considered to represent Experimentalism (examples from Romanticism and Purism are Daumier, Monet, Picasso, Severini, Kandinsky, Marc, and Ozenfant). These styles of expression, in which the struggle for a new balance, a new harmony between the dualistic elements of life, is revealed most clearly, were experimental, because natural spontaneity, albeit realized in a more abstract manner, was predominant. This entirely prevented such styles from achieving a general architectonic or an organic, constructive artistic expression. Although in these experimental modes of expression the desire to supersede traditional representation predominated, there was no success in arriving at a universal, collective manner of expression, a style. This is confirmed, first and foremost, by the lack of general basic principles, of plastic laws found in these expressions. However, those expressions in art which stem from individualistic approaches cannot produce such laws. The general subject with which these experimental arts also dealt was again the tragic, this time expressed in an abstract lyrical manner. These experimental artistic expressions fluctuate between feeling and intellect as a result of a still imperfect, dualistic view of life. Neither feeling nor

intellect alone can solve the problem of art. The great value of such experimental artistic expressions derives chiefly from the discovery of the power of pure plastic means (colour in painting, volume in sculpture, space in architecture, pure sound in music, and so forth). Thereby they avoided the duality of plastic form and plastic content. In order to understand clearly the problem of art, one must examine works of art from earlier times in reference to the manner in which content of life was transformed into *artistic composition*. One will see that this content of life invariably was manifested in terms of representation or illusionism.

In most cases composition was characterized by subdivision into three areas of the picture-surface – a central part or compositional axis and areas to the right and left part (example: Grünewald's *Crucifixion*). This threefold subdivision was most consciously sought and visibly apparent during the Renaissance (example: Raphael's *The three Graces*). The axis or centre of the composition holds the two halves together by means of which a certain symmetry is established. Consequently, this work of art presents us with a predominantly static expression. The architectural element which prevails in all present-day art can already be found in that earlier period. However, life is not merely static but also dynamic, not merely constructive but destructive as well; both are present simultaneously. It was as a reaction to the static that the Baroque style developed with its predominance of the dynamic (example: Michelangelo's *God creating the Earth*). Let us turn away from those expressions of art in nations where the plastic element prevails, and let us examine those nations where the pictorial element predominates. Thus we can find in

Rembrandt, for instance, that the idea of polarity assumes the form of division by contrast, by dark-light (example: *Jewish bride*). In the example I have chosen here, the synthesis of life still derives its expressive strength from visual illustration. As I have stated above, this painting by Rembrandt established the importance of a supranational will to plastic expression. In this phase of the development of painting the secondary elements of plastic form (the objective) already became primary ones: this is to say, coloured objects were subjected to pictorial composition. During the Impressionist period Rembrandt's principle developed into a system (example: Manet's *Déjeuner sur l'herbe*). The objective becomes increasingly unimportant: instead of contrast by light, as with Rembrandt, colour-contrasts become important for an artist such as Manet. Contrasts are increasingly stressed, as is clearly illustrated in this picture by Manet, which contains continually variable and omnipresent compositional effects based upon its use of light and dark coloration. From the supranational will to plastic expression of successive art periods we can deduce a general need for artistic plastic expression, which in earlier periods presented itself less clearly. The struggle for direct expression was initiated very forcefully by Van Gogh (example: *L'Arlésienne*). With crude certainty he forced his experience of contrast on to the canvas surface. He attempted to annul duality by means of a volumic, well-defined form of structure to balance the static and the dynamic and to impose the spiritual upon the material. However, this annulment of duality (of life as experienced by the unbalanced, imperfect man of the past) could not be achieved without the destruction of the illusion of nature, without the dissolution of

closed form, without the *annulment of the form*. Beginning now the new will to style will consider closed form an obstacle. With artists who post-date Van Gogh, such as Van der Leck and Picasso (example: a. *Beggar*, b. *Harlequin*), form is purposely re-created and subjected to a composition consisting of planes. Hereby the canvas surface, hitherto conceived as a negative entity, is given its true significance. As a consequence of the newly expanded viewpoints of science and technology, the problem of space in painting and sculpture is compounded by another important problem, that of *time*. Whereas earlier periods of art solved the problem of space in terms of perspective which modelled form, the problem of time approached solution in the juxtaposition of form. An exact expression, a true balance of spatial and temporal entities, could be achieved only through the mechanization of the canvas plane. This mechanization of the picture surface already was anticipated by artists like Rousseau (*The Bridge*) and Van der Leck (*Artillery parade*).

The pictorial experience of time is expressed on a predominantly horizontal canvas plane by stressing juxtaposition through the repetition of a certain motif.

Naturally, three-dimensional modelling loses its new significance because of the great stress upon rhythmic juxtaposition. Nevertheless, the element of time is still treated here in a naturalistic manner and not in the manner appropriate to art, which is as a rhythmic arrangement of pure plastic means. I have chosen these various examples only to demonstrate that problems such as those of the plane, of the determination of colour, of space, of time and of mechanization were present already in the art of the pre-

121

architectural phase. Therefore, I do not believe that the art which we consider 'new' is literally or entirely novel, but that it is the outcome of a need for plastic expression which existed within all creative men. In the art of the past all these elements of plastic expression remained veiled behind naturalistic form. The most recent generations of artists have rediscovered and are using these elements regardless of the forces which oppose a monumental synthesis. . . .

With the new art plastic expression becomes more profound, abstract, and related to architecture. The striving for an elementary style based on elementary means – as I have shown before – runs parallel to a progressive development of form in technology. From a primitive tool of the Stone Age (example: a primitive drill) developed the electric boring-machine, so matchless in form and function (especially the latest models of this machine). Similarly, today's elementary work of art developed from primitive Stone Age drawings. When these two developments (in technology and in art) meet in our own times, mechanical form will lend itself automatically to the new style. Indeed, mechanics is the immediate balance of the static and the dynamic – the balance of thought and feeling. If culture, in the broadest sense, implies independence from nature, then it should not surprise one that, concerning the cultural will to style, the machine comes to the fore. The machine represents the very essence of mental discipline. The attitude towards life and art which is called materialism regarded handi-work as the direct expression of the soul. The new concept of an art of the mind not only postulated the machine as a thing of beauty but also acknowledged immediately its endless opportunities for expression in art.

A style which no longer aims to create individual paintings, ornaments or private houses but, rather, aims to study through team-work entire quarters of a town, sky-scrapers and airports – as the economic situation prescribes – cannot be concerned with handicraft. This can be achieved only with the aid of the machine, because handi-craft represents a distinctly individual attitude which contemporary developments have surpassed. Handicraft debased *man* to the status of a machine; the correct use of the machine (to build up a culture) is the only path leading towards the opposite, social liberation. However, mechanical production is by no means the sole prerequisite for faultless creation. Not quantity, but quality is the premise for a correct use of the machine. The machine should be directed by the artistic mind towards the purpose of art. Consequent upon the practical and intellectual needs of our time, constructive precision is postulated. Only the machine can produce this constructive precision. The new possibilities created by the machine resulted in an up-to-date aesthetic, which I once called a 'mechanic aesthetic'. Those who expect to govern nature through the mind while neglecting reality will perhaps never admit that the general aspect of contemporary life is the prerequisite for a style of living and of art in which impersonal religious truths are realized. The coming style will first and foremost be a style of harmony and vital repose. Far from embodying romantic vagueness, decorative arbitrariness and brutal spontaneity, this style will represent the achievement of heroic monumentalism (example: the American grain elevator). In contrast to all former styles, I should like to call this the style of complete man, that is to say, a style which evenly balances the

122

opposites discussed above. It would embrace everything which until now we have called magic, spirit, love and so forth. The magic with which primitive man loved to play can be achieved only through electricity, through mechanical control of the air and the water, by solving technically the problem of space and time. The more the new manifests itself in life and in art, the more distinct do the contrasts between the old and the new appear. These sharp contrasts will disappear as soon as the new has replaced the old. However, every period – even our own times – prolongs the older ideas on art, which explains why characteristics of both attitudes towards life survive.

A few characteristics of the will to a new style and their counterparts in the old art expression are:

definiteness instead of indefiniteness
openness instead of closedness
clarity instead of vagueness
religious energy instead of belief and religious authority
truth instead of beauty
simplicity instead of complexity
relation instead of form
synthesis instead of analysis
logical construction instead of lyrical representation
mechanical form instead of handiwork
creative expression instead of mimeticism and decorative ornament
collectivity instead of individualism, and so forth.

The will towards a new style expresses itself in many ways. Not only in painting, sculpture and architecture, in literature, in jazz or in cinema, but particularly in functional products.

No artistic principle has been postulated for any among these products, which above all must answer practical demands. Nevertheless, such objects evoke our sense of beauty. Iron bridges, for example, are aesthetically expressive in their rhythmic arrangement of parts. This effect was achieved not only through careful and exact calculation but also because of a feeling for harmonic relationships (iron bridges).

Nothing is ornamental, superfluous or artificial as are superficial touches of beauty added afterwards. Only the truth of the thing itself exists. Above all else truth, function and construction are expressed. There are no mistakes such as can result from individualistic tendencies.

In all these products, whether iron bridges, locomotives, automobiles, telescopes, cottages, airport-hangars, funicular railways, sky-scrapers, or children's toys, the will towards a new style expresses itself. The similarity of these examples to the new creations in art consists in the same striving for clear, pure form which expresses truth in the objects. It is therefore not surprising to find that the beauty of mechanical form represents a source of inspiration for the present generation in art.

Art is play, and this game possesses its own rules. As former art generations played with nature, so new artists (for instance Dada artists) play with the machine (for example, Man Ray's *Danger*).

Everyone knows the manner in which our practical daily life involves the mechanical control of natural forces and the conquest of space–time, whenever telegraphy, the telephone, a fast train, the automobile or the aeroplane is used.

The old dream of primitive man to become *the master of his environment* is gradually being realized. Only by completely controlling the cosmic forces will primitive *mythical* man evolve into *cosmic* man.

The latest inventions, for instance that of radiotelephony in a cylindrical hat by the American, Frank Chamber, give proof to what extent the possible control of cosmic forces can be achieved.

It is strikingly apparent that the present generation of artists in Europe, and even in America, is, in fact, striving for a solution to the problem of art and technology. The direction taken by painting, chiefly by Cubism, will be taken in *all arts* and run like a continuous thread throughout the course of this century. Since the arts are going predominantly in a constructive, architectural direction, no one should be surprised if they draw together in order to produce a solution. A solution is to be expected from a monumental synthesis. A similar development has already taken place in architecture, years ago.

Several architects (Viollet le Duc, Peter Behrens, Berlage, Van de Velde) have purified the architectural means of expression and stripped them of any superfluous decorativism.

Plastic architectural form is the result of functional demands which determine the divisions of space. Inner form expresses outer form. In this manner architecture has rediscovered its proper means of expression. With a few slides I shall demonstrate by strong contrasts the difference between the decorative and the monumental approach (example: *The Zwinger* in Dresden).

In the first illustration an excess of decorative sculpture destroys architectural form. The second illustration presents a clear, plastic expression which employs pure, architectural means (example: a house by Van 't Hoff). In this house outer form derives from inner form. Every inner space is expressed through outer form. No preference is shown for any single façade. Form is not absorbed by the landscape and yet represents an intellectual expression which possesses a vital repose superior to nature.

The following illustration provides an example of frontalism in architecture, since all effort is concentrated on the façade (example: the town hall in Münster, Germany). I call this two-dimensional architecture. The façade has been erected like an empty theatre coulisse and does not refer to inner structure.

In contrast to the painterly approach inherent in an architecture of two-dimensional façades, the task of the architect is to annul three-dimensional volume by correctly expressing the relationships involved in the arrangement of space. The four side façades must be comprised in a single monumental plastic expression (as with the Allegonda house in The Netherlands, by the painter Kamerlingh Onnes in collaboration with J. J. P. Oud). The illustration given here provides an idea of contemporary architectural principles. Doubtless architecture faces difficult problems. Moreover, town-planning poses problems different from those of architecture. Yet, a proper solution to architectural problems, which would embody contemporary ideas in plastic expression, can also be applied to large-complex buildings (example: the block of houses in Rotterdam by the architects Pauw and Hardeveld). The same quality is shown in the fast aeroplane from Prague to Paris (example).

The following illustration contains a solution for a street corner, which achieves a beautiful plastic effect through the heavy stress placed on advancing and receding parts. The central chimney serves as the axis for the whole design without creating

124

symmetry (see also J. Wils's hotel in Woerden, The Netherlands).

The spatial rhythm created by repeatedly breaking up the cubic masses is also found in an office block (example: engineering construction). Here functionally determined spaces are expressed constructively in outer form. If we turn our attention from outer architectural appearance to inner form, we may observe that in this example a monumental approach, which is shared by both architect and painter, can produce a clear expression of inner space (the Bersenbrugge Studio in The Hague by Wils and Huszar). In contrast to the decorative expression of the Baroque, painting now stresses architectural features rather than destroying them. To my regret, I can only illustrate this interior in black and white whereas the actual effect of the colours in terms of their spatial relationships and the unity among furniture, curtains and carpets used such harmony that both an artistic and ethical result is achieved. Only the proper, artistic use of colour in space can produce this harmony. For modern architecture the problem of colour in space is the most important and difficult issue of our time. In my opinion, a solution to this issue can be expected only if a total synthesis occurs. A balance between the elements of space and time can be achieved only in terms of coloured plasticism, which is to say, in terms of painted three-dimensional space-compositions. As early as 1916 modern Dutch architecture began concerning itself with these problems. As a result, monumental painters are working again to achieve their own appropriate aim, which is the incorporation of painting into architecture. The following two examples of a bedroom and a consulting room illustrate this principle of coloured plasticism; simplicity, clarity and vital harmony here become the main rules which govern plastic expression and through which a monumental whole is realized. A similar approach is demonstrated in an armchair designed by Rietveld; its simple construction fulfils in a harmonic form the function of sitting. The development which has taken place in technology, architecture and painting can be seen in sculpture as well.

Three examples will make this clear. The first example (*The Dance* by Prof Seger) typifies sentimental, anti-artistic art. Instead of remaining predominantly artistic in function, it possesses outer, physical characteristics through a photographic-plastic arrangement of details.

Rather than realize plastic expression, it represents naturalistic mimetic form, the illusion of rhythm without any relationship to space.

In our second example (*L'Idole* by Rodin) we have a naturalistic sculpture which stresses the duality of matter and form and accentuates rhythm through using volumetric contrasts, but does not balance space and form either.

Our third example, a work by Archipenko, achieves a unity of open space and the expression of closed form in an immaterial harmony and it displays much similarity with the perfected industrial forms of our times (for example, with a porcelain distillery-retort).

In the film medium this expression of movement appropriate to modern art also is sought. Here too the new plastic expression is striven for by means of a combination of the elements of space and time (as in the films of V. Eggeling and Hans Richter).

Two motifs for abstract film composition are shown here – above and below are three

125

'stills' of each motif and, through film technique, these motifs are combined in a plastic expression which allows for simultaneous juxtaposition and succession (light and movement).

This specific use of film technique provides pure plastic painting with a new means of expression which contains an artistic solution to the problem of statics versus dynamics, of space versus time. This solution, moreover, responds to the artistic demands of our epoch. What I have shown you as the beginning of a new expression in art and technology has nothing in common with expressionistic anarchy. Instead of seeking aggressive expressions, the new style demands an impersonal combination of all arts which will achieve a harmonic unity. If old art relates to the new art as does wishing to realization, then one may say that, in the monumental art of the future, all our practical and intellectual needs will be unified in one great harmony.

This demand for a total synthesis effected through pure plastic means has been presented for the first time in Holland by the so-called 'De Stijl' group, and most of the examples of architecture, plastic sculpture and painting which I have shown were made by this group of artists in The Netherlands.

This synthesis of art and life is intended as a reconstruction of European intellectual life.

The striving for a purely monumental plastic expression is equally represented in music and will be illustrated in the following pictures as intensified by pure musical compositions (the musical examples are by Jacob van Domselaer while the Neo-plastic examples are by Mondrian, Van Doesburg, Van Tongerloo, Rietveld and Van 't Hoff).

The musical compositions by Jacob van Domselaer are based upon a principle comparable to that of the Neo-plastic works of art: the expression of harmonious musical form through the relationship of pure sound to silence.

De Stijl vol. v 2, Feb. 1922, pp. 23–32; vol. v 3, Mar. 1922, pp. 33–41

Statement to the International Union of Progressive Artists. Creative demands of De Stijl

I   I am speaking here on behalf of the De Stijl group in The Netherlands, which was formed because it is necessary that the potentialities of modern art be realized; this is to say that *general problems must be solved in practical terms.*

II   For us, construction is the organization of parts into a unity (of plastic expression).

III   This unity can be achieved only if all *subjective arbitrariness in the use of plastic means is suppressed.*

IV   We avoid all subjective choices of form and prepare for the application of objective, universal means of expression.

V   We call those who do not fear the

consequences of this new idea in art progressive artists.

VI The progressive artists of The Netherlands adopted an international outlook from the beginning, including during the war (see the Introduction to *De Stijl* vol. I, 1917).

VII This international attitude derived from actual developments in our artistic activity. Thus it was the result of practical work. Due to developments among the most progressive artists in other countries, similar attitudes were formed.

VIII Encouraged by the certitude that similar problems were arising in all countries (in science and technology as well as in architecture, sculpture, painting, music and so forth), we issued our first manifesto in 1918.

IX This manifesto reads as follows: [*There follows Manifesto I as found in* De Stijl, *1918*]

X This manifesto was the product of a shared attitude among creative artists, including painters, architects, sculptors and poets, and it has met with response among

progressive artists from all contries (see *De Stijl* vol. II, 1918, p. 14 and III, 1919, pp. 1–4). Thus an international organization has proven to be a feasible and necessary project.

My reason for coming here is to cooperate towards the building of such an organization.

The De Stijl Group (The Netherlands)
Düsseldorf, 30 May 1922

Creative Demands of 'De Stijl'

1 The annulment of exhibitions and the substitution of space in which to demonstrate teamwork (Applause).

2 An international exchange of ideas on creative problems.

3 The development of unambiguous, universal means of plastic expression in all the arts.

4 The annulment of the divorce between art and life (Art becomes life). (Applause.)

5 The annulment of the divorce between artist and mankind.

De Stijl vol. V, 4, April 1922, pp. 59–62

The new aesthetics and its realization

Construction does not imply plastic architecture.

Neither does the complete abandonment of all superfluous, common ornamentation in form and colour imply plastic architecture; this merely signifies construction without ornamentation. Plastic architecture means more than that.

Neither does placing of boxes or cells of a predetermined standard type side by side or on top of each other connote plastic architecture. Construction of this nature is based upon the principle of repetition as is photography and the use of earlier styles in architecture.

The (seemingly) economic organization of

space found in standardized town-planning actually is in the way of the progress of plastic architecture.

Plastic, creative architecture bears no relationship to the stiffening of curves and obliques into rectangular forms, nor to the mere exhibition of columns and joints from the building's structural skeleton. This practice represents an anatomical attitude in

architecture as much as did Naturalism in painting.

Such attitudes are merely the prerequisites for a plastic architecture.

To build in a constructive manner is not altogether to imply plastic expression.

To think of architecture as a pile of boxes is, to put it mildly, a 'superficial' approach.

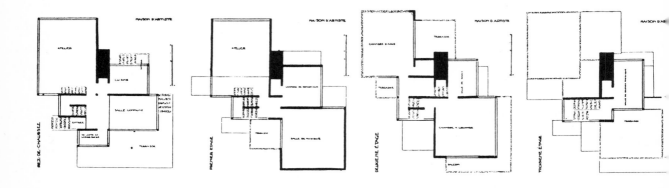

Above Drawings of the groundfloor, first and second floor of the studio house. Theo van Doesburg and C. van Eesteren, 1923

Below Two views of the model (destroyed) of the studio house. Theo van Doesburg and C. van Eesteren, 1923

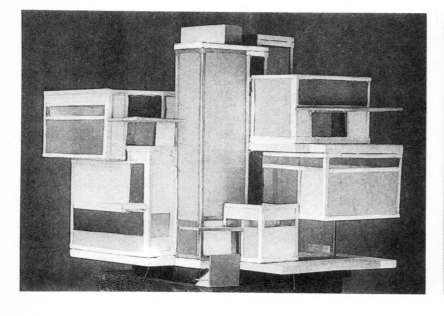

This thinking subsists on the same level as the primitive Southern European concept of plastic expression as an activity solely based on three-dimensional form. Modern man can conceive of plastic architecture as identical with creation, expression (this can also be formless as, for example, if colour only is used), arrangement and organization.

Plastic expression necessarily demands plastic means. The modern view (in contrast to the solely constructive view) conceives of plastic expression as *the organization of plastic means as an unmistakable unity*.

Included in these means I also count space and material.

Anything which destroys this unity reestablishes architecture on the subordinate level from which it derived.

Only in our own times has painting, the most advanced form of art, shown the path by which architecture might reach, like painting and sculpture, the mechanical and disciplined realization in *material* form of what the other arts have already achieved in an imaginary (aesthetic) manner.

It is not surprising that painting, the art which at the beginning of the twentieth century took over the leading role among the arts, first created an ideal aesthetics. The new vision of life demands that the world of duality be abandoned (by a 'world of duality' is meant the common concept of an imaginary world of the mind which is superior and opposed to the concrete world of matter), and it exhibits both a desire for unity, *an indivisible unity of the world*, and the will to materialize in architecture the ideal aesthetics established by the 'liberal' arts.

Not only in The Netherlands, but also in Russia (beginning in 1917) this new movement 'towards the realization of aesthetics' was the result of a consistent development in painting (in The Netherlands of Neo-plasticism, in Russia from Suprematism and Proun).

Only now are architects becoming aware of their appropriate means of expression.

The strong but one-sided belief of dualistically minded people that architecture is the equilibrium of mind and matter originated in the Middle Ages, and this renders completely unfeasible any realistic, clear organization of materials into an unmistakable unity. Only during the Renaissance, when a more scientific attitude towards life replaced the generally accepted religious view of life, were materials and contrasts in material established as a means of expression.

During the Middle Ages matter possessed a symbolic value; with the Renaissance it was used mainly as physical decoration.

Because of the advance of physics in our own times, the concept of matter as solid substance was changed and, as in the field of art, came to be seen as a *unit of energy*.

For the plastic architect, it is essential to experience the differences of energy among various materials in order to achieve, by means of the various contrasts in energy, the pure plastic expression of colour which has been established by painting. (In this writer's book, *Neue Gestaltungslehre*, which will appear shortly, this view is elaborated in four chapters devoted respectively to colour, form, space and plastic expression.)

In my lectures on colour, which were held in Germany, I attempted to explain colour (from an artistic viewpoint) first as 'matter' and second as 'matter in motion'. The rejection in plastic art of colour as prismatic light (even if arranged metrically to a greater or lesser extent) and of colour as a symbolic,

129

literary tool could hardly be contested. Yet the idea of colour as a means of pure plastic expression represented a point of view which made essential demands on the development of architecture.

The plastic architect must treat his problem in handling the material at his disposal as the plastic painter does when arranging contrasting, discordant or complementary energies into an unmistakable unity in two- or three-dimensional space. This must not be achieved in a decorative manner, which is based on the expression of sensuous, personal taste, but in a creative manner, which accords to the contrasting energies characteristic of the material.

Just as in plastic painting yellow and blue express two contrasting energies, in architecture two contrasting materials can accomplish the same thing as, for example:

wood – contraction
concrete – extension.

In contrast, two discordant materials are illustrated by:

concrete – static extension
iron – elastic extension (because of its
        characteristic of expansion).

Only those works in which the engineer has achieved a maximum expression of energy through well-considered creativity are plastic works.

An iron bridge is well-made, which is to say plastic, if the various materials have been organized into a unity which expresses a maximum of energy. A building is well-made, which is to say, that it constitutes plastic architecture, if the various materials (light included) have been organized into a unity which expresses a maximum of energy.

The tremendous possibilities for expression thus made available cannot be summarized in a short article. By beginning with such very strong contrasts as void versus mass and the (open) transparency of glass versus the (closed) opacity of stone, as well as with the relationship between groundplan, elevation and proportion, the constructive architect will be able to discern and to organize the relationships among contrasting, discordant and complementary energies into unity.

In this manner the ideal aesthetics of the one art form are established in the material of the other, due to the comprehension in perfect balance of both ideal and mechanical aesthetics, the well-considered plastic expression of an artistic nature and the expression of constructive utility. This equilibrium constitutes 'Style'.

Thus the domain of plastic expression is open to everyone. It will be everybody's task to organize the material and, if necessary, to create new materials. If the architect creates the plan (without preconceived aesthetics), the engineer must find the material in which it is to be carried out. Architecture will never fulfil the creative potential of its period if the architect timidly and passively contents himself with hitherto available material.

If a certain project demands a specific material, the creative engineer must invent the desired material or transform the material available. Only those who, familiar with the ideal aesthetics, become thoroughly acquainted with the world of matter can discover by reference to mechanics and technology the materials which, due to their contrasting, discordant or complementary energies (colour included), will enable the new plastic expression to be established in architecture.

In observing the use of materials in

contemporary architecture, we notice that, in nearly all so-called architecture, the material has been ignored (for sentimental reasons). Exactly the same thing occurred in painting, where the energy of the material (colour) was also destroyed for sentimental reasons. This criminal ill-treatment of matter (such materials as wood, stone, colour, glass and iron) originated in the caricature-like glorification of a dualistic attitude towards the spiritual hereafter and the material here-and-now. Putting principles of aesthetics into material form creates an attitude towards life which annuls the divorce between reality and the hereafter.

This plastic expression of life as a unity introduces a new civilization.

Weimar 1922
De Stijl vol. VI, 1, March 1923, pp. 10–14

What is dada???????

You probably will be sceptical of learning something about dada from someone who is innocent of dada who is non-dadaist.

Dada: the terror of the easy-chair bourgeois, of the art critic, of the artist, of the rabbit breeder, of the Hottentot, of everybody?

A subject like this scarcely lends itself to serious lecturing, and in fact I do not intend to do so.

I shall be satisfied if, in fulfilling an obligation to friends, I succeed in throwing some light on the dada attitude towards life. This seems especially necessary in a country which since 1880 has been immune to any new expression of life.

Furthermore, it would be arrogant to suggest that I could make the mystery of Dada *comprehensible* on an *intellectual level*.

This would be impossible, and even Dada itself did not achieve this.

Dada is a face.

Dada wants to be lived.

Dada does not want to be understood intellectually.

Dada rejects inexorably any logical association of ideas.

'Dada,' wrote Richard Huelsenbeck, 'has dipped its fingers in all philosophies of life. Dada is the dancer's spirit transcending all terrestial moralities. Dada is the great phenomenon which is parallel to the relativistic philosophies of the present period, Dada is not an axiom, Dada is an attitude of mind independent of schools and theories; it is concerned with the individual himself, without making him predominate. Dada cannot be fixed by laws.'

The question continually put to dadaists, 'What is dada?', can as little be answered as other questions on other phenomena of life.

The answer to the question, 'What is dada?', can only be given by spontaneous action.

It is an error to think that dadaism belongs to the category of new art forms such as impressionism, futurism, cubism, expressionism and so forth.

Dada is not a movement in art.

Dada is an outlook on life, opposed to anything we imagine to be of vital importance.

Dada does not ask questions anyway.

Dada is the denial of the conventionalism of daily life.

Dada is the strongest possible negation of any cultural evaluation. The true dadaist does not adopt anything, neither art, politics, philosophy nor religion.

The dadaist considers all these signs of an obsolete pseudo-culture to be fraudulent trade-marks. Each brand is sold for as long as a new brand has not been discovered.

Dada considers all the hypotheses that have distracted us from reality – whether called Tao or Om, Bramah, Jaweh, God, number or spirit – as simply different labels for one and the same manufacture, which 'having developed from *nought*', is thrust upon humanity with much rah rah and boum boum.

Dada denies any higher, spiritual content of life, art, religion, philosophy or politics.

Dada is the most direct expression of our time as an amorphous era and wishes to be exactly this.

To the dadaist the reason why this ballast exists is based on two things only: publicity and suggestion.

According to the dadaist, humanity, due to fetishistic instinct, is inclined to blind itself with certain characteristic symbols. These serve as advertisements and, as such, are repeated many times, producing an ineffaceable impression: religion by a cross, Odol toothpaste by a curved bottle, Nietzsche by his big moustache, Oscar Wilde by his homosexuality, Tolstoy by his caftan and sandals! Dada does not want to convert. Dada is experienced enough to know that the masses can be won over to 'anything', if only their atavistic instincts are influenced by suggestive publicity.

Dada considers each dogma and each formula to represent a nail with which we try to hold together a dilapidated and sinking boat (our western culture). Dada does not strive for eternality. Dada has arrived at a fifty per cent 'agreement with the world'. Dada was first in exposing the fraud of everything, it has declared the world bankrupt. Dadaism could be called the supra-national expression of humanity's collective experience of life in the past ten years.

Whatever remained latent in modern man is expressed in Dada.

Dada always existed; however, it was discovered only in our own time.

According to Raoul Hausmann, 'the dadaist does not experience the world in a childish way; neither God, nor a father, nor a teacher can punish him. Dada is the practical depoisoning of the self – a modern European situation, anti-eastern, anti-oriental, unmagical. Dada is the germ of a new type of *man*: as opposed to the moralistic, Christian medieval burden of sin, Dada represents the negation of the present meaning of life or culture, which is not tragic but obsolete.' Therefore the dadaist does not accept any responsibility whatsoever for our culture. The dadaist is familiar with all the premises and background of our culture, which to him represents 'humanity and barbarism as one and the same expression'. He knows 'all the ropes' and 'tricks' relating to our most elementary interests in life. He knows exactly how mind is fabricated. Possessing a holy aversion to the ivory towers of our 'Great Men', he does not pretend to be an artist, a philosopher or a renovator. Free from the ambitious wish to be famous or to succeed socially, he is the freest, quietest, most even-tempered man in the world.

Nevertheless, the dadaist credits man with a few positive values: the instinct to dominate

132

and the mutual wish to devour. All ethical motives such as mercy, charity and pity are viewed by the dadaist simply as disguises which hide the true nature of man. Moreover, the dadaist agrees that 'character' can have a positive value, which means that one can have progressed far enough to live and act without false pretexts and hidden motives.

According to Richard Huelsenbeck, 'Dada is based upon itself and acts for itself as does the sun when rising, or a tree when growing. The tree grows without wanting to grow. Dada does not give motives to its acts to serve an "end". Dada does not give birth to verbal abstractions, formulae or systems which it wants to apply to mankind. It is not in need of proof or justification, neither by formulae nor by systems. Dada in itself is the creative act. Dada eliminated the rigid and the rhythm of this time from its mind. Dada is of eminent importance to civilization but is also capable of seeing the limitation to its appearance in time, that is of relating itself to its time.'

II

For the moment it is of little interest how, where and when this phenomenon of all phenomena which we call *Dada* came into being. Dada is rich in data. I could tell you about the first notorious performances in the Cabaret Voltaire in Zürich, the fights in the Gallery Dada, the great manifestations in New York, Paris and Berlin, the dada sermon of the so-called Oberdada in the Dome of Berlin, the dada demonstrations in a Roman Catholic church in Paris, which were kept secret by the press, and much more, but this does not bring you any closer to the essence of *dada*.

Dada has neither country nor nationality. It appeared quite suddenly, due to a general need for spiritual self-purification, in several places far afield: America, Switzerland, France, Germany and elsewhere.

Dada – the word does not mean anything and, as Hausmann remarked, 'Bébé, Sisi or Lollo' could have served just as well – did not stem from any *a priori* or other theory. It was born from a general resistance to our entire way of thinking.

Dada expanded more or less from 'nothing' over a large but limited surface, carrying everything away and finally crystallizing in the negation of all pharmaceutical principles of life.

The dadaists – amongst whom the most outstanding and intelligent people want to be counted nowadays (like Einstein, Chaplin and Bergson)* – declare in almost all manifestos that they do not want anything, nor know anything, nor are anything.

DADA, Picabia writes, does not feel anything, it is nothing, nothing, nothing.

It is like your hope: nothing.

Like your idols: nothing.

Like your paradise: nothing.

Like your politicians: nothing.

Like your heroes: nothing.

Like your artists: nothing.

Like your religions: nothing.

Dada was not made, but came into being.

One cannot become a DADAIST, one can only be one.

During the first notorious days after its birth, the dadaists themselves did not entirely understand what had brought them together. During this first period (about 1915), dadaism was of a predominantly aesthetic character. Gradually this character was lost and finally even art itself was opposed.

According to dada, art has value only as long

* I even learnt from reliable sources that a group of French dadaists are to be admitted to the Académie in Paris.

as it can take advantage of the atavistic and fetishistic sentiments of man. According to the dadaists, art emanates from the need to get rid of these sentiments. However, this has not yet been accomplished.

Dada considers the contemporary view of the world to be a product of the greatest possible contradiction and inconsistency, as the bankruptcy of the effort to explain life from a moralistic viewpoint.

The efforts of Jesus, Buddha, Tolstoy and others have failed. Dada rejects any experiment to organize the infinitely variable, chaotic and heterogeneous mass called humanity.

Dada denies evolution. Each movement evokes a counter-movement of equal force with the one cancelling the other. Nothing changes essentially. The world always remains as it was. Dada completely negates the generally acknowledged duality of matter and mind, woman and man, and in so doing creates the 'point of indifference', a point beyond man's understanding of time and space.

For this reason Dada is able to *mobilize* the optical and dimensional static viewpoint which keeps us imprisoned in our (three-dimensional) illusions. Thus it became possible to perceive the entire prism of the world instead of just one facet at a time. In this connection Dada is one of the strongest manifestations of the fourth dimension, transposed onto the subject.

Dada allows the simultaneous negation of any affirmation, Dada is yes—no, a bird on four legs, a ladder without steps, a square without angles. Dada possesses as many positives as negatives. To think that Dada simply means destruction is to misunderstand life, of which Dada is the expression. To fight Dada means to fight oneself. Dada wants to

annul the divorce of transcendental and everyday reality. Dada is the need of a view of reality of a united world, consisting of discordant and contrasting relationships.

Dada does not see nature as the charming phenomenon we like to imagine, but as a smelling corpse, which spoils our spiritual pleasures and brings everything into immediate decay; everybody from the cleaning-woman to the artist (in essence one and the same person) fights against decay, or nature. I now want to quote the Dutch dadaist I. K. Bonset who expresses this poetically in his THE DRAMADE'S HYPOSTRODON.

The dramade's hypostrodon by I. K. Bonset. dadaistic meditations near a carrion.

appeal to unnatural activities.

it cannot be denied that we are diseased with convictions. No matter to what degree one is schizophrenic, tormented and adorned with mud frills, one thinks himself justified in living life. Observe, however, that 'nature' is a carrion; this is noticeable in 'le grand roue' in Paris, the cornice of your house, the wrinkles of your bride and the good-natured balls of horsedung on the boulevard Saint Michel.

THE DRAMADE'S HYPOSTRODON expresses itself in a floating and naked carrion. Any effort to create a new world of one's invention within a void, to live there unseen and untouched by the cancer of the NATURE DRAMADE, is doomed to fail.

Anything that needs gestures and claims dimension space time and money, is filled with microbes which sooner or later will produce a reactive effect. One can never escape from the inimical counter-image of one's 'spiritual' efforts (oh parody of the parade to paradise).

Whether one is satisfying oneself with luke-warm baths (= poetry), with coloured tin pheasants (= religion), with a Medieval church-window in place of a pair of spectacles (= art), a seesaw in horizontal position (= philosophy) or with many other derivatives, the cancer in one's heart inevitably will expand. Hundreds of generations have slaved to exorcize this cancer, to conquer it or to limit it, while not noticing that their brains and the content of their aspirations are also poisoned with the same bacilli. Dada fights the tyranny of DIRT and thereby distinguishes itself from the impressionists, who had reconciled themselves to Dirt. Whole generations have inhaled eagerly the pernicious fumes of philosophy, religion and art believing the resulting katapepsis to represent the true condition of life.

We neo-vitalists, dadaists, destructive constructivists have laid bare the entire abscess which hides the world's body by crying, 'Look, look, look here here here nothing nothing nothing.' We feel that, without the policeman's truncheon raised above our heads, the leisure we enjoy would be disturbed. The thing we treasure most, dadasophy teaches, is our sleeping-powder. By using this powder carefully and regularly, we do not notice that all life is adorned with mud-frills. No matter how thick the walls may be with which we exclude nature, after a lapse of time, any precision-product such as an elation from our spiritual desire, will be worn out katapeptically.

DO YOU KNOW BY NOW WHAT IS 'DADA'?

What is dada??????? De Stijl, The Hague, 1923, pp. 3–14

Against problem art

An answer to the question of whether or not the new art must serve the community

A form of art which is directed towards one specific social class does not exist. If such art existed, it would be of no relevance to life. I ask those who wish to produce proletarian art, 'What is proletarian art? Is it an art produced by proletarians? Or is it art which serves proletarians and aims to stir proletarian (revolutionary) instincts?'

An art produced by proletarians does not exist because the proletarian, in creating art, ceases to be a proletarian and becomes an artist instead. The artist is neither proletarian nor bourgeois, and his creations belong neither to the proletarian class nor to the bourgeoisie. They belong to *everybody*. Art

is an activity of the human spirit and is dedicated to the aim of liberating man from the chaos of life, from tragedy.

Art is free to choose its own means; however, it is tied to its own laws but *nothing but its own laws*. As soon as a human effort becomes a work of art, it is superior to any class designation such as proletarian or bourgeois. A form of art, however, which serves only proletarians – apart from the fact that bourgeois taste is reflected among proletarians – would be a very limited form, as would be specifically bourgeois art. Such art would by no means represent a universal form of art derived from universal feelings, but would be based upon limited personal, social, temporal and local concepts.

If, on the other hand, art purposely fortifies proletarian instincts, it is using the same means as ecclesiastical and nationalistic art. Painting Trotsky at the head of the Red Guards or Napoleon at the head of the Imperial Guards is one and the same thing, however banal the former scene appears to be. When the painting is considered as a work of art, it is of no importance whatsoever whether proletarian or patriotic feelings are evoked.

From the artistic point of view both feelings are illusory. The task of art is to strengthen, by reference to means peculiar to itself, the creative forces of mankind. Its concern is for *the maturity of man*, not his proletarian or bourgeois status.

Only mediocre talents, who lack a deeper sensitivity and therefore possess no *larger* scope, will produce such a thing as proletarian art (that means *politics in painting*). The true artist is inspired by life and not by any special aspect of social organization.

Art, as we wish it to be, is neither proletarian, nor bourgeois. It produces forces which possess enough strength to influence civilization as a whole but which are not themselves influenced by social circumstances.

Proletarians represent a social status which should liquidate itself. The bourgeoisie also represents a social status which should be abandoned. Precisely because proletarians, in proclaiming their so-called 'Proletarian Culture', are imitating bourgeois culture, they are the very people who unknowingly sustain the present degenerate civilization.

This is to the detriment of art and also of civilization.

It is the proletarian's attachment to old, obsolete forms of expression and his incomprehensible, absurd dislike of modern art which preserve that with which his programme is at war – bourgeois taste in art and bourgeois civilization. This is why sentimentality and romantic vagueness, despite the strongest efforts by radical artists to destroy such qualities, continue to exist and are even cultivated anew.

The idea of renovating art in and through Communism is an error. Communism already is as much a bourgeois affair as parliamentary Socialism; both constitute Capitalism in another form. The bourgeoisie is using the institutions of Communism as a means of renovating its own degenerate civilization (Russia). Thus the so-called 'proletarian' artist is struggling neither on behalf of art nor on behalf of a new way of life but – without knowing or wishing this – on behalf of the bourgeoisie.

Each 'proletarian' work of art is nothing but a poster dedicated to some (future) bourgeoisie.

We modern artists, however, are preparing the monumental works of art which are far superior to all posters whether they be made in order to advertise champagne, Dada or Communist dictatorship.

The Hague, 1923
De Stijl vol. VI 1, April 1923, pp. 17–19

The significance of colour for interior and exterior architecture

I Colour is of extreme importance to the new architecture. It represents an intrinsic part of the material of expression. Colour renders *visible* the spatial effect for which the architect strives. It is in this way that colour makes architecture *complete* and becomes intrinsic to it. Until now colour remained an element of secondary importance. This should cause no surprise since the boxes we live in, which are badly built and knitted together, do not result from a visualization of space. Only when building is transformed into architecture once more, that is to say a monumental synthesis of space, form and colour, will it acquire the significance to which it has a right. It must be admitted that, with few exceptions, until now satisfactory results have not been obtained. Nor should this be a matter for surprise, since a good result can be expected only from the consistent application of colour in interior and exterior architecture. Many a misunderstanding or mistake has resulted when painter and architect did not sufficiently respect one another's field. On the one hand, architects restricted painters; on the other hand they presented them with *too much* freedom. A compromise resulted from the former type of relationship, while painting, which retained a separate function, dominated in the latter (as happened, for example, with Taut and Oskar Fischer in Magdeburg). In both cases, colour led to the destruction of architecture.

The problem of colour's role in architecture is too important to be determined summarily, as is usually done only when the building is finished. A builder's estimate generally does not include the expense of painting, although the results which architects produce are more often than not detrimental rather than beneficial to the solution of the problem of colour. Painting doors or window-frames blue or yellow does not differ essentially from applying paint to timberwork in order to protect it from humidity, which is what house-painters did in the past.

Perspective view of the coloured design for a university hall. In collaboration with
C. van Eesteren, 1923.
Pen, pencil and gouache on paper, 63.5×145.5 cm.
$(25 \times 57$ in.) Collection of Mr C. van Eesteren

137

II   Paint and colour are two different things. Paint is a means, colour an end. One can cover a whole interior or façade with blue, yellow, green, violet or red paint without achieving true colour, no matter how multi-coloured the whole may be. Just as the knitting together of spaces in which to live does not connote architecture, so the unlimited application of 'bright' colours does not provide a solution to the problem of colour.

As always, we are concerned here with balance. Playing with forms, which has become a slogan, is of no use here. Only practice can help.

When starting with the latter we must imagine a completely colourless, neutral, that is to say a grey interior. A limitation of space by means of six neutral, grey planes. This neutral space is not *active*, it *does not reveal its proportions* and the less so the more a free entrance of light avoids opposition with shadowy corners. Such inactive space comprises a *void*. If one places in this interior furniture which uses a neutral, grey material, the result will prove negative or passive. (This contradiction in terms is intentional.) It is impossible to orientate oneself in this interior, to judge the distance between wall and furniture. *Everything fuses together*. Neither space, nor natural objects can be ascertained according to their mutual relationships. *It comprises a visually inarticulate interior*.

I have chosed this negative example deliberately in order to instil in the reader the desire for opposition, for contrast.

Every human being possesses a hidden need to see relationships within his environment visually expressed in terms of oppositions. It is upon this need that the very right of expressing relationships in architecture is based (the plastic element). The need for

contrasts between space and natural objects manifests itself as soon as the demand arises for differentiating furniture from walls through colour by means of either painting, coloured textiles or coloured planes, which do not blend with one another. The fact that colours range from quite grey or neutral (visually inarticulate) to clearly visible contrasts defines the entire problem of colour in architecture. This range moves from the undefined colours, which are without expression, to the well-defined, filled with expression. (In numbers this can be expressed as follows: $0 - 1 - 2 - 3 - 4 - 5$ and so forth.)

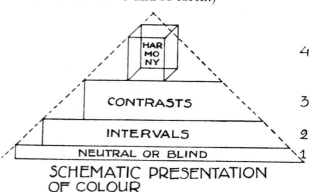

SCHEMATIC PRESENTATION OF COLOUR

This scheme is a presentation of the four phases of development from the quite neutral (or visually inarticulate) towards the most harmonious plastic expression of the interior and the objects which it contains. The relationships between the latter is characterized by intervals (2) and contrasts (3). Within these four phases of development we can imagine various types of interior: for instance using phases 2 and 3, an interior can be imagined which aims at a solution by means of secondary contrasts (as is the case with many modern decorators who apply this

138

to cinemas and coffee shops). However, this has nothing to do with the visualization of relationships through colour.

In phase 4, which is indicated with a cube, a certain neutrality has been produced. This derives in equal measure from the correct use of colour, although it is of a completely different nature from that in phase 1, because of a correct arrangement, proportion and value of the contrasting colours.

An interior which is well-defined in all its parts will present a neutral impression, since it does not possess either a particular form (representing individual caprice) or a particular colour dominating by its fascinating 'effect'. As long as certain details or objects attract special attention through either their form or colour, no unity has been attained. However, if a unity has been produced, then space and the objects contained within it are perceived as a unity in which each colour maintains its individual force of energy.

III Following this more or less idealized explanation of colour as a principle in architecture, we must investigate the practical side of the subject more closely. First, we have to distinguish clearly the three main types of architecture, this being of extreme importance to the application of colour.
1 Decorative architecture
2 Constructive, solely functional architecture
3 Monumental architecture
With decorative architecture colour is used as a means to decorate the constituent planes.

Colour here remains ornamental. It does not achieve a unity with architecture and thus remains a separate element which, instead of *stressing* the architectural factor, camouflages and, indeed, ultimately destroys it (the Baroque period). Almost everything

which our age has produced as examples of modern interior design can be said to belong to this class of architecture. It makes no difference whether or not one is imitating the Biedermeier style, with its motifs derived from nature, creating curved lines or producing forms stylized into rectangular planes (Biedermeier in terms of squares). In constructive architecture which serves material demands alone, colour has no other significance than to accentuate further the common architectural denominator by means of a completely neutral paint (grey, green, brown, neutral colour) and furthermore, to protect wood or iron, from the influence of humidity. Ultimately, this leads towards an anatomical constructive sterility in architecture. Functionalist architecture deals with only the practical side of life or the mechanistic function of life: living and working.

However, something exists beyond the demand for the useful, and this is the spiritual. As soon as the architect or the engineer wishes to visualize relationship – for example, the relationship between a wall and space – his intentions are no longer solely constructive but plastic as well. With the visualization or the accentuation of relationships (including the material), the aesthetic element comes into existence. The conscious expression of relationships constitutes plastic expression.

In this phase of plastic architecture, colour is a material of expression equivalent to other materials such as stone, iron or glass. In this instance, colour serves not only to orientate, by which is meant the visualization of distance, position and direction in reference to space and to the objects which it contains, but even more to satisfy a need for the visualization of mutual relationships in proportion, scale and direction. It is the arrangement of these relationships which constitutes the aesthetic goal of architecture. Once this harmony is established, it manifests style. Needless to say, this balance can be achieved only through an even distribution of tasks between the engineer, architect and painter.

With this phase, architecture has completed the period of constructive purification. No longer satisfied to demonstrate its underlying structure, it will develop into an indivisible, inspired totality.

Bouwkundig Weekblad vol. 44, no. 21, 1923, pp. 232–4

Towards elementary plastic expression

I It is necessary to make a clear distinction between two methods of expression which are diametrically opposed to one another: the *decorative* (ornamental) and the *monumental* (plastics).

The two methods of expression result in completely different concepts of art: one is of the *past* and the other of the *present*. Whereas the *concentrism* is characteristic of the decorative principle, the *eccentrism* is typical of the monumental principle.

The earlier development of art passed through all phases of individualism before attaining the utmost degree of objectivity.

$$\text{individualism} \begin{cases} \text{decoration} & \text{monumentality} \\ \text{the past} & \text{the present} \\ \text{the concentric} & \text{the eccentric} \end{cases} \text{objectivity}$$

Within this tension lies the problem of the new plastic expression in art, of the new style.

With the decorative approach, creative activity was dependent upon personal taste, an arbitrary attitude or the intuitive evaluation of the elements which comprise the work of art. These capricious factors could not possibly satisfy the desire of our time: PRECISION.

For example, those who satisfied this desire, with an intellectual point of view,

believe that they have resolved the conflict by characterizing their work, which is as capricious as speculative, under the heading: 'problem'. They presume plastic art to be no longer concerned with 'creative composition' but with 'problematic construction'. I believe that the difference between *composition* (to put together) and *construction* (to combine) is not to be underestimated as representing a phenomenon of our time. Yet neither the one nor the other will lead towards fruitful endeavour in art *if we cannot agree on the*

140

elementary means of plastic expression.

What we demand of art is UNITY, a demand which will never be fulfilled as long as artists use individualistic means. *Unity can only result from disciplining the means, for it is this discipline which produces more generalized means.* The objectification of the means will lead towards elementary, monumental plastic expression.

It would be ridiculous to maintain that none of this relates to creative activity. If that were true, art would not be subject to logical discipline. It would originate only from spontaneous, impulsive experiences of the individual. The precision, the unity which we demand of a work of art derives from the same sources as does the scientific or technical

perfection that reveals itself in all those functional products which surround us. By examining these objects, which came into existence in answer to the demands of contemporary life, the modern artist can conclude that impulsive and speculative production has come to an end. THE ERA OF DECORATIVE TASTE HAS VANISHED, *the artist of to-day has finished completely with the past.* Scientific and technical developments oblige him to draw conclusions in his own realm. These creative conclusions demand him *to revise his means, to establish laws* creating *a system,* that is to say, *to master his elementary means of expression in a conscious manner.*

Secondary (additional) means	*Primary (elementary) means*
Painting: illusionistic form (the object), the anecdotal, and so forth.	Painting: shape – time – colour.
Sculpture: illusionistic form, the anecdotal, and so forth.	Sculpture: space – time – line, plane, volume.
Architecture: the closed mould, decoration, the symbol.	Architecture: space – time – line – plane.

II   As early as 1916 our first and most important demand was: *the separation of the various realms of plastic expression.* In opposition to the ever-spreading Baroque

(including in modern art), we maintained that the plastic arts should be separated clearly one from another. *Without this clear separation (of sculpture and painting, painting and architecture and so forth), it is impossible to*

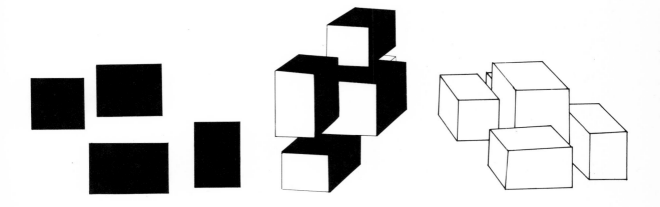

arrive at the elementary means of plastic expression. Until the present the means of plastic expression have been so confused as to make one believe them to be inseparable. This vagueness in the means is *a relic of the Baroque* in which the various arts destroyed one another (by spreading into or being in conflict with related fields of artistic activity) rather than supported one another through

clear, mutual relationships.

A new plastic expression will emanate from the elementary means. Herein, the various arts will be so related as to provide a basis for the greatest possible power of (elementary) expression.

'Material zur elementaren Gestaltung', G □ 1, July 1923

Towards plastic architecture

1 *Form.* The basis for a healthy development of architecture (and of art in general) is the suppression of all *form-ideas* insofar as this concept implies a *predetermined type.*

Instead of using earlier style types as models and thus imitating previous historical styles, one necessarily must pose the problem of architecture entirely anew.

2 The new architecture is *elementary*, which signifies that it develops from the elements of construction as understood in the most comprehensive sense. These elements are for example, function, mass, plane, time, space, light, colour and material, and they are, moreover, also *plastic elements.*

3 The new architecture is *economical*, which signifies that the elementary means are organized either as efficiently and economically as possible or by wasting neither these means nor the material.

4 The new architecture is *functional*, which signifies that it develops from the precise determination of practical necessities which it embodies in a clear groundplan.

5 The new architecture is *formless*, yet defined, which signifies that it is not characterized by any predetermined aesthetic form-type or mould (like those used by pastry-cooks) into which it casts the functional spaces derived from practical living demands.

In contrast to all earlier historical styles, the new architectural method imposes no standard or *basic type.*

The division of functional spaces is strictly determined by rectangular planes which possess themselves no individual shapes, since, although defined (one plane by the other), they can be extended infinitely by the imagination. Thus they can create a coordinated system in which all points correspond to an equal number of points in universal, unlimited open space.

It follows that the planes possess a direct relationship with open (exterior) space.

6 The new architecture has rendered the concept of *the monumental* independent of largeness and smallness (since the word 'monumental' has been abused, it is replaced by the word 'plastic'). This architecture has

Colour construction in the fourth dimension of
space-time. Axonometric of the private house of
1923, Paris, 1924 gouache on tracing paper,
40×40 cm. (16×16 in.)
Collection of Stedelijk Museum, Amsterdam

demonstrated that everything exists in terms of relationships, through the principle of interrelationship.

7 The new architecture possesses no *passive moment*. It has abandoned the use of 'dead spaces' (holes in the wall). The *openness* of the window has an *active* meaning as against the *closure* of the wall-surface. Nowhere does a hole or a void issue forth, everything is strictly determined by means of contrast. See the various counter-constructions, in which the elements of architecture, such as, plane, line and mass, have been freely arranged into a three-dimensional relationship. [*Here Van Doesburg refers to the illustrations given at the end of this programme. They comprise the groundplan and photos of the model for a private house made by C. van Eesteren, as well as four axonometrical drawings of the private house the two of them designed together.*]

8 *The groundplan.* The new architecture has *opened* the walls, thus eliminating the *separateness* of the *interior* and the *exterior*.
 The whole wall no longer carries, it is reduced to points of support. The result is a new, open groundplan, which is completely different from the traditional usage, since interior and exterior space interpenetrate.

9 The new architecture is *open*. The whole consists of one space, which is divided according to the various functional demands. This division is accomplished through the use of *separating planes* (in the interior) or by *projecting planes* (on the exterior).
 The former planes, which separate the different functional spaces, can be *mobile*, which means that the separating planes (formerly the interior walls) can be replaced

by movable screens or slabs (doors can also be treated in this manner). In the following phase of this development in architecture, the groundplan must disappear completely. The principle of two-dimensionally projected space-composition, as *fixed* by a groundplan, will be replaced by exact *calculation of the construction*, a calculation which must transfer the carrying capacity to the simplest but sturdiest points of support. Euclidean mathematics will no longer serve this purpose; yet by using Non-Euclidean calculations in four dimensions, this calculation can be accomplished quite easily.

10 *Space and time.* The new architecture calculates not only with space but also with time as an architectural value. The unity of space and time will give architectural form a new and completely plastic aspect, that is, a four-dimensional, plastic space–time aspect.

11 The new architecture is *anti-cubic*, which specifies that it does not attempt to combine all functional space-cells into one closed cube, but *projects the functional space-cells* (as well as overhanging planes, the volumes of balconies and so forth) centrifugally, or from the core of the cube outward, thereby giving a completely new plastic expression in open space to the dimensions of height, width, depth + time.
 In this manner architecture takes on a more or less hovering aspect (insofar as this is feasible from a structural point of view, which is a problem for the engineer!). This aspect, so to speak, challenges the force of gravity in nature.

12 *Symmetry and repetition.* The new architecture has suppressed symmetry's monotonous repetition as well as the rigid

144

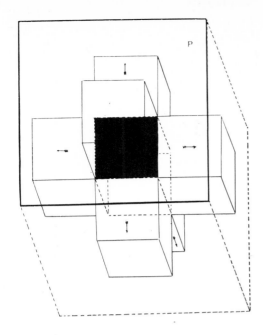 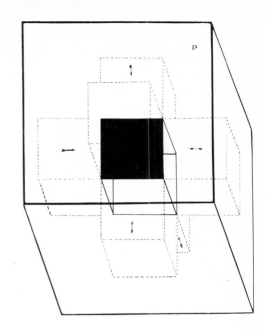

equality which results from division into two
halves or the use of the mirror image.
It employs neither repetition in time, street
walls, nor standardized parts. A block of
houses is as much a whole as a single house.
The laws governing single houses apply also
to both blocks of houses and the city as a
whole. In place of symmetry, the new architecture proposes *a balanced relationship of
unequal parts*; that is to say of parts which,
because of functional characteristics, differ in
position, size, proportion and situation.

The equivalence of these parts is gained
through an equilibrium of unequality rather
than of equality. In addition, the new
architecture has granted equal value to the
'front', 'back', 'right', and possibly also to the
'above' and 'below'.

13 In contrast to *frontalism*, which was born
out of a rigid, static concept of life, the new
architecture offers the plastic richness of an
all-sided development in space–time.

14 *Colour*. The new architecture has

suppressed painting as a separate, illusory
expression of harmony, whether as embodied
indirectly in representational art or directly
in an art of coloured planes.

The new architecture *employs* colour
organically as a direct means of expression
of relationships in space and time. Without
colour, these relationships are devoid of the
aspect of living reality; they are *invisible*.
The equilibrium of the architectural
relationships becomes a visible reality only
through the use of colour. The task of the
modern painter is to integrate colour into a
harmonic whole (by placing it not on a
plane-surface of two dimensions, but within
the new realm of four-dimensional space–
time). In a succeeding phase of development,
colour might also be replaced by synthetic
materials which possess their own specific
colours (this is a problem for the chemical
scientist), but only if practical demands
require such materials.

15 The new architecture is *anti-decorative*.
Colour – and colour-shy people must strive

145

Counter-construction: axonometric
of the private house of 1923, Paris,
1924 ink and pencil on tracing paper,
49.5×40 cm. (19×16 in.)
Collection of Mrs Nelly van Doesburg.
Photo: P. Willi

Counter-construction; axonometric
of the studio house of 1923, Paris,
1924 gouache on tracing
paper, 50×35 cm. (20×14 in.)
Collection of Mrs Nelly van Doesburg.
Photo: P. Willi

to realize this – is not a decorative or ornamental part of architecture but its organic means of expression.

16 *Architecture as the synthesis of Neo-Plasticism.* Construction is only one part of the new architecture; by including all the arts, in their most elementary appearance, the new architecture manifests its very essence.

This architecture presupposes a capacity for thinking in four dimensions, so that the plastic architect, who might also be a painter, must construct in the new realm of space–time.

Since the new architecture prohibits representation (such as easel-painting or sculpture as separate elements), its purpose of creating a harmonic whole from all the above mentioned essential means is inherent in its *very nature*. In this manner every architectural element contributes to the maximum vitality of plastic expression, accomplished on a practical and logical basis, without prejudice to utilitarian demands.

Paris 1924
De Stijl, Series XII 6–7, 1924, pp. 78–83

Towards collective construction

We must understand that art and life are no longer separate domains. The idea that art is *an illusion divorced* from real life must therefore be abandoned. The word 'Art' means nothing to us. We demand that it be replaced by the *construction of our environment according to creative laws* derived from well-defined principles. These laws, which are akin to those of economics, mathematics, engineering, hygiene, and so forth, encourage a new plastic unity. In order to define the interrelationships among these laws, it is necessary to understand and to define them. Until now, the human creative domain and its constructive laws have never been studied *in a scientific manner.*

These laws cannot be produced by the imagination; they exist. One discovers them only through cooperative effort and from experience.

The basis for such experience derives from a knowledge of the elementary and universal

means of expression, which allows one to find a method of organizing them into a new harmony. The basis of this harmony derives from a knowledge of the contrasts or, rather, of a complexity of contrasts such as discord and many orders, which render visible our whole environment. This multiplicity of contrasts produces strong tensions, which, due to the interaction of mutual suppression, create balance and rest.

An equilibrium of tensions is the essence of the new constructive unity. This is why we demand the practical application or demonstration of this constructive unity in the real world.

Our era is hostile to every subjective speculation in art, science, technology and elsewhere. The modern spirit which already controls modern life almost completely is opposed to brutal spontaneity (lyricism), to domination by nature and to scroll-work and other such artistic cuisine.

147

In order to construct the new, we need a methodology, which is to say, an *objective* system. If the same qualities may be discovered in different objects, one has found an objective scale of relationships. One fundamental and fixed law, for instance, states that the modern constructive artist (each one in his own field) makes visible the relationship between *qualities* of objects but not the *relationship between the objects themselves.*

The speculative method – a children's disease – has arrested the healthy development of construction in accordance with universal and objective laws. Personal taste and also admiration for the machine (machine-art) are of no importance whatsoever in establishing unity between art and life. The ideal of the machine in art is as illusory as the ideals which inspired Naturalism, Futurism, Cubism and Purism among other movements, and it remains more dangerous than metaphysical speculation.

Therefore, progress comes about from a predominant use of the elementary means of construction, which suppress all meta-physical illusions. The future, in fact, will witness the expression of a new dimension in the reality of three dimensions.

This does not consist either of dynamics and statics and utility, or of art, composition and construction, but in the *penetration of all elements* in a newly created reality which is the basis for a general principle. Since 1916 the painters, architects, sculptors and others of the De Stijl movement in Holland, through practical experience have arrived at a definition and application of those laws which will lead to a new unity in life.

Because of this new concept, which results from mutual collaboration, individual qualities in works of art will become obsolete.

Only today can one imagine artists constructing a new way of life.

The exhibition of the De Stijl group in the Salles de l'Effort Moderne (Leonce Rosenberg) in Paris aimed at demonstrating the possibility of collaborative creation according to these general principles.

Theo van Doesburg and C. van Eesteren
Paris, 1923
De Stijl, series XII, 6–7, 1924, pp. 89–91

$$- \square + = \mathbf{R4}$$

I In close collaboration we have examined *architecture as the plastic unity of all the arts* (technology and industry excluded), and we have found that the result will be a new style.

II We have examined *the laws of space* and their endless variations (specifically, space contrasts, space discords, complementary spaces and so forth), and we have discovered that all these various spaces can be organized into a balanced unity.

III We have examined *the laws of colour* which operate in space and time, and we have discovered that a balanced relationship among these elements results in a new and positive plastic construction.

IV We have examined the relationship between space and time, and we have found

148

that the plastic visualization of these two elements produces a new dimension through *the use of colour*.

V   We have examined the interrelationships among measure, proportion, space, time and material, and we have discovered a definite method constructing them as a unity.

VI   We have removed the duality of interior and exterior space through the destruction of enclosure (walls).

VII   We have given colour its true position in architecture, and we declare that painting has no reason to exist separately from architectural construction (that is as easel painting).

VIII   The era of destruction is completely finished. A new era begins:

THE GREAT ERA OF CONSTRUCTION.

Theo van Doesburg and C. van Eesteren
Paris, 1923
De Stijl, series XII, 6–7, 1924, pp. 91–2

The end of art

(The other collaborators of this magazine undertake no responsibility for this article)
Against Vienna
Against Paris
Against The Netherlands
Art cannot be renovated.

'Art' is a Renaissance invention which has been carried to a state of extreme refinement in the present day.

This is the so-called *abstract art*!

The production of good works of art was achieved only at the cost of an enormous concentration upon certain matters. This concentration could be achieved only through neglecting *life*, through the very loss of life – just as religion had experienced before.

Today, this situation is no longer tolerable.

Today life is paramount. Modern life in general flatly rejects all tendencies towards isolation and ivory tower-like exclusiveness.

It is absolutely unmodern to concentrate upon just one thing (as did the Middle Ages)!

Modern life is based upon the construction, which is to say, upon a system of tensions or the neutralization of the system of carry and support.

In agreement with this concept we too must distribute our vitality over the whole range of life taken in the broadest possible sense. All other attitudes towards life produce tragedy.

This can be called progress and it excludes concentration on one interest.

This is the primary reason why art is impracticable.

Secondly, the development of a true life is hampered by art, just as in the Middle Ages scientific development was limited by religion and its official representatives.

The position which religion then took is now taken by art.

Art has poisoned our life.

Aesthetics has infected everyone (we are ourselves not excluded). No single object remains uninfected (in the Netherlands every cobble-stone is painted with an ornament or a rectangle). No pile can be driven into the ground without the priests of art raising

Sketch for a small flower-room at Hyères, France.
A – ceiling, B, C, D, E – walls; colour-construction, 1924–1925
ink, pencil and gouache on tracing paper, 54 × 61 cm. (21 × 24 in.)
Collection of Mrs Nelly van Doesburg. Photo: L'Art en photographie

objections and complaining about the resulting damage to the harmony of town-planning or landscaping.

If one chooses to put a typewriter or a sewing-machine in the living room, the housewife says: 'Please take it away; it destroys the harmony of the room.'

Post-cards, stamps, pouches, railway-tickets, pots, umbrellas, towels, pyjamas, chairs, blankets, handkerchiefs and ties – everything is 'arty'. How much more refreshing are those articles which are not called art: bathrooms, bath-tubs, bicycles,

automobiles, engine-rooms and flat-irons.

There are still people who can make beautiful things without art.

They are the progressives.

However, such people are frustrated; their activities are prescribed by ministers of art and their invention is hampered by art.

For the sake of progress we must suppress the notion of 'art' as an aesthetic speculation.

Paris 1925
De Stijl, series XII, 9, 1924–5, pp. 135–6

Painting: from composition towards counter-composition

Memorandum In 1912 I published my first articles on the new art under the title 'Essay of a New Criticism of Art'. I attempted to compare as objectively as possible my personal development with the general development in art and described the universal as its new content and rectilinearity as its new, future means of expression. In my view, these two elements would produce a new style.

I terminated this period in my development with an abstract composition which derived from naturalistic form (*Girl with buttercups*). Upon being demobilized in 1916, I founded *De Stijl*, not without enthusiasm. If the war had not prevented me from doing so, I would have founded De Stijl in 1914, since only in 1916 could I begin to develop my artistic production and conceptions (during this two-year interval perhaps they had been purified and refined) from the point at which I had left them in 1914. In an article, 'From Nature towards Composition'

(published in *De Hollandsche Revue* in 1918), I summarized my views by means of a series of pictures – abstractions from a subject – and demonstrated how I had travelled from naturalistic to plastic composition.

With the foregoing example (which ended in a composition composed of discords), I terminated this early period.

In writing down the title of the present article, I thought it advisable to relate the preceding information, since this article can be understood as a continuation of 'From Nature towards composition'.

With the *Composition in White, Black and Grey* of 1924, which is reproduced in the present issue of *De Stijl*, I terminated the period which in my view represents that of classical-abstract composition.

Doesburg, Paris, 1926

I The term COUNTER-COMPOSITION is not an artificial one, since it *arose naturally* rather

Counter-composition XVI 1925
oil on canvas, 100 × 180 cm. (39 × 71 in.)
Collection of Gemeente Museum, The Hague

than being selected either by chance or arbitrarily. It defines a phase of work and of plastic thought (or vision) which must be explained after the event.

Admittedly insofar as painting itself represents a way of thinking and of plastic thought or vision, all explanations are superfluous. Nevertheless, an explanation *a posteriori* (if it excludes all theorizing) can reinforce this vision. The time is past in which the painter, architect or composer need not think during his work nor live during his thinking.

On the one hand, the notion of 'counter-composition' is opposed to the classical, it is an 'abstract' notion of composition and plastic expression.

On the other hand, counter-composition is opposed to the fact that fundamental structural elements of nature and architecture are predominant everywhere.

Such elements, of course, were important to evolution; indeed, man needs a long time in order to acknowledge himself and his time. Our time has produced a need for contrast. This has been achieved not only in the external appearance of plastic expressions of colour and matter, but also, and chiefly, in the tempo of life and in the techniques related to the daily, mechanical functions of life; namely standing, walking, driving, to lying and sitting – in short, every action which determines the content of architecture.

This analysis is sufficiently confirmed by the verticals of our houses, by the horizontal planes of ceilings and floors and by the

152

horizontal and vertical planes which are contained within tables, chairs, cupboards and beds. These objects, in as much as they were once related to handicraft, have now become related to the machine. . . .
In conclusion, we perform our physical movements in horizontal and vertical directions.

These natural movements have become more or less mechanical through constant repetition. Instinct has been mechanized. In this process our spirit plays no role. To the degree that spirit has not become as 'stiffened' as our physical life, it opposes itself to this 'natural' mechanization and assumes a completely different dimension.

Our entire environment demonstrates the fundamental polarity of the horizontal and the vertical in natural structures. Perhaps more elementarily in our houses and cities than in the forest or in the landscape, but, in any case, the tension of this natural duality can be observed to a greater or lesser degree everywhere.

Our predecessors, like ourselves, expressed this throughout their work, either figuratively, by means of the *Standbein* and *Spielbein*, or symbolically, by means of the cross. All classical construction (load support) was based upon this principle.

The horizontal-vertical constitutes the basic content of physical, real or optical nature. The classical notion of art consisted of the plastic expression of this polarity as a balanced unity, but this solution has proved inadequate to the expression of the modern spirit which is characterized by an unavoidable strong opposition to nature, to physical structures and to all symbolic romanticizations thereof. [See Fig. 1, p. 154.]

Since our physical function in life is determined by the horizontal and the

vertical, it follows that, as long as this function has not been assumed by the machine, the most superior architecture is that which bases itself completely on the horizontal and the vertical.

II There are no objective and absolute laws which are *independent* of that vision which is becoming increasingly profound and variable (and if they were, would lead only to dogmatic sterility). Although there is no fundamental, objective truth, no truth at all, the specific quality of our work, nonetheless has become measurable.

Had optical perception not evolved into something more than sensory perception, into super-sensory perception, then the present period would never have had the courage to discover the spiritual in matter. There would have been no fundamental difference between a painting by Picasso (from his so-called 'abstract' period) and one by Paulus Potter, or between one of Brancusi's latest sculptures (*Sculpture for a blind man*) and an artificial egg from the bazaar.

Nature has not changed independently of us but we have made an ever-changing use of nature.

If this were not true, then natural forms – because of the character of the human spirit – would not have been converted into mechanical and impersonal forces. The same factors account for the individual and organic function of life. We are convinced that the conversion of these organic functions into mechanical functions represents a characteristic of a 'higher' culture and already we hold in contempt those who, by remaining utterly natural, function merely organically. This contempt is based mainly upon a feeling of complete unity with organic nature; the qualities which we do not find in 'natural'

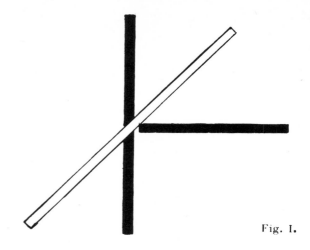

Fig. I.

man are opposition, contrast, resistance and struggle, or, in one word, spirit.

Without minimizing the natural by the adoption of a medieval stoicism, we actually *observe* that the human spirit possesses a structure completely different from that of organic nature and that the natural represents only the opposite (and not the counterpart) of spirit within the general aspect of the *technique of life* (which was formerly called 'drama').

Even an aeroplane flight can already convince one of the great difference between nature and the human spirit if one only compares the *landscape* with the *city*. In the latter environment and in each area wherein the human spirit has triumphed, a completely different order has been established, which is based on entirely different laws which are expressed in totally different forms, colours, lines and tensions.

With the same hostility as the city is related to the countryside, so is the structure of the human spirit related to that of nature.

Spirit is the natural enemy of nature although no duality is created, no matter how paradoxical this may seem.

The differences between the sigh of the wind, the rustling vibrations of water and the electrifying sound of a negro jazzband are bridged by the human spirit.

III I understand spirit to be entirely different from that which it represented for our predecessors or, until this very day, for witches, fortune-tellers and Theosophists.

Through its use in clichés, the word 'spirit' – as equivalent to the superior characteristic in man – has lost its significance and therefore its expressive power. Hence, it is difficult to designate that element in plastic expression which is achieved in a

direct manner. If the tension between extreme opposites, as we conceive them – for instance the polarity of nature-spirit – is neutralized through a satisfactory plastic equilibrium, then, due to the ineluctable need for evolution, it is still necessary to establish a new point of view towards this equilibrium. If this were not so, then the spirit would become crippled within the established equilibrium and would then represent a dead end (to quote Roland Holst, for once). No matter whether this equilibrium is conceived as representing a new culture, a new construction, a new religion or a new attitude towards life, if it represented the one and only goal, it would contain and epitomize everything which the human spirit could possibly seek. A new culture which was based on such an equilibrium would not permit any further evolution. If this equilibrium were to be manifested in a new construction or a plastic expression, these products could neither be improved upon nor developed. The established equilibrium would then be of an absolute instead of a relative nature, or of a stable instead of an unstable one: it would be eternal and immutable.

Naturally, this ideal is impracticable and, yet, no matter how absurd it may seem, all traditions and dogmas whose fundamental precepts were firmly believed to be immutable and which therefore became conventional and finally died, were based upon the hope of such permanence.

However, the need for evolution and the disturbance of the existing equilibrium (achieved through revolution) – a disturbance necessary to that evolution (which is a supreme and ineradicable characteristic of the human spirit) – have dictated another course of development.

Similarly, an attempt has been made to broaden the concept of space in terms of mathematics, providing a new dimension to our imagination (intuition or consciousness), and through continually novel attitudes to the already broadened concept of plasticism. This attempt has awakened our consciousness to a new *polarity* between nature and spirit, which operates, however, on an entirely different and much higher level than did the preceding classical conception.

If we define the principle of balanced relationship as exclusively the outcome of the conservative notion of art, then this new polarity is demonstrably made up of a unity of nature and spirit with the new superior notion of life as its opposite.

We include a diagram of this inherently changeable equilibrium, in which one easily can follow the line of evolution described above (see Fig. II, below).

IV   These considerations are only rather inexact explanations for the plastic expression by means of the oblique (in reference to natural and architectural structure). The new manner of painting as a process of spiritual expression is significant only in opposition to and not if homogeneous with organic-natural and architectural structure. This homogeneity expressed itself solely in a horizontal-vertically determined painting which functioned within the horizontal-vertically determined construction of archi-tecture. The former reinforced the latter. The development of the coloured plane and the line served the same natural, or functional, architectural structure. Thus, in Figs. III and IV, the shaded beams represent the natural or architectural structure based on the horizontal-vertical, the black lines the structure of classical abstract painting. In the case of contrast-painting (the counter-composition) the coloured plane and the line develop in opposition to the natural or architectural structure, which is to say that they contrast with it.

Both of these radical potentialities offer a great number of additional possibilities to art. It is plastic intuition, controlled by a scientific idea, which is needed by the new man.

In a future article I intend to discuss the degree to which technique and method will change in consequence of this new level of creation. Indeed, with reference to technique, it will be necessary to abandon illusionism (for instance through the suppression of illusion or romanticizing achieved by the use of value, tone and so forth) and to accept pure MATTER as the most precise and superior means of expression.

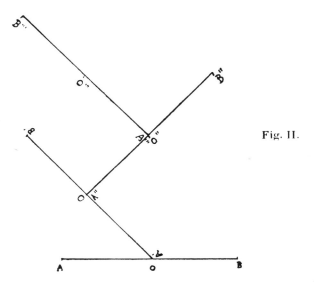

Fig. II.

155

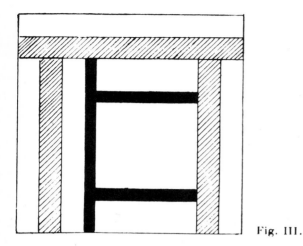

Fig. III.

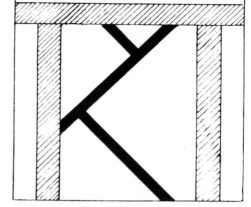

Fig. IV.

With the following list of definitions I have tried to circumscribe more closely the meanings which I attach to various, frequently used expressions. I believe that this should prevent a great deal of misunderstanding.

Spirit: man's capacity to think and thus to distinguish himself from animals; the superior quality of any substance, of which the soul is the essence.

Instinct: the first impulse, which derives from a purely animal need for selfpreservation or to protect oneself from and to respond to a natural phenomenon.

Intuition: the immediate understanding of values, truths and phenomena, without the use of preconceived thought.

Intellectual: that which is understood by the spirit apart from intuition alone.

Intelligence: the activity of the spirit itself, which integrates and governs all other functions of feeling.

De Stijl series XIII, 73–4, 1926, pp. 17–18, 23–7

Painting and plastic art

On Counter Composition and Counter-Plastic Elementarism (A Manifesto fragment)

Terminology
According to Marinetti it would be better to replace the term 'counter-composition' with 'anti-static painting'. However, his term could also be applied to architecture since architecture likewise can manifest an anti-

156

static character, if optically conceived, with new materials and new construction methods (for example, construction based on tension). That which belongs in essence to painting only seemingly belongs in architecture. Whatever construction is used, matter remains subject to the force of gravity. It makes no essential difference whether architecture uses load-and-carry construction, that based on tension or no construction at all (one thinks of the future possibilities provided by light skeletons in reinforced concrete and of modern methods of synthesizing which make a *chemical architecture* possible).

We operate within a kind of 'constellation of contrasts' in order to determine the precise relationship of man to the universe. Man controls the natural characteristics of matter through the mechanical production methods of bending, pressing, twisting, rolling and flattening. Modern technology transforms matter, *denaturalizes* it. The forms thus created completely lack the decorativeness of antique forms. Our own period's style is largely based on this *de-* or, rather, *transnaturalization*.

The term '*Neo-Plasticism*' (new plastic expression) unfortunately suggested a new plasticity in the sense of tangible three-dimensional sculpture. 'Plastic', as understood since its first use in my essay, 'The New Movement in Painting' (published in the periodical, *De Beweging*, 1916), meant the opposite of 'picturesque' and representational and, later on in *De Stijl*, stood for an immediate, elementary expression of aesthetic relationships. Consequently, it is a term which does not bear the Latin meaning of 'plastic'. I have replaced it by an all-embracing, more universal expression: *Elementarism*.

In addition, elementarism is real instead of abstract. The use of the term *abstract* also caused much misunderstanding. This is easily explained, if one adopts the point of view set forth in the present article.

As used in connection with visual methods of expression, the term 'abstract' is extremely relative. 'To abstract' something implies one of those mental activities (in contrast to emotional spontaneity) through which certain (aesthetic) values are isolated from the world of reality. However, when such values were realized visually and applied as purely constructive means, they became real. Thus the abstract was transformed into the real, thereby illustrating the relativity of the former term.

Hence, the term 'abstract-real' (Mondrian) was a fortunate invention, although in reference to a new orientation, the term '*real*' is sufficient.

The period of abstraction is at an end.

Is not an elementary painting, which is to say a certain composition of plane-linear colours, organic in itself, more concrete than a similar composition which is nonetheless veiled by the illusion of natural-organic form? Indeed, this instantaneously static, rigid composition, which is isolated within the four boundaries of the plane, is more abstract than the organic form which is composed of realistic colours in a so-called 'abstract' painting. In fact, abstraction is precisely that which takes place within the boundaries of individual thought. An unfolded newspaper is a manifestation of utter abstraction, since its content becomes real if a man bends over it in order to absorb and to translate the variety of events cinematographically and with tremendous velocity. The newspaper is real only if seen as a division of black and white. To the printer, a newspaper represents a reality completely different from the readers'. Abstract and real are relative, if not arbitrary, terms.

There is no doubt, however, that an increasing desire for *visual reality* has caused the tremendously increased popularity of the cinema, illustrated newspapers (one is reminded of the growing popularity of magazines), photography and so forth. This desire for visual reality is part and parcel of the style of our times. The printer's block represents as real a means of communication as does the train. We already enjoy a plastic, film-technical reign over space and time, and we are not far from achieving a chemical and radiomechanic elimination of the remaining dependence upon nature.

V   In order to achieve a new orientation in art, it is absolutely necessary to acknowledge this increasing need for reality. It has developed from our having an isolated abstract religious culture no longer suited to our emotional life.

The separation of religion from politics, of art from religion, of architecture from decoration and of politics from economics transpired during distinct, separate phases of this development.

This need for reality also left traces for many decades in the development of both art and architecture.

Whenever they were kept separate, pure construction and pure art, permitted a better opportunity for achievement in architecture. On the one hand, architecture had to become detached from the superabundances of earlier art forms, 'to abstract' in order to become independent. On the other hand, painting liberated itself from architecture, from the anecdotal, illusionist and classic notions of composition. Orthogonal composition, which

neutralized the extreme tension between the horizontal and the vertical, retained a certain similarity to static (carry-and-load) architecture, since both retained vestiges of conservative composition.

Counter- (or anti-static) composition has completely detached itself from this similarity. Its contrasting relationship to architecture can be compared (on another level) to the relationship of contrast between a white, planar-linear architecture and the grey curvilinearity of nature.

Elementarism has truly liberated painting from all convention. A quick review of the historical development of composition which begins with pure classicism, will convince us of this.

I   CLASSIC, SYMMETRICAL COMPOSITION

An equal division between and arrangement of halves flanking the central axis of a plane (for example, *The Three Graces*). Previous to the Christian era, painters often deviated from the method of symmetrical composition; after Christ, however, when the 'figurative' centre, Isis, Apollo and other such subjects were replaced by Mary or Christ, the symmetrically 'centred' type of composition achieved a formal, methodical significance which lasted until the beginning of the twentieth century.

II   CUBIST CONCENTRIC COMPOSITION

In the course of time symmetrical composition became more and more centred around the vertical axis of the plane, and so much so that the composition was arranged in an entirely axial way leaving the borders of the canvas white and thus void. Christ, Mary and the Cross were replaced by Guitar, Bottle and Newspaper.

III *NEO-PLASTIC, ECCENTRIC COMPOSITION*

A very important, genuine renovation of compositional methods. Gradual elimination of the centre and any passive voids. *Composition develops in the opposite direction. Composition gravitates towards the extreme boundaries of the canvas, instead of towards the centre*, and indeed, implies continuation beyond these limits. This approach also implied the possibility of a compositional development in three dimensions.

IV *ELEMENTARY (ANTI-STATIC) COUNTER-COMPOSITION*

This type adds a new, oblique dimension to orthogonal, eccentric composition. *Thus it eliminates the tension of the horizontal and the vertical in a realistic manner*. It introduces oblique and discordant planes which are opposed to gravitation and architectural-static structure.

In counter-composition the equilibrium within the place of the canvas plays a less important role. Each plane is related to eccentric *space*, and the construction must be regarded as a *phenomenon of tension* rather than a *phenomenon of planar relationships*.

This produces a larger variety of new possibilities for plastic expression. Apart from orthogonal and oblique constructions and their combination, simultaneous constructions can be produced as well. Colour is introduced as an independent energy.

V   *Elementarism* acknowledges Time as an element in modern plastic expression. Thus it offers new possibilities to *film, plastic art and theatre*. It is here that the *synoptical* effect achieves fundamental significance ('Synoptical' represents the simultaneous, optical combi-

nation of various parts which belong to a whole).

Elementarism represents a quite universal method of plastic expression and production. It is opposed both to compromise and to any dogmatic one-sidedness. It can be considered the most vital manner of expressing the modern spirit. It is the product of *Neo-plasticism* as well as of a new orientation in the fields of modern science and technology.

Elementarism comprises all expression in its most essential and elementary appearance. It demands that everything be determined and acknowledges the pure elementary existence of all separate phenomena: nature as nature, culture as culture, art as art and architecture as a functional, practical method of construction. All earlier systems thought themselves able to neutralize the hostility between organic nature and human intelligence through keeping them either alternate or in balanced relationship.

Elementarism rejects these systems and, because of the prevailing spiritual and social chaos, is confirmed in its basic principle concerning the complete difference in structure between the state of nature and the individual spiritual man.

It supports any destructive force which contributes towards true liberation and the ascent to a higher level of human spiritual activity. Because of its new orientation towards former efforts to renovate life and art (which include Futurism, Cubism, Expressionism, Dadaism, Neo-plasticism and so on) *Elementarism* contains all truly modern elements (which one-sidedly have often been ignored!).

Therefore, *Elementarism* may be viewed as a synthesis of the new plastic notions of our times. The 'isms' of recent decades went bankrupt largely through one-sided, dogmatic

159

limitations or compromises and due to chauvinism. They no longer possess any value or vitality that could lead to renovation.

Elementarism is the equivalent of relativity, of the latest discoveries about matter and of phenomenological definitions concerning the unlimited, yet latent, omnipotence of human intelligence. In contrast to religious dogmatists, the Elementarist considers life only as 'a perpetual transformation', whereas the creative artist represents a phenomenon in contrast with this perpetual transformation.

VI   The subject matter of counter-composition. Due to the increasing need for an understanding of reality, which expresses itself in the gradual suppression of all illusionistic means and transitional phases of approach, the *independence of matter* becomes increasingly apparent.

The same observation applies to colour.

Elementarism rejects the colour arrangement which stems from illusionism. Each colour – as pigmentation or as matter – possesses an independent *energy, an elementary force*. This applies to the three most positive colours – yellow, blue and red – and to their negative equivalents – white, black and grey. Neither Cubism nor Neo-plasticism could do without 'value'.

Admittedly Cubism (Picasso), Futurism (Carrà) and 'Merz' (Schwitters) each made an effort to use novel materials (such as newsprint, coloured matter, tin, metal and glass) in order to master the determination of value or, rather, its *material independence*. Post-Cubist styles of expression ignored their intuitive approach. Only by Neo-plasticism were the abstract approach and the expression of relationship consistently promoted.

In addition to using novel materials, Cubism both maintained the values obtained

through colour theory and also used letters, figures and monotonously dotted planes.

Elementarism rejects the use of these substitutions, while admitting their great value. It juxtaposes the positive colours with the negative white, black and grey, and, whenever these do not suffice, it adds elementary *variations* of colour or line (see the diamonds in my *Counter-composition XV*, 1925, illustrated in *De Stijl*, issue 73–74). Very elementary earthen colours and ochres can also serve as 'variations'.

In my now-completed 'Theory of Plastic Colour', I have dealt in a very direct way with colour as a means of creating *energy* and also *discord, contrast* and *variation*.

VII   Counter-plastic form: it is much more difficult to construct in an elementary manner through plastic form conceived as an independent, plastic expression, which is to say, in terms of painting, poetry and so forth. For instance, although on the one hand orthogonal plastic form is perhaps purer and more consistent than Cubist or Orphist plastic form, on the other hand it accentuates the force of gravitation in nature more than did its predecessors (which might be the explanation for its tragic default). It is understandable why – in order to avoid this either through the use of moving figures or more elementary forms – there arose a need for dynamics, which is another way of saying that a desire was born to create a form which contrasts with the orthogonal axis of static form.

Elementarism is preparing for the realization of elementary counter-plastic form, and we must first destroy the use of a static axis in contempt for the Euclidean view of life (which relates to the static point). With the use of a relief medium, this goal should prove easily

attainable; however, this relief medium calls
to mind too specifically an ornamental plate
and, by extension, the art of Russia. (The
Russian sculptor, Tatlin, called his bent-metal
reliefs 'counter-reliefs'. They nevertheless
possessed no quality of counter-plastic form,
since Tatlin, who was a romanticist,
understood neither the problem of modern
plastic form nor that of architecture. This is
sufficiently proved by his spiral, baroque
monument, which by reason of the illogical
composition of its spaces and elements, is
actually symbolic! (Russian
muddle-headedness and snobbish braggadocio
aimed at impressing teenagers!).

Several important works in the figurative
manner already point the way (one thinks of
several good sculptures by Archipenko, such
as *The Dance*, which was reproduced in *De
Stijl*, vol. I, and his *Gondolier*, as well as many
works by Boccioni, Brancusi and Laurens)
but, from an Elementarist's point of view,
hardly anything exists which can be
designated as an example of counter-plastic
form. Optical illusion seems to play a
dangerous and inevitable role in relation to
this problem.

Rome, July 1926
De Stijl, series XIII, 1 75–6, 1926, pp. 35–43

The other face. To be (I. K. Bonset)

He who is above cannot be below
Not to show one's colours is to be like flotsam
not to be consistent (to be oneself) is not being
inconsistent
but never being true
hate all flag-heroism but incite to
being oneself
suffering the consequences of being:
to be hard to be cold to be cruel
To kill to hurt
to disturb tranquillity
to distort harmony
from truly being `
that is heroic being
to be oneself is
being neither under bond nor borrowed nor sold nor hired
to be
means
to be spiritually free

De Stijl vol. XIII, 75–6, 1926, p. 64

161

The other face. Preface, Chapter one (I. K. Bonset)

abstract, sur-humanistic novel

preface

literature possesses its own reality, its own
system. 'reality' measures in seconds and
millimetres; the new literature does not
acknowledge such reality. It contains neither
'sense' nor purpose. its contents are words.
its medium is the method of writing. this new
method of writing, now applied for the first
time to the dutch language, is 'automatic'; it
is intuitive. in it a logical coherence is not to
be found.

each suggestion of continuation and
coherence has been terminated as in a
fraction of a second. in this automatic
procedure the entire field of inner
presentation is laid bare. the skeleton
becomes visible.

the dream is a banal form of literature. the
dream, however, possesses one advantage if
compared with literary forms of poetry. it
excludes reason. through this accomplishment
it acts upon the 'reader'.

we like dreaming because it makes us feel
free (we even wish dreams to be 'lascivious').
from the slavery of existence we flee into the
dream.

the new literature is at its best if like this.

the new poetry was born during the reign
of reason, as a relaxation which is opposed to
reason.

keep your ridiculous reason only in order to
check the bills of your tailor.

chapter one

after the nocturnal eclipses of the sun had
vanished and I had experienced the pleasant
sensation of dying, it became clear to me –

for the first time in my life – how dependent
was the fabric of my being. two unequal
parts, which showed no similarity whatsoever
to one another. each part invariably wished to
do very opposite things. despite this relative
hostility in disposition, structure, and sex, my
life had expressed itself in an undeniable
balance. at the moment of my death, time
had solved itself through matter and the
'nothingness' of which my double-being
largely consisted had assumed such enormous
proportions that entirely different dimensions
were required in order to contain it.

why?

and for the first time, through glazed eyes
my awakened consciousness perceived the
tremendous size of this pregnant body which
had been created from nothingness; the entire
mechanism of my being was dismounted
screw by screw and bolt by bolt. each part
was cleaned and polished; the whole was
carefully and thoroughly examined under
the microscope and then placed beneath
immaculate glass hemispheres, clean and
shining, as if I must perceive the complicated
organization of a world unfolding before my
petrified eyes. everything which gained
existence within the two of us – coloured
skeletons in swallow-tail coats, discoloured
mummies, perfumed or smelling of
putrefaction, or adorned with scarlet tin
flowers, mummies transparent as gelatine,
elastic as tape-worms and nourished by
luxurious vegetation, brains silvery,
ulcerated and sometimes decorated with
burning chalk candles or mummies swathed

162

in lace and silk sheets, decorated with flowers of blood – all fell apart in front of the frozen windows of my early consciousness and melted and washed away beyond recall in the immense abyss of nothingness. 'this is not the place to disturb and to deplore pleasant things', I was thinking at the moment when the razor sharp steel of an invisible guillotine split me into two unbalanced parts, preventing me from expressing an accumulation of contempt and horror for a world justified only thanks to its brothels.

De Stijl, series XIII, 77, 1926, pp. 66–7

Painting and plastic art: Elementarism

Elementarism (fragment of a manifesto)

Elementarism has been born partly in reaction to an over dogmatic and often narrow-minded application of Neo-plasticism, partly as its consequence but ultimately from what is primarily a radical correction of Neo-plastic ideas.

I   Elementarism rejects the demands of pure statics which lead to sterility and to the laming of creative potentialities.

Instead of denying Time and Space, Elementarism acknowledges these elements to be the most elementary means for creating a new plastic expression. Just as Elementarism attempts to bring both elements, statics and dynamics (rest and movement) into a balanced relationship, so it also attempts to combine these two elementary means within a new dimension. In contrast to the Neo-plastic manner of expression, which is restricted to two dimensions (the plane), Elementarism acknowledges a form of plastic expression in four dimensions, the realm of space–time.

In opposition to the orthogonal style of plastic expression, which is *homogeneous* with natural construction, Elementarism postulates a *heterogeneous*, contrasting, unstable manner of plastic expression based upon planes oblique in relation to the static, perpendicular axis of gravitation.

If Neo-plasticism introduced new ways of eliminating the compositional centre, Elementarism completely renovates our optical impressions, does not permit the work of art to consist of a left and a right half and radically destroys classical, optical frontalism in painting.

Although all human physical movement may be based upon the horizontal and the vertical, it is, in fact, only an accentuation of our *physique*, of the natural structure and functions of the organism, if the work of art *intensifies* this dualism of nature in our consciousness, even if in a manner appropriate to art.

After Neo-plasticism rejected symmetry because of its association with our external, physical structure (and rightly so), it should also have rejected the orthogonal because of its association with our physical, organic structure *as the exclusively practicable manner of expression*. This is precisely what is being done by Elementarism, which, through the suppression of rigid statics, evokes in us a

163

new spiritual emotion that goes with the new optics.

Elementarism is therefore the purest and most direct manner of expressing the human spirit, since it is bound neither to the left nor the right, to symmetry nor to statics and is based on neither the horizontal nor the vertical alone, but is always revolting against and contrasting with nature.

II   The method of construction in Elementarism is based on neutralizing the positive and the negative through the use of the *oblique* and, in relation to colour, through dependence on the *discord*.

Balanced relationship is not its final goal. Elementarism rejects arrangements of colours which accord with one another and each with the whole (the classical notion of composition!)

Elementarism acknowledges *colour as matter and independent energy*.

III   Elementarism rejects all artificial value and postulates the counter-value instead, which is to say, the variation opposing the invariable, the discord opposing the contrast, and, finally, combined lines and materials.

In opposition to the composition of balanced relationship in Neo-plasticism, Elementarism postulates *unbalanced counter-composition*, which is a phenomenon of temporal-spatial tension in colour, line or plane and always in opposition to natural and architectural structure.

Elementarism entirely rules out architecture as an art. Experience and research over the years have shown art and architecture to represent two completely different and incompatible entities.

Elementarism consciously strives for the end of applied art and is hostile towards all decorative application of the new principles. The basics of Elementarism, whenever applied to architecture, produce an architecture free from any aesthetic intention.

IV   Elementarism is directed not only at Art, Architecture and Design, but also concerned with man and his joy in life and the community. It seeks to provoke and strengthen the revolutionary spirit of the coming generations and counts on a larger group of younger people for the collective realization of a truly inner renovation of human attitude. This stimulation, since it is much more psychological than political, demands heroic spontaneity. Elementarism which is undertaken as psychological stimulation is called *profoundism*.

Renovations in art during the last twenty years have not prevented the individual and the community from concerning themselves solely with material interests. Material (natural) prosperity for the individual and the community was and still is used as mankind's criterion for success. Entirely different means than art can provide are needed to release man from his debased condition (which is supported by religion) and to lead him towards a new optimistic notion of life. Elementarism offers these means and sympathizes with all those movements (even those which advocate different principles in art) which make sacrifices to achieve this renovation, liberation and broadening of our notion of life.

The growing need to experience *reality* is not to be confused with an increasingly materialistic view of life.

The experiencing of reality can be seen as *resulting* from the old and almost entirely obsolete belief in a dualism between matter and mind.

Matter and mind are in essence qualitative ideas similar to those of the positive-negative, velocity-inertia and active-passive polarities.

In the experience of reality as set forth here, these qualitative ideas are neutralized and presumed to be a unity. Whether or not this experience of reality is 'abstract' is, from an Elementarist point of view, a technical question and, in fact, a matter of secondary importance, at least to the Elementarist. Since he regards universal movement (not to be confused with actual motion) as the cause of multiple relativity, matter and mind, reality and supra-reality and abstract and concrete represent nothing but *formulae*, which the development of consciousness in the thought process has *established and which exist at this very moment*.

This thought process, or this development of consciousness, is the sole reliable manifestion of polydimensional movement. 'Objective' and 'subjective' belong equally to the *type* of notion *Elementarism* has abandoned.

Elementarism begins where philosophy and religion leave off. As spontaneous, vital manifestations of consciousness, the latter disciplines have become sterile and obsolete. Each individual consciousness requires intellectual instead of perceptual activity. The Elementarist flatly denies all objective activity; he knows that everything became, becomes and will become real through subjective recognition. Feeling (art), labour and intellect were the three vehicles of consciousness. The artist's notion of life was based on an emotion, that of proletarians on labour and that of intellectuals on analysing intellect.

The great struggle which began with Elementarism consists in the complete destruction of the illusionistic view of life in all its aspects (which include the predominance of religion, nature and art) and, simultaneously, the reconstruction of an elementary world of reality full of beauty and precision. It is the task of Elementarism to demolish one by one those decorative reliefs which veil our image of the world such as the remnants of religion and of all other traditional forms.

The Elementarist is a spiritual rebel, an agitator who sacrifices his own tranquillity and who intentionally disturbs the peace, the regularity and routine, of bourgeois life. He does not abandon form on a piece of canvas measuring a half yard square; rather, he unrelentingly abandons form on the gigantic plane of human tragedy.

He understands that man is a tragic animal who lives only in terms of tradition, conservatism and the constant repetition of everyday routine. He comprehends this situation, this form of mercy seeking, as based upon one or another delusion which is variously called religion, duty or honour. If one abandons this delusion, one destroys at the same time the possibility of life for the bourgeoisie and even for those who think themselves above such delusion.

The Elementarist recognizes that all the various styles of life are temporal, relative and transitory, and of interest more as a phenomenon of fermentation than of culture. A new cultural phenomenon, however, was the discovery that ideas such as spirit, body and soul do not express any essential quality of life and that such characterizations of consciousness no longer possess any essential elementary value.

Elementarism advocates the complete destruction of traditional absolutism regardless of the guise in which it appears

165

(the nonsense of rigid oppositions like those of man and woman, man and god, good and bad and so forth). The Elementarist considers life a vast infinity wherein such polar characteristics as these continually interchange. Absolute differences are merely mental, symbolic and imaginary concepts, which are entirely neutralized and unified through reality. In opposition to this uniformity, the Elementarist postulates an absolute notion of universal movement. Even the individual 'I' is included in this notion. Thus, Elementarism is the purpose or end of life (the completion of consciousness) and necessarily plays an elementary role in life.

Paris, December 1926 – April 1927
De Stijl, series XIII, 78, 1926/7, p. 82–7

Elementarism and its origins

The fundamental polarity of natural structure found in everything which surrounds us is based upon horizontal and vertical positions. The entire machinery of common life is based upon an orthogonal system. The vital functions (to stand, to walk, to encounter, to move, to sit, and so forth), which is to say, everything involved in architectural structure, is also based upon this system.

Since the accelerated rhythm of contemporary life has gradually suppressed all sense of intervening intervals, elementary forms were bound to appear. The architecture engendered by this idea uses only the straight line and horizontal and vertical planes for expressing the notion appropriate to its period. Elementary means of expression in architecture and painting have not been applied arbitrarily, but have resulted from a series of psychological, biological and economic considerations. The straight line corresponds to the velocity of modern traffic, the horizontal and vertical planes to the most subtle manipulation or the most simple functions of life and industrial technology.

It is true that such functions have largely been taken over by the machine; nevertheless, the natural duality of the horizontal and the vertical remains dominant. Formerly this duality expressed itself in individual works of art as well as in collective productions (the good and the bad, the static and the dynamic or load and support).

The concept of classical art is based equally upon some duality. In painting it produces either representational or abstract composition. The human spirit, already deformed by the twin forces of symmetry and duality (feminine–masculine; space–time, and so forth), confounded the spiritual by using the natural. A confluence of primordial values ended in chronic decadence.

Modern man has left this era completely. Although he uses the machinery of modern life, his mind does not thereby become enslaved. He grasps the universe through projections and transverse sections. Without separating himself physically from the world, he liberates himself spiritually therefrom. *For him, the universe is only a system of relations.* He regards it as possessing a new dimension. He constructs a new world from the residue of the old world and challenges the orthogonal

166

View of the festivity hall in the Aubette,
Strasbourg, France, 1928 (destroyed)

system with an oblique one.

This oblique dimension not only nullifies
ancient modes of orthogonal expression (in
music, architecture, painting, sculpture, dance
and so forth) but simultaneously creates a
new system of optics and phonetics. These
elementary renovations find their equivalent
in the theory of relativity, in the new research
on the nature of matter and in a fresh
attitude towards the unlimited intelligence
and creative initiative of human beings.

Unlike defenders of religious dogmatism
and absolutism, the Elementarist experiences
life as a perpetual transformation and
spiritual activity as a phenomenon of
contrast.

167

View of the staircase in the Aubette,
Strasbourg, France, 1928.
Design by Theo van Doesburg;
colours by Hans Arp (destroyed)

168

Elevations and axonometric drawing of the private house.
Theo van Doesburg and C. van Eesteren, 1923

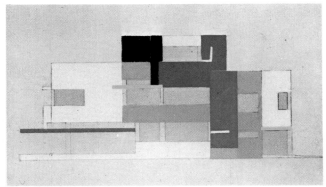

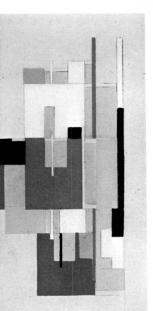

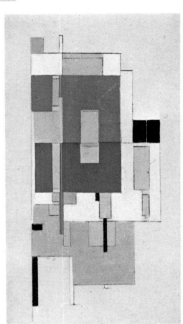

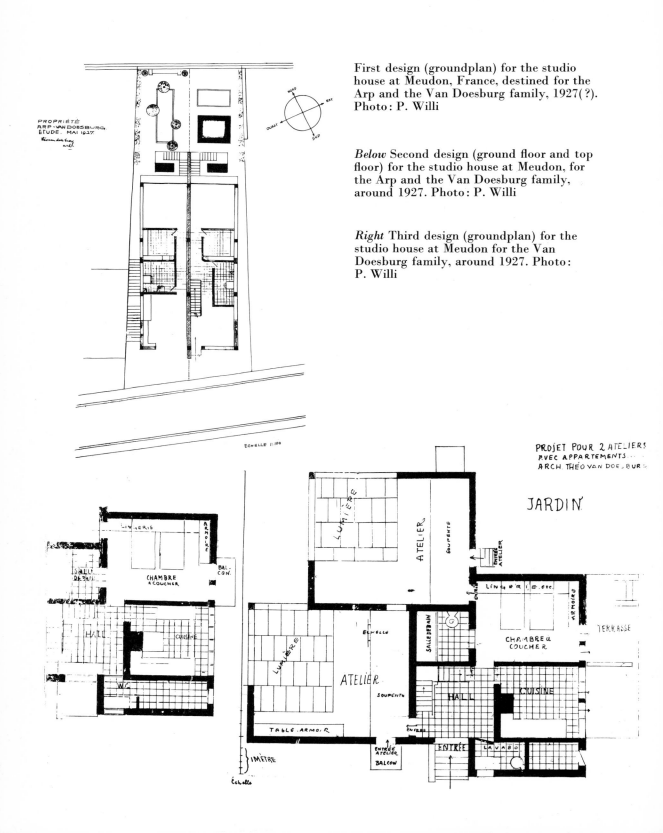

First design (groundplan) for the studio house at Meudon, France, destined for the Arp and the Van Doesburg family, 1927(?). Photo: P. Willi

Below Second design (ground floor and top floor) for the studio house at Meudon, for the Arp and the Van Doesburg family, around 1927. Photo: P. Willi

Right Third design (groundplan) for the studio house at Meudon for the Van Doesburg family, around 1927. Photo: P. Willi

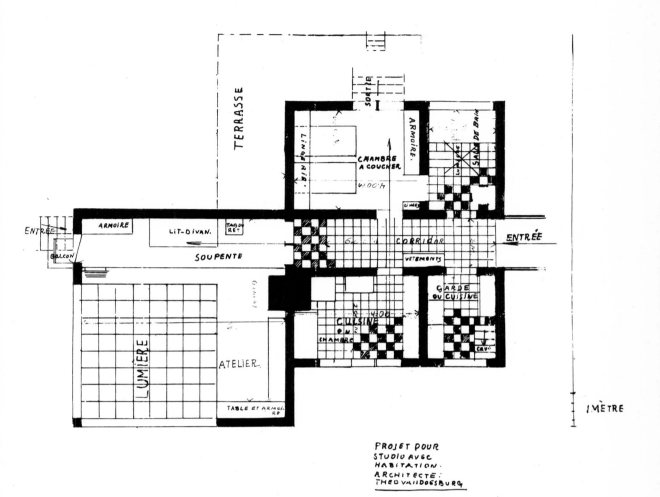

PROJET POUR
STUDIO AVEC
HABITATION.
ARCHITECTE:
THEO VAN DOESBURG

The Elementarist seeks to unify in a new method of expression the two main factors in creative activity, which is to say, rest and movement or space and time.

The Elementarist acknowledges times as an important value in the plastic work of art; in this manner he has presented film, music,

drama, sculpture and architecture with new possibilities.

This provides a universal method both for art and for industrial production.

Elementarism is opposed to compromise, to decadence, to contemporary aesthetic confusion (Neo-classicism, Surrealism and so

Design for the ceiling of the cinema and dance hall
in the Aubette, 1927 gouache on tracing paper,
72×109 cm. $(28 \times 43$ in.)
Collection of Mrs Nelly van Doesburg.
Photo: P. Willi

Design for a wall of the cinema and dance hall in
the Aubette, 1927 gouache on tracing paper,
45×105 cm. $(18 \times 41$ in.)
Collection of Mrs Nelly van Doesburg.
Photo: P. Willi

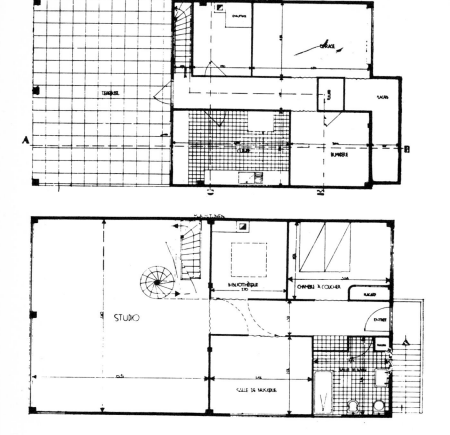

Fourth and final design for the studio house at Meudon (ground floor and top floor), 1929

forth) and to narrow-minded dogmatism.

It reduces all spiritual and technical activity to its most elementary form. It stems from functional thought, acknowledges the latent energy of matter (in colour, glass, iron, concrete, sound and word) and discovers for architecture a construction method which synthesizes all functions of human life. Elementarism was born in 1924 in The Netherlands (from the De Stijl group) and since then has won adherents in many countries.

Georges Antheil in music, Cesar Domela, Vordemberghe-Gildewart and the author of the present article (founder of the movement) in painting, Constantin Brancusi in sculpture, Mies van der Rohe, Van Eesteren, Rietveld and the author in architecture, I. K. Bonset in literature and Fr. Kiesler in the renovation of the theatre, all are Elementarists.

The Elementarist abandons all preceding systems and finds the confirmation of his basic principles in the spiritual and social chaos and the lack of style which predominate to-day and which result from the cardinal structural difference between *nature and society or between spirit and the individual*. It is for this reason that Elementarism defends those destructive movements which seek a true liberation of the human spirit by leading the individual and collective mankind towards a final higher level of existence.

All 'isms' which originated here in recent decades have failed largely because of the narrow-mindedness of their dogmas, compromise, or a chauvinistic tendency. All the gains in aesthetic insight of the last twenty years could not dislodge either the individual or collective mankind from its exclusive interest in material prosperity. Only material and physical well-being has served, and still serves, as a criterion of success. Much stronger means than those supplied by art will be needed to save man from debasement and to lead him towards a consciously held and more optimistic view of life. The Elementarist, with this purpose in view, seeks to develop the means which will serve this end and, for that reason, sympathizes with every movement which does not fear sacrifice in order to renovate and liberate itself and to render the new concept of life more profound. The great struggle engendered by Elementarism revolves around the destruction of the old concept of life, which is

based upon illusionism in all its aspects (which satiates both nature and art, for example); on the other hand, Elementarism seeks to reconstruct an elementary world of *super-sensible* reality. It accepts its task of suppressing the love of decorative frills, which is spreading throughout the entire world, as well as the remnants of religion and the clichés of tradition. Elementarism does not restrict itself to art, architecture and utility, but is also concerned with the human being and collective mankind. It will reawaken and reinforce the spirit of heroism in future generations in order to establish the essential renovation of contemporary viewpoints. This activity, which is much more psychologically than plastically based, demands *heroic disinterest and spontaneity*.

It is with all this in mind that I have undertaken the extensive piece of work involved in the *Aubette* at Strasbourg, which is intended to realize the *plastic expression* of Elementarism.

De Stijl Aubette Issue, series xv, 87–9, 1928, pp. 20–25

Space–time and colour

The plastic expression of space is inconceivable without light. Light and space complete one another. In architecture light represents an element of plastic expression – in fact, the most important one. An organic relationship between *space* and *material* is possible only with the aid of light. The highest achievements in architecture can be accomplished only if light also is treated as

plastic form. Plastic expression in architecture is inconceivable without colour. Colour and light complete one another. Without colour, architecture is expressionless, blind.

This truth has been expressed in every period in a different manner and according to different needs. If the Functionalists wish to suppress colour completely, then this merely proves that they never understood the

175

Design for a wall of the cinema and dance hall in
the Aubette, 1927 gouache on tracing paper,
44×93 cm. (17×37 in.)
Collection of Mrs Nelly van Doesburg
Photo: P. Willi

Design for a wall of the cinema and dance hall in
the Aubette, 1927 gouache on tracing paper,
44×86 cm. (17×34 in.)
Collection of Mrs Nelly van Doesburg.
Photo: P. Willi

importance of colour as an *architectural element*, as a means of plastic expression, no matter whether used with iron, glass or concrete. It does not make any fundamental difference whether one is concerned here with paint that has been applied to something or with the colour inherent in the materials used. Naturally, architecture does not become art merely through the use of colour, and it is therefore understandable that revolutionary and Constructivist architects wish to restrict themselves to the use of strictly architectural means. Colour was misused in architecture because it was applied decoratively. However, colour is as indispensable to man as is light. The plane in modern architecture demands intensified realization, which is to say plastic expression in terms of spatial, pure colour. The correct use of modern materials remains subject to the same laws as those governing colour in space and time, even if applied paint is completely abandoned. Just as the various colours (for example, red, blue and yellow) each have an energy of their own, the modern materials (for example, concrete, iron, glass) each possess an energy of their own. Blue and yellow, for instance, produce two entirely opposed energies. I call this opposition a *tension*.

A similar tension is produced by the two materials iron and glass. The application of this tension in space and time is as aesthetically and architecturally relevant as the application of two colours on a plane or in space. In order to orient ourselves correctly to the use of colour in space (while not as yet touching upon the notion of 'time'), we must agree upon the various manners of relating painting to architecture.

We shall list the following:
1 the decorative, ornamental manner;
2 the Rationalist or Constructivist manner;

3 the creative manner or plastic expression.

In the *decorative use of colour* one is concerned with a tasteful effect of colour in space. Space is decorated with colour (the ornament) without achieving any organic relationship to the construction. Colour merely serves to hide construction. (The Dutch architect, Berlarge, in his theories, has even indicated where ornament must be applied in architecture.) Construction and painting are never truly related. They co-exist, rather than penetrate one another, and, therefore, they do not evoke a 'synoptical' result. The principle of decoration and ornamentation is based fundamentally upon repetition of the pattern, a repetition established by the element of 'time'. THE SOLUTION OF THE PROBLEM OF COLOUR IN ARCHITECTURE IS IDENTICAL TO THE SOLUTION OF THE PROBLEM OF TIME IN PAINTING!

Only to-day, in the twentieth century, have we understood that the practice of repeating an ornament is the result of spiritual poverty. Oriental tapestries and wall-paper which is derived from them are subject to the same weakness of repetition. All painting in the past implied continuation into space and therefore, being subject to the continuation of time, possessed the character of repetition. This applies to painting and architecture, to music and poetry. The problem remains; only the means and the styles of expression have changed. They have become *realistic* instead of illusionistic. The repetition of a musical theme is as decorative as the regular repetition of certain architectural parts. Similarly, the element of symmetry, which is retained to-day by some modern architects (Le Corbusier, Loos, Oud, and others) has its roots in decorative and ornamental habits.

177

About fifteen years ago, when there was a reaction against decorativism, a demand was made: 'Return to rational construction. Down with the ornament.' The ornament was considered criminal and colour was banished completely from architecture. Only the creation of 'grey in grey' remained. When construction ended, the world of colour ceased to exist. Architecture was rendered naked, consisting of skeleton and skin.

Some time ago (about 1918), I described this architecture which dealt only with naked structure as 'anatomical' architecture. Indeed, in Germany, one spoke of a 'skeleton and skin' architecture and was not prepared to discuss aesthetic speculation or problems of plastic form. One healthy phenomenon in this movement was the suppression of predetermined form in architecture. The new definition of architecture could be summarized as organization of materials according to function. Form was considered secondary and independent of function. There was no room for colour. Painting was 'finished'.

The Russians were the first to return to 'painting' and even to 'art for art's sake'.

Subsequently (or, rather, in practice), one admitted that this elementary, grey architecture was expressionless and blind. Through the fanatic glorification of 'pure utility' and the 'purely functional', one was restricted to practical or factual considerations and prone to neglect the 'optical, tactile and spiritual' factors. In modern man the desire for colour is as indispensable as that for light. Movement (the dance) and even mere noise have become essential elements in the life of modern man, in the modern 'nerve-system'. Any attempt at renovation that stresses only one factor and, consequently, leaves out all other factors, is weak and bound to perish.

Thus, Functionalism would have perished, too, if it had not acknowledged human spiritual needs. However, the functional romantic was willing to accept colour only as functional colour. A second manner of using colour thus came into existence, the rationalist or Constructivist method. I must stress here that this debasement of colour into functional colour occurred at a time when the very existence of the artist as such was in danger. A virtue was made of the necessity by declaring that the poster, the emblem and the advertisement were the consequence of a new 'abstract' art in painting. However, only results possess meaning within the field of creative activity.

The basis for painting does not lie in its purpose. Nor can the suppression of colour in architecture be considered the basis for modern architecture. On the contrary, since painting and architecture developed increasingly a common denominator, a more coherent relationship between colour and space was manifested. It was at this moment that the problem of the creative use or the plastic expression of colour in space was born.

During my collaboration with the young architect C. van Eesteren (1923), I myself sought to employ colour as *an element which stressed* the architectural expression of space. In this attempt any artistic or compositional approaches were barred. The planes which determined space were painted in a certain colour according to their positions in space. Height, depth, and width were emphasized by red, blue and yellow, whereas volume was conceived in grey, black and white. In this fashion the dimensions of space became quite expressive and architecture was reinforced instead of destroyed.

What is it, in the end, that we believe the plastic use of colour in space to represent?

Simultaneous Composition XXIV 1929
oil on canvas, 50×50 cm. (20×20 in.)
Yale University Art Gallery, Gift of Société
Anonyme

Since the founding of the so-called De Stijl movement, we have attempted to solve this problem in both practice and theory. The solution has presented itself as the logical result of the consequences of two-dimensional painting. After illusion had been eliminated from painting and the picture had ceased to limit itself to the representation of the individual expression of personal experiences, painting achieved a relationship to space and, more important still, to MAN. The relationship of colour to space, and of man to colour, sprang to life. Through this relationship of 'dynamic man' to space, a new notion was established in architecture, the notion of time.

The movements of man in space (from left to right, from in front of to behind and from above to below) gained an importance fundamental for painting's role in architecture. Whereas man had remained fixed in a certain position in reference to static painting, and although decorative or 'monumental wall-painting' had already made him susceptible to a kinetic, 'linear' termination of the picturesque in space, the plastic expression of SPACE–TIME PAINTING would enable him to experience the full CONTENT of space in a pictorial (Optical-aesthetic) manner. This experience was just as novel as the first flight by aeroplane.

This manner of painting did not propose to direct men along the coloured planes of the walls with the purpose of allowing them to perceive the pictorial development of space from wall to wall, but rather to evoke a *synoptical effect* between painting and architecture. In order that this could be achieved, the coloured planes had to be related in both an architectural and a pictorial manner. The whole had to represent the plastic expression of a *tangible object*.

Construction and composition, space and time, and statics and dynamics were welded into a unified organism.

Fundamentally architectural space must represent nothing but expressionless and inarticulate *emptiness* so long as colour has not transformed it into the true expression of plastic space.

The plastic expression of space–time painting in the twentieth century enables the artist to realize his grand vision of placing man *within* painting instead of in front of it.

In the final analysis it is only the exterior surface which defines architecture, since man does not live within a construction but within an *atmosphere* which has been established by the exterior surface.

De Stijl Aubette Issue, series xv, 87–9, 1928, pp. 26–7, 31–34

Art Concret. The basis of concrete painting

We state:

1   Art is universal.

2   The work of art should be fully conceived and spiritually formed before it is produced.

It should not contain any natural form, sensuality or sentimentality.

We wish to exclude lyricism, dramaticism, symbolism and so forth.

3   The painting should be constructed

completely with pure plastic elements, that is to say, with planes and colours. A pictorial element has no other meaning than what it represents, consequently the painting possesses no other meaning than what it is by itself'.

4 The construction of a painting and its elements should be simple and direct in its visualization.

5 The technique should be mechanical, that is to say, precise rather than impressionistic.

6 Absolute clarity should be sought.

Carlsund, Doesburg, Hélion, Tutundjian,
Wantz
Art Concret April 1930, p. 1

Comments on the basis of concrete painting

1 We speak of *concrete* and not *abstract painting*, because we have finished with the period of research and speculative experience.

In their search for purity artists were obliged to abstract from *natural forms* in which the plastic elements were hidden, in order to eliminate natural forms and to replace them with *artistic forms*.

To-day the idea of *artistic form* is as obsolete as the idea of *natural form*. We establish the period of pure painting by constructing *spiritual form*. Creative spirit becomes concrete.

We speak of concrete and not abstract painting because nothing is more concrete, more real than a line, a colour, a surface.

A woman, a tree, a cow; are these concrete elements in painting? No. A woman, a tree and a cow are concrete only in nature; in painting they are abstract, illusionistic, vague and speculative. However, a plane is a plane, a line is a line and no more or no less than that.

Concrete painting. Spirit has arrived at the age of maturity. It needs a clear, intellectual means of expression in order to manifest itself concretely. The domination of individualism and narrow-mindedness were always a serious hindrance to the birth of a universal art.

Whenever the means have been liberated from all particularity, they correspond to the very aim of art: to embody a universal language.

2 The work of art is not created with the fingers nor by the nerves. Emotion, sentiment and sensitivity have never advanced art towards perfection. Only thought (intellect), which doubtless possesses a speed superior to that of light, is *creative*.

Lyricism, dramaticism, symbolism, sensitivity, the sub-conscious, dreams, inspiration and so forth are substitutes for creative thought.

Intellectuality is effectively important in all realms of human activity. The evolution of painting is nothing but an intellectual search for the truth by means of a visual culture.

Beyond the creations of thought there is only the baroque, Fauvism, animalism, sensualism, sentimentality and that super-baroque testimony of weakness:

181

phantasy. It is quite the contrary with the era which is now beginning; this is the era of certitude, that is to say, of perfection.

Everything is measurable, even spirit with its one hundred and ninety-nine dimensions. We are painters who think and measure.

3 In painting colour represents the only truth. Colour is a permanent energy which is determined in opposition to another colour. Colour in painting is the one element which possesses only the meaning inherent in its own nature. Painting is a means through which thought is expressed in a visual manner; every painting is a colour-thought.

4 Construction in accordance with the plane of the canvas-surface, as well as the space created by colours, can be controlled by the eye. This process of construction differs completely from those of arrangement (decoration) and tasteful composition.

Most painters work like pastry-cooks and milliners. In contrast we use mathematical data (whether Euclidean or not) and science, that is to say, intellectual means.

Before it is physically made material, the work of art is fully conceived by the spirit. Thus its production must reveal a technical perfection equal to that of the concept. It should not reveal any trace of human weakness such as trembling, imprecision, hesitation, nor any unfinished parts.

In the name of humanism one has tried to justify quite a lot of nonsense in art. If one cannot manage to draw a straight line with the hand, one may use a ruler. Typewritten print is much more clear, readable and beautiful than handwritten script.

5 We reject artistic handwriting.
If one cannot draw a circle by hand, one

Cover of the magazine *Art Concret*, 1930
18.5×13.9 cm. ($7 \times 5\frac{1}{2}$ in.)

may use a compass. All instruments which were created by the intellect due to a need for perfection are recommended.

6 A work of art thus conceived will manifest the principle of clarity which will serve as the basis for a new culture.

Paris, January 1930
Art Concret April 1930, pp. 2–4

Towards white painting

'Brown', 'Blue', and 'White' correctly express the three phases of the development of humanity and of all its activities: science, art, religion, technology and architecture.
WHITE   This is the spiritual colour of our times, the clearness which directs all our actions. It is neither grey nor ivory white, but pure white.
WHITE   This is the colour of modern times, the colour which dissipates a whole era; our era is one of perfection, purity and certitude.
WHITE   It includes everything.

We have superseded both the 'brown' of decadence and classicism and the 'blue' of divisionism, the cult of the blue sky, the gods with green beards and the spectrum.

White pure white.

Looking around us, we see only manure, and it is in manure that filth and microbes live.

Let them amuse themselves, down there in the depths; we want more, we want to mount the heights of truth where the air is pure and can be withstood only by metallic lungs.

Our spirit has muscle, which is why we dare to paint, to live. It has been forgotten what painting means; the cards have been stacked, and even the most humble spectator will understand that this is foul play. These tricks of embellishing things and imitating hysterical hallucinations are too well-known and easily come by. We are not searching for 'Luna-park' sensations, nor sadistic or sexual attractions in order to tempt a snobbish and surfeited bourgeoisie. Those pictures which devour the onlooker . . . we are through with them.

All such pleasantries we leave to those who need them. We don't believe in wonders, we are realists.

There is a greater 'miracle' in the tension between concrete colours or the balance of lines than in all the diseased exaltations which are presented to us to-day as modern painting. We have seen enough painting which possesses a nauseating character. *There is nothing to be read in painting: there is only something to be seen.* In the vigour of its youth, painting displayed a certain fever in the use of brush work or selection of subject. However, painting has arrived at the age of maturity. To-day man is more consciously intellectual, profound and spiritual than ever before. His art reveals this new attitude which displays greater simplicity, firmness and regard for science. In the future art will be based upon science and technology rather than upon the dream.

We have the experiments of the falsifiers in painting as proof that the dream is a misleading guide to the plastic realm. The aim of painting is not to exhibit vices or to undress before the spectator. These 'impressive' canvases, which are presented as modern painting in all art galleries are the cork to the bottle of individualism.

This bottle contains nothing, not even poison.

Painting which is done in the manner of Jack the Ripper can interest only detectives, criminologists, psychologists and psychiatrists. It is and will remain outside modern life, outside our social and artistic demands; it shows no relationship whatsoever to our architectural spirit and constructive intelligence.

Paris, December 1929
Art Concret April 1930, pp. 11–12

183

Elementarism (the elements of the new painting)

What is it about which the painter of to-day cares most?

He cares most to feel as if he himself is like colour, or eventually is colour. Without this attitude the work of art will remain achromatic, even if it is multi-coloured.

To be white, red, yellow or black is to be a painter. To-day it is not sufficient for the painter to think of colour; he should be colour, feed on colour and transform himself into painting. That is the essential thing.

To feel like colour means to carry within oneself the entire range of colours, not as a treasure, but as a trust.

In reference to form, a single element for instance, the square is sufficient.

The square represents a stable element which must be arithmeticized if it is to be animated. The line is functional, it separates and unites simultaneously. It bestows power on the work of art and provides the onlooker's eye with direction. 'Composition' is no longer prevalent in painting. Composition represented a transition to a universal form, the form of the spiritual. The true work of art is created only by those who did not hesitate when faced with the complete destruction of their former visual modes of perception. The complete and definitive work of art is created beyond one's individuality; one therefore must not hesitate even to renounce this individuality. The universal transcends such a level. Mere spontaneity has never created a work of art which possesses a lasting cultural value. The method leading to universal form is based upon calculations of measure and number. The Pyramid of *Cheops* was based upon a similar approach. Individuality had a *raison d'être* along with

'composition'; however in the present period of 'construction', individuality has become an obstacle and a subject for satire. Composition means individual variation of form and colour or balanced relationships (the painter functioning as an equilibrist). Construction means stabilization and the synthesis of form, colour and relationships which is a supra-individual approach. To prefer a certain colour (for instance, yellow) or a certain direction (for instance, the vertical) is similar to preferring a certain kind of nourishment. Art is more than a type of cuisine. To change the direction (for instance to the oblique) is to change and renew the perception of the onlooker. 'A miracle' was never created by means of spontaneity, since this approach was based upon superficial fantasy. Nothing is more dangerous than fantasy! Fantasy represents a music-hall mentality. Only profound and disciplined work is of significance.

Hasty or hurried work, executed without discipline or control, can only produce fugitive impressions. Works of art created in this fashion will not create in the onlooker any desire for contemplation.

A cool and tense surface will be more significant than a nervous touch of the brush or warm colouring. Spiritual maturity will be more effectively demonstrated through the use of grey, yellow and green than through red and brown (one may use ochres, if these are conceived as representing material reality). One must always paint in opposition to nature, and to one's own 'mood'. To let oneself go is a weakness, a sort of hysterics.

If you are full of red, choose a green or a blue; if you feel like yellow, choose grey or black. In this continuous opposition lies the entire secret of plastic creation.

To create presupposes, in any case, that we ourselves are opposed to matter, nature and the surrounding environment; otherwise, plastic art would not possess meaning. To create a great work of art demands self-mortification.

Choose white, always much white and black, for the significance of colour emanates only from the opposition of black and white. A single colour is sufficient to create a work of art, provided that this colour possesses such power, such mathematical significance, that it is able to evoke all other colours through the power of measure, direction and position.

The best handicraft is the one which displays no human touch. Such perfection is dependent upon an environment of absolute cleanliness, constant light, a clear atmosphere and so forth. These characteristics of our environment are transformed into the qualities found in our work. The artist's studio will be like a glass-bell or a hollow crystal. The painter himself must be white, which is to say, without tragedy or sorrow. The palette must be of glass; the brush must be square and hard, dust-free and as immaculate as a surgical instrument.

Doubtless there is much to learn from a medical laboratory. Do not artists' studios usually smell like monkey-houses? The studio of the modern painter must reflect the ambience of mountains which are nine-thousand feet high and topped with an eternal cap of snow. There the cold kills the microbes.

Paris, 13 July 1930
De Stijl Van Doesburg Issue (last issue),
January 1932, pp. 17–19

From intuition towards certitude

1 Speculative and random methods in art have become obsolete. Intuition leads us to adventure and to the dream.

2 Paintings cannot be realized through a juggling-trick or by sleep-walking. It was this type of decadence which forced us to arrive at that formidable guide: intuition.

3 That which to-day bestows a cultural value on painting is mathematical or, rather, arithmetical control. Mathematics has represented not only the basis of all science but also the foundations of art during the great epochs. As soon as the artist uses elementary forms as a means of expression, his work is not merely 'modern', but universal.

4 After having passed through the various phases of plastic creation (the phases of arrangement, composition and construction), I have arrived at the creation of *universal forms* through constructing upon an arithmetical basis with the pure elements of painting.

5 This universal form contains a *number of plastic events* and, at the same time, is the

185

starting point for a multiplicity of constructions.

6 The relationships of each construction can
be controlled arithmetically and always
correspond to the first theme.

7 Here we have a means for arriving at a
serious and universal art. All artists who think
in these terms may use these methods.

Paris, 1930
Réalités nouvelles, 1947, no. I, p. 3

Unpublished material

The struggle for the new

Aims

1 To promote a radically new type of plastic expression through the development of common basic principles.

2 To strip the means of expression of all individualistic characteristics.

3 To develop a collective-creative personality.

4 To create upon a common basis (not to be confounded with dogma) a system which makes it possible to organize the entire realm of plastic expression and, thus, to apply the creative means of expression in a correct non-morphoplastic way.

5 To dispense completely with decorative and other such forms of applied art.

6 To distribute various tasks among architects, painters, engineers, chemical scientists and other designers (such as the cabinet-maker).

7 To mechanize methods of production in reference to both the details and the product as a whole.

8 To dispense with every individualistic, arbitrary manner of production or handicraft.

9 Point 8 can also be applied to music in reference to mechanical performances with newly created instruments.

10 Research on materials in laboratories of plastic expression.

11 Research on construction in experimental spaces and specialized studios.

12 To unify the real (construction) and the ideal (aesthetics).

Systematics

Just as for centuries individualistic morpho-plasticism has created a system of form and feeling, so universal, formless, elementary plastic expression will create a system in accordance with a new mentality. Although this system will destroy the still predominant individualistic morphoplasticism, it will not effect individuality. Some characteristics of the De Stijl system are given as examples here:

1 Orthogonality, definition and directness.

2 The plane, pure colour and pure sound

(pure colours are red, blue and yellow or black, grey and white).

3 The strongest opposition (for example, horizontal-vertical), but also the opposition-less: the oblique, the discord.

4 Openness.

5 The use of the fourth dimension or time (film, music and architecture).

6 Harmony and disharmony by means of an opposition of planes and colours (contrasts).

7 Utmost concentration: the suppression of the (predominant) individualistic approach.

8 Mechanization, automatization and elementary construction (as opposed to naturalism).

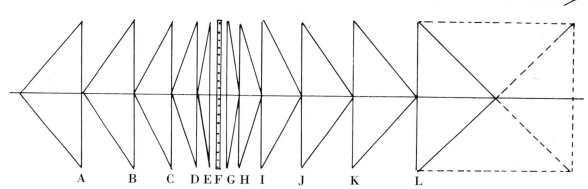

A   B   C D E F G H I   J   K   L

Graph of the development from perspective illusionism towards the plane (F) and onward to the creation of new realms

A–F the suppression of perspective in favour of the plane

F the plane

B C D E some phases of development, for example:

B Impressionism

C Fauvism

D Futurism

E Cubism

F the New Plastic Expression (a psychological change)

With the mastering of the plane, which is the basis of a new creative expression, the entire consciousness of plastic expression is reversed.

The illusionistic representation of space and time in terms of volumes (of objects) gradually will disappear until the plane has supplanted it.

F The realms of space and time, which previously were expressed through illusion only, are now established as a real-plastic manner of expression.

Commentary: it is already generally acknowledged that since 1905 painting has led in the entire development of the new art.

However, it is an error to confine the new possibilities of expression to painting. Each form of art must be renovated according to its intrinsic function. It would be folly to introduce a system of three tones in music because painting has established a system of three colours.

It would be equally senseless to demand a flat show-box for the theatre because painting possesses only two optical dimensions. Neither medieval frontalism nor Renaissance three-dimensionality concerns us to-day; De Stijl regresses to neither.

De Stijl progresses towards unimagined possibilities in four, five or six dimensions (plural dimensionality).

The *counter-construction* is of first importance here. In Graph I, this has been indicated with G.

H The mastering of space–time (problematic,

four-dimensional possibilities of expression).

I The mastering of tactile space (fifth dimension).

J Qualitative differences of space and the possibilities of expressing it, which, until now, have remained unimagined.

Marinetti's Tactilism can be seen as an instinctive effort in this direction even if it presents only the sensuous-tactile expression of space through using various materials.

Picasso's earlier compositions in various materials also concern us here. The Russian artists (Tatlin and Lissitzky) also appreciated the exterior quality of the plane, not only optically, but also in a tactile manner.

The creative possibilities contained between F. and J. are dependent upon scientific and technical progress. Intuition already produced a foreknowledge of these new realms, but they can be established fully only by science.

De Stijl always has striven for a harmony between the realms of intuition and scientific determination. If one looks once more at the realms which precede F., one can see that art is becoming increasingly linked with real life. Thus it can be understood why architecture (the plastic expression of life as a whole) is increasingly important.

1929–30

The new architecture and its consequences

Until now, architecture has been approached from two opposite points of view. Either it was examined from a rationally constructive,

utilitarian position or a speculative, aesthetic one. On the basis of the rational-constructive point of view, the architect has rejected all

189

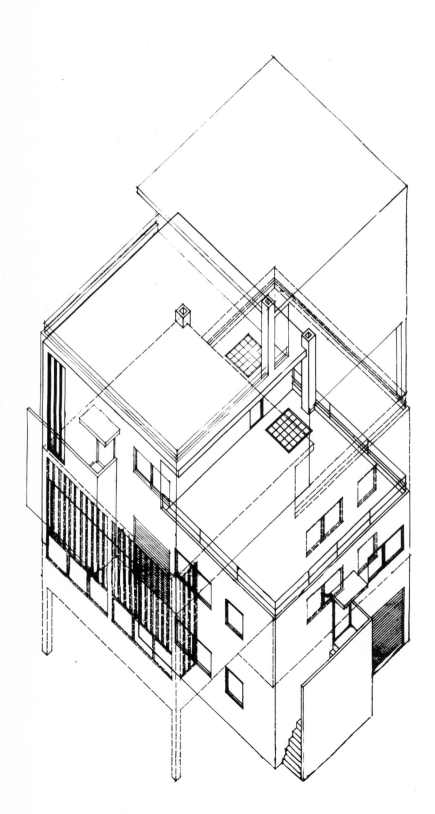

Design (axonometric) for a
vertical projection of the
Meudon house, 1929.
Photo: P. Willi

aesthetic speculation and renovated architecture through building functionally which demands the industrialization of architecture as an ultimate consequence. The speculative-aesthetic approach has produced an ordinary ornamental manner of building, an architecture decorated by the applied arts: Hoffmann-ism in Austria and 'Wendingen' in Holland, which represent an approach in architecture exclusively based upon aesthetic speculation. These two approaches are mutually inimical to such a degree that fusion is impossible. In my view, the correct approach to architecture is to be found neither in the materialistic-constructive efforts of the former, nor in the decorative-speculative attitude of the latter of these two approaches.

Architecture is a scientific problem, the solution of which depends on social and bio-genetic circumstances. Renovation should respond to the demands which are produced by the evolutionary development of life itself.

If it is said that a house is 'only to live in', one must ask how 'living' is defined. Living is a function of life which is concerned not only with our physical but also with our spiritual activities. These two activities cannot be divorced, and thanks to this fact, architecture has gained a new task, which, since 1916 we have called its plastic aim. 'Plastic' must be understood here in the sense of the constructive-creative combination of all concrete and abstract values in architecture.

From this point of view the concept of architecture is no longer restricted to the house but comprises our entire environment as well and culminates in the idea of 'the city'. Therefore, if one approaches architecture from a single point of view, for example by adopting either the rational-constructive or the pure creative attitude, the result will be unilateral and impoverished.

Architecture does not comprise merely a house, a factory, a block of houses or a town quarter, but implies *the complete expression of all our physico-spiritual demands, or, in short, the full expression of* our life. It comprises all problems of detail, construction, creativity and economics.

What matters is to consider all these elements in relation to architecture rather than to consider each a separate *form* of architecture. Each element must be maintained in its proper place and not exchanged for another as is still being done. It is here, I believe, that the mistake lies. The mutual control of various arts is indispensable to a correct application of those architectural means which produce an elementarist architecture.

The development of modern architecture in Holland, for instance, was influenced by parallel developments in painting.

Remarkably, the various arts mutually influence and control one another at all periods of development. For example, in about 1910 the Cubists were extraordinarily interested in music and architecture. In these arts they encountered principles which were similar and fundamental to those of painting. Recent efforts in Constructivism and Neo-plasticism likewise reveal an interest in technology, science, industry, hygiene and even in modern life as a whole. However, neither in Cubism nor in Constructivism were artists aiming at the fusion of various manners of expression. For both movements mutual control served only to purify the means of expression. Cubism remained a form of painting which differed from earlier painting through its constructive-architectural character.

It can easily be understood why more recent movements, namely Constructivism

191

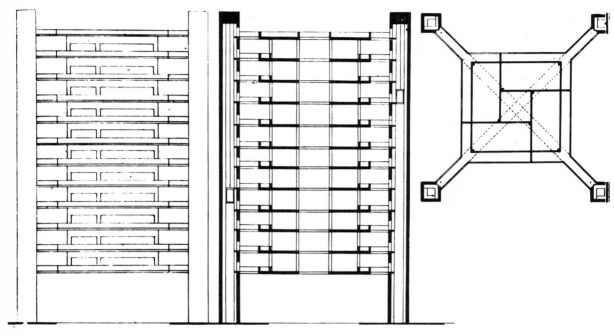

Design for a traffic town: façade, cross-section,
groundplan and axonometric view, 1929.
Photo: P. Willi

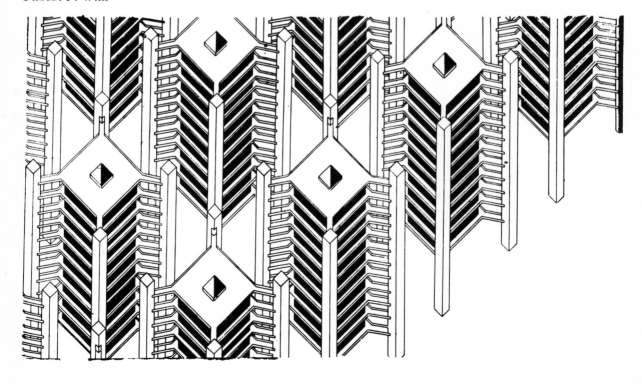

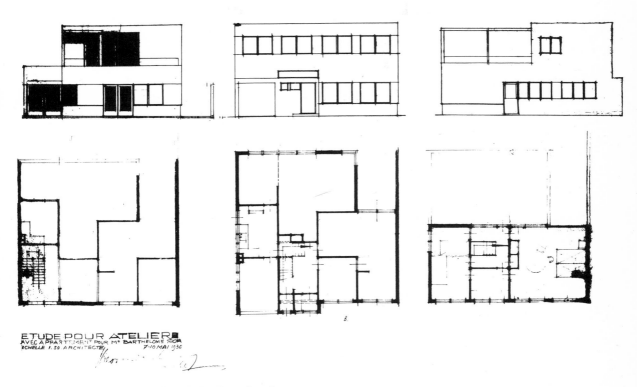

ETUDE POUR ATELIER
AVEC APPARTEMENT POUR M. BARTHELOME POR
ECHELLE 1.50 ARCHITECTE/   7-10 MAI 1930

Design for a studio house for Mr B. Por; façades,
ground floor, first and second floor, 1930.
Photo: P. Willi

and Neo-plasticism, were brought into close
contact with architecture. Architecture,
which had already become more abstract in
its means of expression, never struggled with
the illusion of natural form as did painting
and sculpture. Thus architecture could
embody much earlier than painting and
sculpture the new forms of plastic expression.
That which was criticized in painting or
sculpture proved acceptable in architecture.
This was especially true in countries in which

development was unhampered by any
'famous' tradition, such as America,
Holland, Germany and Czechoslovakia.
In Holland, where progressive painters had
to struggle against an old tradition in their
medium, it was much easier than elsewhere
for architects to demand, and even in part to
produce, a new architecture. However, a risk
remained that arbitrary or capricious forms
would be casually bestowed upon architecture.
An example where this occurred is the

so-called Amsterdam School.

The first major steps towards the renovation of architecture in Holland were taken by the architect Cuypers in his *Central Railway Station* in Amsterdam and by Berlage in his *Stock Exchange building*, which is also in Amsterdam. These first steps produced the initiative for liberating architecture in Holland from its imitative character.

Yet a great difference remained between the demands of modern architects and those of the transitional period.

In fact, the blocks of architecture by Oud in Rotterdam represent a major advance in spite of the repetition of a standard-unit.

Because of their knowledge of painting, the Dutch architects Van 't Hoff, Rietveld, Oud and Wils and others, have developed an Elementarist architecture both in practice and theory. Its principle had already been propagated by the magazine which is devoted to the new plastic expression, *De Stijl*.

With this architecture a new era began, and already one can say that Holland possesses an architecture that is independent of tradition.

The above-mentioned demand was first posited in painting and stimulated the development in architecture which took place in the following order: painting, houses, blocks of houses and town-planning.

In all countries a principle of architecture with general validity came into being purely due to practice. From the new and collective plastic expression derived a demand for the abolition of individualism. Without this the collective plastic expression could not have been fulfilled. For the sake of a better understanding I would like to state some of the fundamentals upon which the new 'architecture' is based.
[*Here follows Van Doesburg's architectural programme, 'Towards plastic architecture', which is almost exactly the same as that of 1924. The most important change is that he takes the discussion of time from point 10 and makes it into a new point 11, bringing the total number of points to seventeen.*]

Since these principles are generally valid and thus provide a common basis for artistic creation, a correct distribution of tasks will be necessary. Unless the creative forces are organized, a collective effort will be impossible. Thus it will be necessary to distribute the various creative tasks; the discipline of colour goes to the painter, the discipline of space to the architect, the discipline of the objects to the sculptor and to the cabinet-maker and so forth.

Although it is correct that these principles were first developed by the so-called De Stijl artists, in fact, in all countries architects struggled for the development of a new style at the beginning of this century. Witness Van der Velde in Belgium, Perret in France, Peter Behrens in Germany, Adolf Loos in Austria, Saarinen in Finland, and Wright in America.

Fifteen or twenty years ago one could discover in all these countries a predominantly constructive approach. Each country had its 'constructive conscience' which was represented by one of these architects, all of whom, in practice or in theory, were struggling for the best approach to architecture. For the sake of renovation these pioneers revolted against ornamental and decorative architecture which was already decadent at the time. Ornaments were stripped off; what mattered was design only. Everything superfluous to *the essence of architectural* form was done away with.

However, this renovation is limited in its turn. It ends where architectural form ends.

As we have seen from the principles which I have summarized in the seventeen points presented above, we are no longer concerned with the problem of form, but with the problem of building. This problem is universal, finding its representatives in all countries – a situation similar to that of fifteen years ago.

We do not know any form but only problems in building. Form is not the aim but the result of our work. Form does not exist by itself – form as an end represents formalism and this we reject. (*G II* – 1924)

This statement was written by an architect who was working in Berlin, Mies van der Rohe. However, form and style are not to be confounded. An architecture which limits itself to the horizontal and the vertical elements of building, to this strongest opposition permitting the balance of the greatest tensions, and possessing elementary 'form', has nothing in common with form as a mould. One could as well call it a 'formless' architecture. In France, where this approach also has won many followers (such as Le Corbusier Saugnier, Mallet Stevens, Guevrikian, du Four, and others), the 'formless style' is called 'the orthogonal style'. It resulted from elementarization of the architectural means of expression and not (as it is often mistakenly said) of the simplification in form, which began to develop earlier this century. The resulting simplification, in Germany as well as in other countries, produced a purely constructive, *anatomical* architecture, which displayed its skeleton on the inside and its skin on the outside.

Flourishing pre-war industry provided architecture with new challenges: the factory, the office and the department-store. Modern architects thus were obliged to abandon romantic and aesthetic speculation.

This explains why architects such as Peter Behrens, Berlage, Wright and Walter Gropius, though romantics at heart, developed a functional, sober architecture.

I do not believe that exclusively rational or constructive architecture is the criterion of modern building. In my view, the basic opposition between constructive and speculative-aesthetic architecture will never be resolved. Neither the former nor the latter will be able to satisfy us completely, which is to say in all respects, both spiritual and practical. In order to advance a better understanding, I would like to offer an illustration. Imagine a house which is well designed from a material or practical point of view. Everything in it will satisfy our material demands. If we lived in this house, we should feel happy only from a physico-functional point of view. Our house would respond to only a certain part of our life.

Apart from these physico-functional demands, there are also *psycho-functional* demands which correspond with our optical, phonetic and tactile experiences. Until now, mankind has attempted to satisfy these 'supra-material' demands with a painting on the wall or a sculpture in a room. Furniture provided an 'aesthetic' plastic expression and our houses were changed into museums or concert-halls.

The architecture of the future will have to destroy this duality. Its task will be to express completely and fulfil all our demands. Thus its task automatically will become expression through a *creative-constructive* manner, rather than through a rational-constructive or speculative-aesthetic manner.

In order to develop this principle, it is important to pay attention to the newest

195

advances in architecture. To aid the purification of the architectural means, one must subject everything to *open space*. The material must serve a double function, which is firstly elementary-constructive and secondly elementary-plastic. When these two functional values interpenetrate, the quality of mechanical precision will logically result. Instead of production by handicraft, manufacture of single parts will be demanded. The machine limits the production by handicraft to a minimum with building. Naturally, the forces present in the materials will have to be adapted to the creative forces as expressed with such materials. If it is true that culture in the widest sense of the word represents independence from nature, one need not be surprised that the machine becomes prominent with the modern cultural will to style. The machine is a phenomenon of spiritual discipline *par excellence*. Materialism, as a view of life and of art, always considered that handicraft functioned as the direct expression of inner emotion. The new spiritual view of art not only allowed the machine to be experienced as beauty but also acknowledged its infinite potential for expression in art. A style no longer imposes the task of creating individual objects, such as paintings, decorative objects or private homes, but of studying collectively and in accordance with economic circumstances entire town quarters, sky-scrapers and airports; style is no longer related to handicraft. Here the machine serves as the sole criterion, since handicraft corresponds to a predominantly individualistic consciousness of life which has become obsolete through progress. Due to the predominance of materialism, handicraft has led *mankind* to a debased use of the machine; the correct use of the machine (in producing a culture)

is the only manner of bringing about the opposite, social leisure. However, mechanical production by no means represents the sole means of faultless creation. Quality, rather than quantity, should be the principle for a correct use of the machine. Its use must be guided towards creative ends by creative spirit. Constructive precision is necessarily consequent upon the spiritual-practical demands of our time. The machine alone can ensure such constructive precision. The new possibilities provided by the machine have created an aesthetic which is inherent to our time and which I once called the 'mechanical aesthetic'.

A common approach to architecture is establishing itself in all countries today; already the characteristics inherent in both of the above mentioned attitudes to life have become visible.

The characteristics of the new will to style which oppose those of earlier times are, for example:

precision	instead of inaccuracy
openness	instead of closedness
clarity	instead of vagueness
truth	instead of beauty
simplicity	instead of complexity
relationship	instead of form
synthesis	instead of analysis
logical construction	instead of lyrical imagination
mechanics	instead of handicraft
plastic expression or ornamentation	instead of imitation
collectivity	instead of individualism

Judging by the points presented above, it follows that architectural creation results from the functional demands which determine the subdivision of space. The interior provides the exterior with its plastic expression. Thus architecture has regained its appropriate means of expression. The entire exterior is the result of the interior. Each inner space extends itself plastically to the exterior. Nowhere does a predominant façade exist. Although it is not fused with the landscape, architecture remains the expression of a vivid repose, since the exact calculation of extreme tensions of load and support express a balance of matter and mind.

Contrary to frontalist architecture, which concentrates on the façade, architecture in the future will reveal a richness of dimensions which until now has remained imaginary. Now the modern architect will no longer be satisfied with an architecture which projects in only two dimensions upon his drawing-table. In contrast to the painterly approach inherent in architecture of two-dimensional façades, it will become the task of the modern architect to master three-dimensional space through correctly relating arrangements of space-cells, which means that the four sides will have to be under consideration simultaneously. This will be possible only when the architect is capable of thinking and feeling in a *spatio-temporal* (multi-dimensional) manner.

Life represents a *function* which is inconceivable without motion. And motion cannot be conceived without time or continuity. The function of life does not allow for projection in two dimensions on the drawing-table. Walking, sitting, eating, drinking, sleeping and working are functions which are subject to a certain rhythm, a measure in time. This *measure in time*, or *succession*, produces an arrangement in *juxtaposition*.

In the future architecture will search for the *intrinsic unity* of both realms. I am restricting myself here to the 'physical' functions, but, as a matter of course, our 'psychological' functions play an equally large role.

Naturally, the new ideas in plastic architecture should influence the education of artists. Until now, no institution has recognized these new demands. Either one finds teaching restricted to classical examples with students copying in two dimensions that which originally was created in three dimensions, or else students are allowed to combine numerous materials without method according to their own taste. These students thus design houses from 'inspiration', which is referred to generally as modern education or free expression.

However, all speculation is considered dangerous in modern education and almost a crime when used as a means to educate the students in practical work.

All the architectural rubbish that has been produced throughout the past fifty years is the result of this so-called 'creative intuition'. In the De Stijl courses which I began in 1922 I have attempted to find a way out of this labyrinth. In so doing I used a rigid method which was analogous to searching the alphabet beginning with the letter *a*. Modern man is not satisfied with a superficial knowledge of the plastic means of expression; he demands scientific research into them. Since the technical side of architecture is based upon science, a *science of plastic expression* arises. It is sentimental to maintain that, on the contrary, creative activity results only from creative impulse. At present the theory of intuitive plastic expression is producing an entire generation of ornamentors, opportunists and snobs.

I have attempted to explain how the ideal of the new constructive aesthetics may be realized in architecture, by which is meant a unified plastic expression of environment. If this expression is to be established completely, it will be necessary not only to acknowledge the objective laws of plastic expression presented above, but also to experience them genuinely. Once this has been achieved, *collective plastic* expression will be possible. The present divorce of art from life will then automatically cease to exist. Art will participate in the general process of work and cease to be illusionary.

If we view architecture as the synthesis of all creative activity, in the sense set forth in the beginning of this article, it becomes clear that the architect of the future will have a new task which corresponds generally to that of a conductor. He will 'conduct' material colour and objects in space with the aim of producing total construction. This approach will provide town-planning with unimagined possibilities.

Our present distance from this collective style is easily proved by the purely formalistic and intellectual products of the Swiss architect, Le Corbusier Saugnier, who designed a town at his drawing-table without paying any attention to the complexity of the functions which are involved. Needless to say, such amateurish games have nothing to do with a collective style as we see it. Town-planning is a problem in itself and will continue to be based upon arbitrary speculation as long as we do not solve the problem of housing.

All object-form emanates from function, the best form being the one which corresponds with its function in as economical a manner as possible. Though the 'orthogonal style' may provide the most useful forms and express our age most clearly, curved form is more suitable to objects of illumination, lamps or wheels. If functional form is confounded aesthetically with creative form, decoration replaces the architectural constructive principle. *Function* and *decoration* are diametrically opposed.

These two incompatible ideas represent a polar contrast between the new and the old consciousness in architecture.

1930

Fundamental principles

Part II from 'The Fundamental spirit of contemporary architecture', lecture held in Madrid and Barcelona, 1930, representing a final, revised edition of Van Doesburg's architectural programme of 1924.

For the examination of new methods of construction, it may be useful to draw attention to the principles which underlie the organization of a new architectural unity.

These principles, which have been developed and applied in almost every conceivable manner since 1916, when they were first tested in Holland, provide the basis for the development of a new European architecture.

I Form
The new kind of architect, instead of using a predetermined form, restates the problem of construction for each new project. Form is *a posteriori.*

Two views of the studio house at Meudon, 1931

Overleaf
Two views of the interior (studio part) of the
studio house at Meudon, 1931.
Photo: Gemeente Musea van Amsterdam

199

The interior of the studio house in Meudon
showing built-in concrete table with original
steel-framed windows.

II   The elements
The new architecture is Elementarist; it develops from the very elements of construction: light, function, materials, volume, time, space and colour. These elements are simultaneously the creative means.

III   Economy
The new architecture is economical; it employs those elementary means which are most essential, without waste of means or materials.

IV   Function
The new architecture is functional; it is based on a synthesis of practical demands. The architect fulfills such demands in a clear and legible groundplan.

V   Formlessness
The new architecture has no *a priori* scheme, no mould into which all functional spaces must fit. In contrast to all former styles, the new architectural method uses no basic types. The division and subdivision of interior and exterior spaces are rigorously determined by planes which possess no individual form.

VI   The monumental
The new architecture is not monumental, but is more an architecture of transformation, of lightness and of transparency.

VII   The window
The window is no longer a penetration in the wall. The window is actively important for its relative position within the two-dimensional surface of the blind wall. No penetration or gap is visible anywhere, because everything is determined strictly in terms of contrasts.

VIII   The groundplan
The new architecture has 'opened' the walls so that the separateness of interior and exterior is suppressed. Walls no longer sustain since the system of construction is based upon the use of columns. This results in a new type of groundplan, an open groundplan, which is totally different from classical ones, since interior space and exterior space are interrelated.

IX   Subdivisions
The new architecture is 'open' instead of 'closed'. The whole building comprises a single general space, which is subdivided with separating planes into different spaces, either mobile or static in accordance with the practical demands of the building. In a later phase of development of the new architecture, the groundplan will disappear. The composition of space through two-dimensional projections upon a horizontal section, the groundplan, will then be replaced by exact calculations of construction.

X, XI and XII   Time
The new architecture considers not only space, but also time to be an architectural value. The unity of space and time will give architecture a new form of appearance, which is more complete. This is what is meant by 'active space'. Dissimilar spaces are not combined within a single closed cube. On the contrary, the dissimilar space-cells develop eccentrically from the centre to the borders of the cube, thereby granting a new plastic quality to the dimensions of height, width, depth and time. In this manner and especially due to its system of columns, the new dwelling will give the impression that it consists of planes which are suspended in air in contradiction to the force of gravity.

XIII   Symmetry and repetition
The new architecture has suppressed monotonous repetition and destroyed the equality of two symmetrical halves. It does not allow for continuous repetition. A block of houses is as much a whole as an independent house. Balance and symmetry are two entirely different things. In place of symmetry the new architecture proposes a balanced relationship of unequal parts or parts which differ (in position, proportion, size and materials) in functional character.

XIV   Frontalism
In contrast to frontalism, which was born from a static conception of life, the new architecture will achieve great richness by developing a multilateral plastic use of space and time.

XV   Light and colour
More than ever light and colour have become basic elements of architecture. Light creates space, and colour is one of the elementary means of rendering visible the harmony of architectural relationships. Without colour, relationships of proportion cannot be visualized; through colour or through contrasts of 'denaturalized' materials (such as glass, nickel, ebonite and aluminium) architecture in the future will attain the perfection within the contemporary style, which signifies the synthesis of all our research.

XVI   Decoration
The new architecture is anti-decorative. Instead of dramatizing a two-dimensional surface or serving as a superficial ornament, colour like light becomes an elementary means for pure architectural expression. This is literally what we must master in the new process of creating architecture.

Modern architects in almost all countries have already designed many buildings stimulated by these principles which demonstrate the fundamental spirit of our architecture. They have not restricted themselves to the construction of country houses, hotels, streetplans and factories, but have expanded the problems related to the single house to include those related to *urbanism*.

1930

Bibliography

Complete writings by Theo van Doesburg

Books

De maskers af Portfolio with caricaturist drawings,
Vennootschap Letteren en Kunst, Amsterdam
(1916?), 20 ills.

De schilder De Winter en zijn werk Psycho-
analytische studie. J. H. de Bois, Haarlem,
1916, 15 pp.

De nieuwe beweging in de schilderkunst Technische
Boekhandel en Drukkerij J. Waltman, Delft
1917, 44 pp., 21 ills.

Drie voordrachten over de nieuwe beeldende kunst
Maatschappij voor goede en goedkoope lectuur,
Amsterdam 1919, 104 pp., 39 ills.

Klassiek-barok-modern De Sikkel, Antwerp 1920,
31 pp., 17 ills.

Wat is Dada De Stijl, The Hague 1923, 14 pp.

Grundbegriffe der neuen gestaltenden Kunst
Bauhausbücher no. 6, Albert Langen Verlag,
Munich 1924, 40 pp., 32 ills. Reprinted in
Neue Bauhausbücher, ed. H. M. Wingler,
Florian Kupferberg, Mainz 1966. English edition
Principles of Neo-plastic Art Lund Humphries,
London; New York Graphic, Greenwich, Conn.
1969. With an epilogue by H. L. C. Jaffé.

Die Scheuche In collaboration with K. Schwitters
and Käte Steinitz. Aposs Verlag, Hanover 1925,
12 pp.

Unpublished books

Werdegang der neuen Malerei German translation
of three lectures held in Utrecht 1928, titled
'Hedendaagsche stroomingen in de kunst'.

Beeldende Constructie-leer Deel I. De Kleur. Also
called: *Gestaltende Farbenlehre*. Versuch zu
einer kunstwissenschaftlichen Gestaltungslehre.
1924–1927/29.

Im Kampf um das Neue Entwicklung der Stijl-
Bewegung seit 1916. I Einführung; II Die
Prinzipien (published in *Neue Schweizer
Rundschau* 1929, called *Kampf um den neuen
Stil*); IIa Die Architektur als Synthese einer
neuen Gestaltung: Die Stijlarbeit; Ziele;
Möglichkeiten; Paedagogische Möglichkeiten;
Systematik; Merkmalen des alten und neuen
Systems; Litteratur; Grafische Darstellung der
Entwicklung perspektivischer Illusion nach der
Fläche (F) und von dort die Eroberung neuer
Gebiete. (Part IIa is unfinished and unpublished.
Van Doesburg planned the parts I, II and IIa as
a 14th Bauhausbook with illustrations, a list of
which is among these papers), 1929–30.

Das Bild der Gegenwart, around 1929.

Europäische Architektur, around 1930. This
manuscript consists of a German translation of
his articles in *Bouwbedrijf*. Its last page was

published in exhibition catalogue no. 81,
De Stijl, Stedelijk Museum, Amsterdam 1951,
p. 120.

Articles

1912
'Proeve tot nieuwe kunstkritiek' I 'Over schilder-
en beeldhouwkunst. N.a.v. Intern. tentoonstelling van schilderijen en beeldhouwwerken
in't Sted. Museum te Amsterdam', *Eenheid*
no. 111, 20 July; no. 112, 27 July; no. 113,
3 Aug; no. 115, 17 Aug; II 'Religie en kunst'
no. 116, 24 Aug; III 'Over beeldhouwkunst'
no. 118, 7 Sep; IV 'Japansche kunst' no. 120,
21 Sep.
'Futurisme' ibid., no. 127, 9 Nov.
'Over moderne kunst N.a.v. tentoonstelling van
schilderwerken der "Moderne Kunstkring" in
't Sted. Museum te Amsterdam' ibid., no. 129,
23 Nov.

1913
'Onafhankelijke bespiegelingen over de kunst',
'Inleiding' *De Avondpost* 1 Aug; 'Mensch en
kunstenaar' 12 Oct; 'Slot' 18 Oct.
'Het ontstaan van een beeldend kunstwerk' ibid.,
23 Oct.
'Het ontstaan van het kunstwerk' ibid., 8 Nov.
'Opstanding. Een historisch gedachtenspel van
schoonheid en liefde' *Eenheid* no. 146, 22 March;
no. 147, 29 March no. 148, 5 Apr.
'Proeve tot nieuwe kunstkritiek', 'Aziatische
kunst' ibid., no. 147, 29 March; no. 153/4,
17 May; 'Tent. van Broeckman bij Dorens en
Zn., Amsterdam' no. 156, 31 May; 'Over
moderne kunst. N.a.v. tentoonstelling van
schilderwerken der "Moderne kunstkring" in
't Sted. Museum te Amsterdam en de "Erster
deutscher Herbstsalon' te Berlijn' no. 182,
29 Nov; 'Over moderne kunst. Kandinsky'
no. 183, 6 Dec.
'De verboden beelden. Een sprookje' ibid., no. 166,
9 Aug.
'De kunstenaar een schoonheidsdienaar?' ibid.,

no. 176, 18 Oct.
'De legende van Bimbisara' ibid., no. 179, 8 Nov.

1914
'Onafhankelijke bespiegelingen over de kunst.
De evolutie en zending der kunst' *De Avondpost*,
24 Jan; 7 Feb; 'Van oude en nieuwe waarden'
28 Feb.
'Schilderkunst. De modernen en de kunstkritiek'
De Controleur, no. 1251, 18 July
'Uit den tempel der schoonheid', 'I Het verhaal
van Vrouw Koome' *Eenheid* no. 204, 2 May;
'II Het verhaal van den hond' no. 205, 9 May;
'III Het verhaal van den valschen rijksdaalder
en den gouden berg' no. 207, 23 May; 'IV Het
verhaal van den Karkeeme' no. 211, 20 June;
'V Het verhaal van de ganzen' no. 220, 22 Aug.
'Over tentoonstellingen St. Lucas' ibid., no. 208,
30 May
'Pensées sur l'art moderne' ibid., no. 218, 8 Aug.
'De oorlog. Het lied van het wilde beest' ibid.,
no. 218, 8 Aug.
'Nog eens 'n "Ode aan de dieren" ' ibid., no. 234,
28 Nov.
'Het Varken. *Het Volksblad*', issue not known

1915
'Meditaties aan de grenzen', 'I Inleiding; Over den
oorlog' *De Avondpost* 16 March; 'II De oorlog
in verband met de menschelijke natuur' 20
March; 'III De oorlog en zijne verdwijning
(vervorming) in verband met de cultuur'
2 Apr; 'IV Vervolg' 17 June; 'V Vervolg'
29 June; 'VI Slot' 3 July
'Algemene beschouwing over de moderne schilderij,
N.a.v. de najaarstentoonstelling, Nov.–Dec.
1915, der "Onafhankelijken" te Amsterdam'
ibid., 20 Nov.
'Fabricius onder 't mes' *De Controleur* no. 1315,
9 Oct.
'Knaap aan de galg?' ibid., no. 1316, 16 Oct.
'Prof. Dake (vermoord)' ibid., no. 1317, 23 Oct.
'Een nieuw middel voor zelfmoordenaars' ibid.,
no. 1320, 13 Nov.
'Een professor in het nauw' ibid., no. 1320, 13 Nov.
'Zoo zijn onze manieren, manieren . . .' ibid.,

no. 1323, 4 Dec.
'Een verfijnde verrassing in loopgravenstijl' ibid.,
   De Controleur no 1304, 24 July
'Mijne liefde . . .' *Eenheid* no. 243, 30 Jan.
'Uwe Liefde . . .' ibid., no. 246, 20 Feb.
'Meditaties aan de grenzen', 'Inleiding. I Over den
   oorlog' II De oorlog in verband met de
   menschelijke natuur' ibid., no. 251, 27 March;
   'III De oorlog en zijne verdwijning (vervorming)
   in verband met de cultuur' no. 254, 17 Apr;
   'IV Vrede door denken' no. 266, 10 July
'Achter het huis van Baal' ibid., no. 252, 3 Apr.
'De liefde' ibid., no. 257, 8 May
'Aan de redactie van "De Blijde Wereld" en van
   den "Dageraad" ' ibid., no. 261, 5 June
'Aanteekeningen over moderne kunst. N.a.v.
   "De Onafhankelijken", 5e Jury-vrije tentoon-
   stelling te Amsterdam' ibid., no. 263, 19 June
'Kunstenaar en publiek. 'n Kleine, oude historie'
   ibid., no. 271, 14 Aug.
'Uit den tempel der schoonheid', 'VI De rose kapel'
   ibid., no. 274, 4 Sep.
'De vijand. Een sprookje' ibid., no. 280, 16 Oct.
'Over kunst- en natuurkritiek' ibid., no. 282,
   30 Oct.
'Kunst-kritiek. Moderne kunst: Stedelijk Museum,
   Amsterdam. Expositie Mondrian, Leo Gestel,
   Sluiters, Schelfhout, Le Fauconnier' ibid.,
   no. 283, 6 Nov.
'Kunst. Opgedragen aan den heer August Heyting
   en zijn vrienden' ibid., no. 286a, 27 Nov.
'Oproep. Ten behoeve van J. de Winter' ibid.,
   no. 288, 11 Dec.
'Sociologie. Egoisme, individualisme, anarchisme'
   Het Volksblad issue not known

1916
'Het wezen der moderne schilderkunst' *De
   Amsterdammer* vol. 29, 29 July
'De nieuwe stijl in de schilderkunst' *De Avondpost*
   23 Jan; 2 May
'De nieuwe beweging in de schilderkunst'
   De Beweging vol. 12; no. 5, pp. 124–31;
   no. 6, pp. 219–26; no. 7, pp. 57–66; no. 8,
   pp. 148–56; no. 9, pp. 226–35
'Pornografische schilderwerken en dito kritiek'

De Controleur no. 1327, 1 Jan.
'Een "Lampje" zonder . . . licht' ibid., no. 1328,
   8 Jan.
'Weer een misdaad' ibid., no. 1341, 8 Apr.
'Een ontdekking uit het ongeziene' ibid., no. 1348,
   27 May
'Tijdbesparing' ibid., no. 1348, 27 May
'Het schilderij. Historische twee-acter. Speelt zich
   af in het einde van het tijdperk der Hessies'
   ibid., no. 1365, 23 Sep.
'Beeldende kunst' ibid., no. 1375, 2 Dec.
'Uit den kritischen mallemolen' ibid., no. 1378,
   23 Dec.
'De natuur der liefde' *Eenheid* no. 292, 8 Jan.
'De priester-kunstenaar' ibid., no. 294, 22 Jan;
   reprinted in exhibition catalogue Theo van
   Doesburg, Van Abbemuseum, Eindhoven, 1969
'Vincent van Gogh. N.a.v. een tentoonstelling van
   diens werk in "Voor de Kunst" te Utrecht'
   ibid., no. 297, 12 Feb.
'Victor de Budt. Tentoonstelling bij de Firma
   Regnault, Keizersgr. 792, Amsterdam' ibid.,
   no. 298, 19 Feb.
'De expressionisten en kubisten' ibid., no. 305,
   8 Apr.
'Kunst en kunstnijverheid. N.a.v. een expositie
   van Fransche etsen te Apeldoorn, "Op den
   Paschviever" ' ibid., no. 306, 15 Apr.
'Tentoonstelling H. E. Boot en D. Roggeveen'
   ibid., no. 312, 27 May
'De ontwikkeling der moderne schilderkunst'
   ibid., no. 312, 27 May; no. 315, 17 June;
   no. 316, 24 June; no. 319, 15 July; no. 320,
   22 July; no. 323, 12 Aug.
'De onafhankelijken. Indrukken van een bezoeker'
   ibid., no. 318, 8 July
'De heilige steen' ibid., no. 327, 9 Sep.
'Bedelaar zalig. Verhalen en sprookjes van onzen
   tijd' ibid., no. 334, 28 Oct.
'Over beeldhouwkunst. N.a.v. een tentoonstelling
   van beeldhouwwerken in het Kunstnijverheids-
   museum te Haarlem' ibid., no. 337, 18 Nov.
'Algemene beschouwing over het werk van A. de
   Winter' *De Nieuwe Amsterdammer*, 12 Aug.
'De revolutie in de schilderkunst' ibid., 9 Sep;
   23 Sep; 11 Nov; 23 Dec.

'Ingezonden stuk over dagblad-kunstkritiek'
  Nieuwe Arnhemsche Courant, 3 Jan.
'Iets over schilderkunst als beeldende kunst.
  Ingezonden' *Nieuwe Courant*, 14 May
'Daumier als caricaturist' *Oude Kunst* II 2, pp.
  52–6
'De allermodernsten' *De Telegraaf* issue not
  known
'De schilderwerken en batiks van Djurre Duursma'
  Twenthe, 4 March

1917
'Ingezonden brief aan H. C. Verkruysen' *Architectura* XXV 5, 3 Feb.
'De Onafhankelijken. 9e Juryvrije tentoonstelling'
  De Controleur no. 1400, 24 May
'Weg met de dilettantenkritiek' ibid., no. 1415,
  6 Sep.
'Schilderkunst. N.a.v. eerste tentoonstelling van
  de Leidsche Kunstclub "De Sphinx" ' *Eenheid*,
  no. 348, 3 Feb.
'Grootmeesters der beeldende kunst', 'I Frater
  Giovanni da Fiesole genoemd Beato Angelico'
  ibid., no. 357, 7 Apr; no. 361, 5 May; no. 368,
  23 June; no. 376, 18 Aug; 'II De Renaissance'
  no. 385, 20 Oct; no. 392, 8 Dec.
'Schilderkunst. Notities over Impressionisme'
  ibid., no. 362, 12 May
'Thijs Maris' ibid., no. 380, 15 Sep.
'Beeldende kunst'(?) *Holland Expres*, 4 April
'Open brief aan Bernard Canter' ibid., 12 Sep.
'Ingezonden brief n.a.v. Bernard Canters kritiek
  over "De Onafhankelijken" ' ibid., 20 Dec.
'De revolutie in de schilderkunst' *De Nieuwe
  Amsterdammer* 23 June
'Schilderkunst en ornamentale kunst? Aan
  Laurens van Kuik en zijn richtinggenoten'
  ibid., 25 Aug.
'Ter inleiding' *De Stijl*, I 1, 1 Oct.
'Bij de bijlagen' ibid., I 1, 1 Oct.

1918
'De nieuwe kunst en de kritiek' *Algemeen
  Handelsblad* 6 Oct.
'Grootmeesters der beeldende kunst', 'II De
  Renaissance' *Eenheid* no. 400, 2 Feb; no. 429,

22 Aug; no. 434, 26 Sep.
'Schoonheids- en liefdesmystiek' *Het Getij* July,
  pp. 180–90; Aug., pp. 212–15; Sep., pp. 242–50
'Rekenschap der nieuwe beeldingswijze in de
  schilderkunst' *Nieuwe Courant* 19 Sep., and
  De Nieuwe Amsterdammer 16 Nov.
'Daumier als schilder' *Oude Kunst* IV 1, pp. 15–19
'Ingezonden stuk' *De Wiekslag* March
'Hamer en zaag; stillevenkompositie door
  V. Huszar' *De Stijl* I 3, Jan.
'Fragmenten' I ibid., 4, Feb.
'Antwoord aan mejuffrouw Edith Pijpers en
  allen, die haar standpunt innemen' ibid., I 6,
  April
'Bij bijlage II. Ruimte-plastische binnenarchi-
  tectuur' ibid., I 6, April
'Fragmenten' 2 ibid., I 7, May
'Aanteekeningen bij bijlage 12. De zaag en de
  goudvischkom van P. Alma' ibid., I 8, June
'Moderne bouwkunst bij noodwoningen in
  gewapend beton' ibid., I 8, June
'Aanteekeningen bij twee teekeningen van Piet
  Mondriaan' ibid., I 9, July
'Open brief aan den architect Huib Hoste' ibid.,
  I 9, July
'Inleiding bij den tweeden jaargang' ibid., vol. II 1,
  Nov.
'Manifest I van "De Stijl", 1918' ibid., II 1, Nov.
'Aanteekeningen over monumentale kunst; naar
  aanleiding van twee bouwfragmenten, hall in
  vacantiehuis te Noordwijkerhout; bijlage 1.
  ibid., II 1, Nov.
'Guillaume Apollinaire' ibid., II 2, Dec.
'Denken- aanschouwen- beelden' ibid., II 2, Dec.

1919
'Moderne tuinplastiek. Bloemenvaas' *Bouwkundig
  Weekblad* XL 51
'Grootmeesters de beeldende kunst. II De
  Renaissance' *Eenheid* no. 469, 29 May
'Expressionistisch-literaire komposities' *Het Getij*
  Feb.
'Godenkultuur' ibid., April
'Een belangrijk kunsttijdschrift' ibid., June
'De vrijwilliger' ibid., August
'Van "natuur" tot "kompositie" ' *De*

Hollandsche Revue, XXIV 8
'Grondbegrippen der nieuwe beeldende kunst'
    Tijdschrift voor Wijsbegeerte XIII 1, pp. 30–49;
    no. 2, pp. 169–88
'Eenige losse gedachten over moderne architec-
    tuur in verband met het zomerhuis te Huis ter
    Heide, architect R. van 't Hoff' *De Stijl* II 3,
    Jan.
'Moderne wendingen in het kunstonderwijs' ibid.,
    II 3, Jan; 4, Feb; 5, March; 6, April; 8, June;
    9, July; 11, Sep; 12, Oct.
'Over het zien van nieuwe schilderkunst' ibid., II 4,
    Feb.
'Fragmenten' '3. Beelding van innerlijkheid en
    uiterlijkheid' ibid., II 4, Feb.
'Valori Plastici' ibid., II 6, April
'Over het zien van nieuwe kunst. Aant. bij bij-
    lagen 11, 12 en 13 ibid., II 6, April
'Rondblik' ibid., II 6, April; 9, July; 12, Oct;
    III 1, Nov.
'Antwoord aan F. M. Huebner' ibid., II 8, June
'Slotbemerkingen' ibid., II 10, Aug.
'Aanteekeningen bij de bijlagen' ibid., II 11, Sep;
    12, Oct; III 1, Nov; 2, Dec.
'Overzichtelijke beschouwing bij de intrede van
    den derden jaargang' ibid., III 1, Nov.
'Aanteekeningen over de nieuwe muziek' ibid.,
    III 1, Nov.

1920
'L'art monumental' *Bleu*, 1, July
'Images-X' ibid., no. 2, Aug. (I. K. Bonset)
'La letteratura. Manifesto no. 2–1920, lanciato
    dalla rivista olandese d'arte De Stijl' ibid., 2,
    Aug.
'Is een universeel beeldingsbegrip thans mogelijk?'
    Bouwkundig Weekblad XLI 39
'De taak der nieuwe architectuur' ibid., XLI 50,
    pp. 278–80; 51, pp. 281–85
'De zwarte vlek. Simultaneïstische schets' *Het
    Getij* V
'De belangstelling voor de moderne kunst' *De
    Loods*, 12 Aug.
'L'Art monumental' *Lumière* April
'De ontwikkeling van het "schilderachtige" en
    "monumentale" en hun verhouding in de

nieuwe beeldende kunst' *De Nieuwe
    Amsterdammer*, 3 Jan; 17 Jan; 3 April
'Dada' ibid., 8 May
'Images-X' *Poesia*
'L'art monumental' *Terramar* II 23/4
'L'arte nuova in Olanda' *Valori Plastici* II 1/2
'Aanteekeningen bij de bijlagen' *De Stijl* III
    3, Jan; 5, Mar; 7, May; 8, June; 12, Nov.
'Rondblik' ibid., III 3, Jan; 5, Mar; 8, June;
    9, July; 10, Aug; 11, Sep; 12, Nov.
'Schilderkunst van Giorgio de Chirico en een stoel
    van Rietveld' III 5 Mar.
'La littérature. Manifeste II de "De Stijl"' III
    6, Apr.
'X-Beelden' (I. K. Bonset) ibid., III 7, May;
    9, July
'De beteekenis van het vlak in de nieuwe
    schilderkunst' ibid., III 7, May, pp. 62–4
'Over het nieuwe vers en het aaneengeknoopte
    touw' (I. K. Bonset) ibid., III 8, June
'Het andere gezicht' (I. K. Bonset) ibid., III
    10, Aug; 11, Sep.
'Het Picasso'sche kubisme en de Stijlbeweging'
    ibid., III 11, Sep; 12, Nov.
'Lijstenaesthetiek ibid., III 11, Sep.

1921
'De betekenis der mechanische esthetiek voor de
    architectuur en de andere vakken' *Bouwkundig
    Weekblad* XLII 25; 28; 33
'De taak der nieuwe architectuur' ibid., XLII 1
'La littérature d'avant-garde en Hollande' *Ça ira*
    12, Mar.
'Beeldende kunst' *Het Getij* VI 2, pp. 73–6
'De nieuwe woordbeelding' ibid., VI 1
'Revue der avant-garde' ibid., VI, 1, pp. 109–12;
    pp. 193–200; 2, pp. 25–8; pp. 138–141;
    VII 1, pp. 13–15
'X-Képek' (I. K. Bonset) *Ma Aktivista Folyóirat*,
    VI, Apr.
'De nieuwe beelding in Holland' *De Ploeg* III 25
'Inleiding tot de nieuwe verskunst' (I. K. Bonset)
    De Stijl IV 1, Jan; 2, Feb.
'Rondblik' ibid., IV 1, Jan; 2, Feb; 4, Apr; 5, June;
    6, June; 9, Sep; 10, Oct.
'Over het moderne schilderen' ibid., IV 3, Mar.

'Het andere gezicht' (I. K. Bonset) ibid., IV 4, Apr.
'Caminoscopie. 'n Antiphylosofische levensbeschouwing zonder draad of systeem' (Aldo Camini) 'Inleiding' ibid., IV 5, June; 'I Een hoofdstuk zonder hoofd' 5, June; 'II' 5, June; 'III Een hoofdstuk zonder armen en benen. De radioelectrische mensch' 5, June; 'IV De laatste poot van den hemelstoel' 6, June; 'V Het identiteitsprinciep' 6, June; 'VIII De natuur van den geest en de temperatuur van Dada' 7, July; 'VIII IX Dynamisch hoofdstuk' 8, Aug; 'X XI Hydrologisch hoofdstuk' no. 12, Dec.
'Abstracte filmbeelding' ibid., IV 5, June
'Open brief' ibid., IV 5, June
'Kritische tesseracts' (I. K. Bonset) ibid., IV 6, June; 12, Dec.
'Grondslagen tot een nieuwe versbeelding' (I. K. Bonset) ibid., IV 7, July
'Letterklankbeelden' (I. K. Bonset) ibid., IV 7, July; 11, Nov.
'Het kubistisch probleem zijn gronden en zijn consequenties' ibid., IV 10, Oct; 12, Dec.
'Manifest III. Tot een nieuwe wereldbeelding' ibid., IV 8, Aug.
'X-Beelden 1920' (I. K. Bonset) ibid., IV 11, Nov.
'Uit de serie "Soldaten" 1916 en uit de serie "Stillevens" 1914 en 1915' (I. K. Bonset) ibid., IV 11, Nov.
'Balans van het nieuwe' ibid., IV 12, Dec.

1922
'Monumental art' (title in Russian) *Bewb* (Objet, Gegenstand), no. 1/2, Mar./Apr.
'Van de esthetiek naar het materiaal' *Bouwkundig Weekblad* XLIII 38
'Het kubisme voor het laatst' *De Bouwwereld* XXI 35
'Une plastique nouvelle en Hollande' *Ça ira* 18, May.
'Az épitészet mint szintetikus müvészet' (Hungarian: Architecture as the synthesis of the plastic arts) *Ma. Aktivista Folyóirat* 7, July
'A hollandi Stijl-esoport beszámolója' (Statement to the international union of progressive artists by the Stijl-group Holland), ibid., no. 8, Aug.
'La nouvelle conscience poétique et ses nouveaux moyens d'expression' *La vie des lettres et des arts* 25
'Rondblik' *De Stijl* V 1, Jan; 5, May; 9, Sep.
'Aanteekeningen bij de Rotterdamsche betonwoningen. Architecten Pauw en Hardeveld' ibid., V 1, Jan.
'X-Beelden' (I. K. Bonset) ibid., V 1, Jan; 5, May
'Der Wille zum Stil. Neugestaltung von Leben, Kunst und Technik' ibid., V 2, Feb; 3, Mar.
'Kort overzicht der handelingen van het internationale kunstenaarscongres te Düsseldorf, 29–31 Mei 1922' ibid., V 4, Apr.
'Rechenschaft gegenüber der Union internationaler fortschrittlicher Künstler' ibid., V 4, April; reprinted in *Grundbegriffe der neuer gestaltenden Kunst*, Florian Kupferberg Verlag, Mainz 1966; and *The Principles of Neoplastic Art*, Lund Humphries, London 1969; New York Graphic, Greenwich, Conn. 1969
'Caminoscopie. 'n Antiphylosophische levensbeschouwing zonder draad of systeem' (Aldo Camini) Boek II, 1, ibid., V 6, June
'Beeldende verskunst en hare verhouding tot de andere kunsten' (I. K. Bonset) ibid., V 6, June
'Carrément contre les artistes imitateurs' ibid., V 6, June
'Balans van het nieuwe' ibid., V 7, July; 9, Sep.
'De consequentie van de pen en de teekenhaak' ibid., V 9, Sep.
'De Stijl 1917–1922 en zijn beweging in: schilderkunst, architectuur, plastiek, monumentale beelding, muziek, litteratuur, anti-phylosophie, machinisme, voorwerpen, dans' ibid., V 12, Dec.
'Antikunstenzuivereredemanifest' (I. K. Bonset) *Mecano* yellow number
'Citaat' ibid., yellow number
'Archachitektonica' (I. K. Bonset) ibid., blue number
'Dada/Hollande I.K.B.' (I. K. Bonset) ibid., blue number
'Chronique scandaleuse des Pays-Plats' (I. K. Bonset) ibid., red number
'Madapolan' (I. K. Bonset) ibid., red number
'Chroniek-mecano' (I. K. Bonset) ibid., red number

1923
'Voorwaarden tot een nieuwe architectuur'
   Architectura XXVII 27
'De invloed van de Stijlbeweging in Duitschland'
   Boukkundig Weekblad XLIV 7
'De betekenis van de kleur in binnen – en
   buitenarchitectuur' ibid., XLIV 21
'Zur elementaren Gestaltung' *G* □ I July
'Pariser Neuheiten. Motiv :nur' ibid., II Sep.
'Az ideális esztétikától a materiális megvalósitás
   felé' (The new aesthetics and its realization)
   Ma. Aktivista Folyóirat IX 1
'Dadaisme' 'I Dada vormt zich' *Merz* Jan; 'II De
   veelvormigheid van Dada' Apr.
'Manifest Proletkunst' ibid., Apr.
'Das Schiffchen: Dada Nachrichten' ibid., Apr.
'Dadaisme' *Het Vaderland* 3 Feb.
'Huszar's beeldend tooneel' ibid., 23 Feb.
'Von der neuen Aesthetik zur materiellen
   Verwirklichung' *De Stijl* VI 1, Mar.
'Anti-tendenzkunst' ibid., VI 2, Apr.
'Caminoscopie' (Aldo Camini). Boek III ibid., VI
   3/4, May/June
'Symptomen eener reconstructie der dichtkunst
   in Holland' (I. K. Bonset) ibid., VI 3/4, May/June
'Licht-en tijdbeelding. Film' ibid., VI 5
'Rondblik' ibid., VI 5
'9 × B' (I. K. Bonset) *Mecano*, white number
'Tot een constructieve dichtkunst' (I. K. Bonset)
   ibid., white number
'Karakteristiek van het Dadaisme' ibid., white
   number
1924

'Architectuur-diagnose' *Architectura* XXVIII 15.
   17 May
'Odnowienie architektury' (Polish: The
   renovation of architecture) *Blok* 5
'Vernieuwingspogingen in de Fransche
   architectuur' *Bouwbedrijf* I 4; 6
'De nieuwe architectuur' *Bouwkundig Weekblad*
   XLV 20
'Réponse à notre enquête: Où va la peinture
   moderne?' *Bulletin de l'effort moderne* 3, Mar.
'Vers un style collectif' ibid., 4, Apr.
'Vers une construction collective' ibid., 9, Nov.

'La signification de la couleur en architecture'
   La Cité IV 10
'C'est le spirituel . . .' *G* III June
'Das Problem einer aktiven Ausstellungsmethode'
   Neues Wiener Journal 31 Oct.
'Vers une construction collective' *Pasmo* 2
'Vyzna!–Aufruf!' ibid., 7/8
'Obnova architektury' (The renovation of
   architecture.) *Stavba* III 2
'K. elementární tvorbé' (Towards elementary
   plastic expression.) ibid., III 2
'Ke kollektivni konstrukci' ibid., III 2
'Nová architektura Holandská' ibid., III 5
'Caminoscopie' (Aldo Camini). Vervolg Boek III.
   De Stijl XII 6/7
'Tot een beeldende architectuur' ibid., XII 6/7
'Vers une construction collective' ibid., XII 6/7
'– □ + = R4' ibid., XII 6/7
'Surrealisme. Realistische samenspraak' ibid..
   XII 8
'Alphabetische informatie. Tijdschriften-boeken-
   artikelen enz. A–C' ibid., XII 8
'Tijdschriften en boeken' ibid., XII 8

1925
'L'évolution de l'architecture moderne en
   Hollande' *L'architecture vivante* III 9
'Vernieuwingspogingen in de Fransche
   architectuur' *Bouwbedrijf* II 1
'De voorbereidingen der "Exposition des arts
   décoratifs" Parijs 1925' ibid., II 4
'Vernieuwingspogingen der architectuur in
   Duitschland en Oostenrijk' ibid., II 5
'Het Hollandsche paviljoen op de "Exposition des
   arts décoratifs" te Parijs' ibid., II 6
'Vernieuwingspogingen der Oostenrijksche en
   Duitsche architectuur' ibid., II 6, pp. 225–7;
   7, pp. 262–5; 10, pp. 363–6
'Classique-baroque-moderne' *Bulletin de l'effort
   moderne* 20 Dec.
'L'architecture moderne en Hollande' *Le Home*
   4, Apr.
'Evolution of modern architecture in Holland'
   The little review XI 1
'The literature of the advanced guard in Holland'
   ibid., XI 1

'Voorbijtrekkende troep; ruiter' (I. K. Bonset)
    ibid., XI 1
'Das Ende der Kunst' *Pasmo* 13/14
'Das Ende der Kunst' *Periszkop* June/July
'Vers une construction collective' *Punct* 8, 9 Jan.
'Neue Gestaltung in der Architektur von heute'
    Sächsische Staatszeitung 13 Feb.
'De dood der modernismen. Diagnose van het
    Futurisme, Kubisme, Expressionisme,
    Purisme, Dadaisme, Constructivisme enz.'
    De Stijl XII 9
'Rondblik' ibid., XII 9
'Aanteekening bij de reproduktie eener
    glas-in-lood compositie XIII 1924' ibid., XII 9
'Het einde der kunst' ibid., XII 9
'Appel de protestation contre le refus de la
    participation du groupe "De Stijl" à
    "l'Exposition des arts décoratifs" à Paris'
    ibid., XII 10/11
'Het fiasco van Holland op de expositie te Parijs
    in 1925' ibid., XII 10/11

1926
'Olanda. Stazione dell'Aja. Vers un art
    élémentaire' *L'Antenna* I 1, 25 Mar./9 Apr.
'L'Arte elementare' ibid., I 3, 1–14 May
'De architect André Lurçat' *Bouwbedrijf* III 4
'Architectuurvernieuwingen in het buitenland.
    Frankrijk, Duitschland, Oostenrijk, Tjecho-
    slowakije etc.' ibid., III 2, pp. 74–8;
    5, pp. 191–4; 6, pp. 228–31; 7, pp. 266–8;
    8, pp. 296–8; 10, pp. 346–9; 11, pp. 371–2;
    12, pp. 424–7; 15, pp. 477–9
'Classique-baroque-moderne' *Bulletin de l'effort
    moderne* 21, Jan, pp. 1–3; 22, Feb, pp. 1–3;
    23, Mar, pp. 1–2
'Ku sztuce elementów' (Towards elementary art.)
    Praesens 1
'Vers un art élémentaire' *Vouloir* 19, Mar.
'Toelichting "Glasbild", Paris 1924' *Das Werk* July
'De Stijl' *Zenith* 38, Feb.
'Van de beeldende letteren' (I. K. Bonset) *De Stijl*
    XIII 73/4
'Schilderkunst. Van kompositie tot contra-
    kompositie. I, II, III, IV' ibid., XIII 73/4
'The end of art' ibid., XIII 73/4

'Schilderkunst en plastiek. Over contra-kompositie
    en contra-plastiek. elementarisme. Manifest-
    fragment' ibid., XIII 75/6
'De rechte lijn als vernietigster der "artistieke
    ambachten" en der decoratieve architectuur'
    ibid., XIII 75/6
'Het andere gezicht. Zijn' (I. K. Bonset) ibid.,
    XIII 75/6
'Het andere gezicht. Abstracte, sur-humanistische
    roman. Voorwoord, hoofdstukken 1 en 2'
    (I. K. Bonset) ibid., XIII 77
'Over den zin der letterkunde' (I. K. Bonset)
    ibid., XIII 77

1927
'Actividad de la moderna arquitectura holandesa'
    Arquitectura 98, June
'Architectuurvernieuwingen in het buitenland'
    Bouwbedrijf IV 20; 'De architectuurtentoon-
    stelling "Die Wohnung" te Stuttgart' 24;
    'Frankrijk, Duitschland, Oostenrijk,
    Tsjechoslowwakije, Italië, Zwitserland, Rusland,
    Polen' IV 2, pp. 40–4; 4, pp. 88–91; 9, pp. 217–20;
    15, pp. 352–5
'Naschrift bij "Die neue Baukunst in Oesterreich –
    eine Entgegung" door Alex. Popp' ibid., IV 6
'Über das Verhältnis von malerischer und
    architektonische Gestaltung' *Der Cicerone* XIX 18
'The progress of the modern movement in
    Holland' Ray. *Art Miscellany* 2
'The end of art' *Shin Kenchiku* June
'L'Art collectif et son importance sociale'
    Vouloir 25
'Schilderkunst en plastiek. Elementarisme.
    Manifest-fragment' *De Stijl* XIII 78
'Het andere gezicht. Abstracte, sur-humanistische
    roman' (I. K. Bonset); 'Hoofdstukken 3 en 4'
    ibid., XIII 78; 'Hoofdstukken 5, 6 en 7' XIV 79/84
'10 Jaren Stijl. Algemeene inleiding' ibid., XIV
    79/84
'De gouden druppel' (I. K. Bonset) ibid., XIV 79/84
'Van het woord en de letterkunde 1917–1927'
    (I. K. Bonset) ibid., XIV 79/84
'Data en feiten (betreffende de invloedsont-
    wikkeling van "De Stijl" in 't buitenland) die
    voor zich spreken' ibid., XIV 79/84

212

'Brancusi' ibid., XIV 79/84

1928
'Actividad de la moderna arquitectura holandesa' *Arquitectura* 105, Jan.
'Die Moderne in Holland' *Die Bauschau* III 21
'De beelding van het interieur' *Binnenhuis* X 21, pp. 279–83; 26, pp. 345–51
'Kunst en architectuurvernieuwing in Sovjet-Rusland' *Bouwbedrijf* v 20, pp. 395–400; 22, pp. 436–41
'Eenige nieuwe architectuurdemonstraties in Tjechoslowakije' ibid., v 26
'L'Architecture moderne en Hollande' *La construction moderne* XLIII 15, pp. 169–76; 36, pp. 421–6; XLIV 13, pp. 152–4
'Avant-garde literature in Holland' *Transition* II Feb.
'Answer to inquiry among European writers into the spirit of America' ibid., 13, Summer issue
'Hugo Ball' *De Stijl* XV 85/6
'Het andere gezicht' (I. K. Bonset) 'Hoofdstukken 8, 9, 10, 11 en 12' ibid., XV 85/6
'Notices sur l'Aubette à Strasbourg' ibid., XV 87/9
'L'Elémentarisme et son origine' ibid., XV 87/9
'Farben in Raum und Zeit' ibid., XV 87/9

1929
'Die Verkehrsstadt' *Architektur der Gegenwart* 3
'De beelding van het interieur' *Binnenhuis* XI 3, pp. 29–31; 4, pp. 39–42; 5, pp. 54–6; 6, pp. 67–70; 10, pp. 111–14; 13, pp. 145–8; 16, pp. 181–4; 18, pp. 205–8; 21, pp. 241–3
'Het glas-in-lood in de oude en nieuwe architectuur' ibid., XI 24, pp. 279–81; 26, pp. 301–04
'Kunst– en architectuurvernieuwing in Sovjet-Rusland' *Bouwbedrijf* VI 3, pp. 49–52; 13, pp. 263–6; 17, p. 341
'De ombeelding van de Aubette in Straatsburg' ibid., VI 6
'Kunst– en architectuurverniewing in Italië' ibid., VI 9, pp. 179–81; 10, pp. 201–3; 13, pp. 263–6; 16, pp. 305–8; 17, pp. 341–4
'Kunst– en architectuurvernieuwing in Italië en

Spanje' ibid., VI 20
'Architectuurvernieuwingen in Spanje, Polen, Japan enz.' ibid., VI 24, pp. 472–3
'Het glas-in-lood in de oude en nieuwe architectuur' ibid., VI 26
'L'Architecture moderne en Hollande' *La construction moderne* XLIV 29
'Farben im Raum' *Form* IV 2
'Film als reine Gestaltung' ibid., IV 10
'Das Buch und seine Gestaltung' ibid., IV 21
'Der Kampf um den neuen Stil' *Neue Schweizer Rundschau* 1, Jan, pp. 41–6; 3, Mar, pp. 171–5; 5, May, pp. 373–7, July, pp. 535–41; 8, Aug, pp. 625–31
'Orientaćní poznánky', 'I Historie hunti de Stijl'; 'II Elementarismus' *Red* II 7 (The second part was probably in preceeding issue.)
'Fernand Léger et le cubisme' *Sélection* III 8

1930
'De beelding van het interieur' *Binnenhuis* XII 9, pp. 97–101; 14, pp. 157–61; 16, pp. 181–4
'Het glas-in-lood in de oude en nieuwe architectuur' ibid., XII 3, pp. 26–9; 5, pp. 49–52
'Interieurbeelding' ibid., XII 26
'Terrassenarchitectuur' *Bouwbedrijf* VII 1
'Het glas-in-lood in de oude en nieuwe architectuur' ibid., VII 2, pp. 40–2; 6, pp. 122–5; 10, pp. 202–5
'Architectuurvernieuwingen in Spanje, Polen, Japan enz.' ibid., VII 3, pp. 60–2; 7, pp. 145–9
'Buitenlandsche architectuur' ibid., VII 9
'Architectuurvernieuwingen in Spanje, Polen, Servië, Japan enz.' ibid., VII 11, pp. 219–22; 13, pp. 259–62; 18, pp. 358–61
'Belangrijke nieuwe uitgaven over nieuwe architectuur' ibid., VII 20
'Het meubel in den ouden en den nieuwen tijd', 'Le meuble dans les temps anciens et dans les temps nouveaux' *Intérieur* XLVII 271, pp. 1567–74; 272, pp. 1609–15
'Oude en nieuwe textielkunst', 'L'Art textile jadis et aujourd'hui' ibid., XLVII 273, pp. 1651–7; 274, pp. 1695–7; 276, pp. 1783–7
'L'Architecture nouvelle en Hollande' *Monde* III 108

'Was will die neue Malerei?' *Neue Züricher Zeitung* 26 Jan.
'Base de la peinture concrète' *Art Concret* Apr.
'Commentaires sur la base de la peinture concrète' ibid., Apr.
'Vers la peinture blanche' ibid., Apr.

1931 and later
'Kunst– en architectuurvernieuwing in Polen' *Bouwbedrijf* VIII 5
'Oude en nieuwe textielkunst', 'L'Art textile jadis et aujourd'hui' *Intérieur* XLVII 277, pp. 1826–33; 278, pp. 1867–74; XLVIII 279, pp. 17–21; 280, pp. 65–70
'Surrealistische letterkunde in Frankrijk' *Groot-Nederland* 2, Feb, pp. 201–11; 3, Mar. pp. 290–307
'Obnova umjetnosti i arhitekture u Evropi' (The renovation of art and architecture in Europe.) *Hrvatska Revija* 8
'Elémentarisme' *De Stijl*, last issue, Jan 1932
'Elémentarisme. Les éléments de la nouvelle peinture' ibid.
'Uit de dagboeknotities van Theo van Doesburg' ibid.
'Uit het "journal d'idées" van Theo van Doesburg' ibid.
'Das andere Gesicht. Abstrakter surhumanistischer Roman. Kapitel 8' (I. K. Bonset) ibid.
'Caminoscopie' (Aldo Camini) ibid.
'Elémentarisme' *Abstraction-creation-art non-figuratif* 1932
'Fernand Léger *Cahiers d'art* 1933 3 and 4
'Neoplasticisme-Elementarisme' *D'Aci i d'Alla* 1934 XX 179, Dec.
'Brief aan Paul Citroen' *Prisma der Kunsten* 1936, May
'Sobre pintura' *Cercle et Carré* 1937, Feb.
'De l'intuition à la certitude' *Réalitées nouvelles* 1947 1
'Aus "Der Wille zum Stil"' *Werk* 1951, XXXVIII 11, Nov.

Unpublished articles

'Amersfoortsche Brieven. Aan mijn Agnita. – Indrukken bij aankomst; 's Avonds. Een gezicht in het "Paviljoen"; Uit de colonne; Onder het gevechtsschieten' 1908
'Amersfoortsche Indrukken, I en II' 1908
'Amsterdamsche Brieven. Aan mijn lieve vrouw' 'I Over deugd; Over harmony' 'II Ik en de kritiek; Een schets' 1908
'Over sexualisme. Fragment voor het werk over hetero - en homoliefde' 1908
'De Spin' 1908
'Hoe er een mensch in de wereld kwam' 1908
'De domme' 1908
'Het evenbeeld' 1908
'De dag van den vrome' 1908
'Jan, Piet en de beesten' 1908
'Het monster' 1908
'Het gebluste vuur' 1908
'Het pennetje en het zwaard' 1908
'De wonderpot' 1908
'De broeders' 1908
'De kunst van den mensch' 1908
'De drie stokken' 1908
'De herder en de wolven' 1908
'De kaars' 1908
'De leeuwerik en de musch' 1908
'De uitspraak' 1908
'Jan Jansen had een ezel' 1908
'Het zevende muisje' 1908
'De parel' 1908
'Het puistje' 1908
'Het goudstuk, 1908
'Engelenbeeld 1908
'De liefde' 1908
'De stem van de duivel' 1908
'De veter' 1908
'Het graankorreltje' 1908
'De potten' 1908
'De zwanen op het land' 1908
'Het was een koning die uit den hemel viel' 1908
'Waar dient de mensch voor?' 1908
'De leugenaar' 1908
'De kleine en de grote pot' 1909
'Het meesterstuk van den duivel' 1909

'De pijp en de tabak' 1909
'Duivels drinkwater' 1909
'De oude schoenen' 1909
'De ruiter en zijn paard' 1911
'De held des vredes' (From the series 'De tempel
    der schoonheid') 1912
'De Japansche schilderkunst van Onono Tofu tot
    Hokusay' 1912/1913
'De last van het paard' 1913
'Het leven is een vraag waarop de dood antwoord
    geeft' 1913
'Nieuwe woordbeeldingen', 'Kubistische en
    Expressionistische verzen', 'Soldatenverzen',
    'Letterklankbeelden', 'X-beelden' (Several of
    these poems were published in *De Stijl*; or
    reprinted as in Carola Giedion-Welcker, *Poesie
    der Abseitigen*, Bern, 1946; and exhibition
    catalogue *Theo van Doesburg*, Van
    Abbemuseum, Eindhoven 1968)
'Het kind' 1914
'Franske. Document tot de menschelijke natuur'
    1914
'De zon en de schaduw' 1914?
'Van God' 1914
'Brieven aan Lena. Ster; Liefste, grootste vriend'
    1914
'Ik dacht . . .' 1914–15
'Document C. Gedenkschriften van een milicien;
    Gedenkschriften van een landweerman; De
    gelijkenis van de muur en dé kamer; Het riet
    en de mensch' 1914–15
'De denker. Aan mijn blanke muze' 1915
'De boer' 1915
'M'nsieur Cabinet' 1915
' "Ik" en "God" ' 1916
'Fragmenten IV' 1918–19
'Slampang. Manifeste métallique de shampooing
    néerlandais' 1921
'Gerade heute □ 2' 1922
'Ribemont-Dessaignes und die Tendenzen der
    neuen Litteratur in Frankreich' 1926
    'Film und Abstraktion' 1926
'Bilanz der Kunst in 1926' 1926
'La situation de l'art moderne en Italie' 1926
'Quelques notices biographiques sur le peintre et
    architecte Theo van Doesburg' 1928

'Die Stadt ohne Strassen' 1930
'Die neue Gestaltung in der Spanischen Architek-
    tur' 1930
'Le planisme de Torrès Garcia' 1930
'Die neue Architektur und ihre Konsequenzen'
    1930
'Die Kunsterneuerung der "Stijlgruppe" '
    (incomplete), 1930

Lectures

'Paedagogisch-aesthetische voordracht over de
    moderne schilderkunst' I and II, Tilburg 1915
'Tot Stijl' Brussels, Weimar 1921
'Der Wille zum Stil' Jena, Weimar, Berlin 1922
    (published in *De Stijl*)
'Neo-plastische Monumentalität' Weimar 1922
'Der Aufstellung meiner Grundbegriffen in 1916'
    Weimar 1922
'Katagorien der Gestaltungswerte' Weimar 1922
'De schilderkunst en haar omgeving' (incomplete)
    n.d.
'Wat wil het dadaisme' 1923
'Die Kunst als Hemmung des Fortschrittes'
    Hanover 1924
'Die Entwicklung der modernen Architektur in
    Holland' Berlin, Prague, Brno 1924
'Hedendaagsche stroomingen in de kunst'
    Utrecht, 24 Jan; 31 Jan; 7 Feb. 1928
'Eenige punten ter verklaring der moderne
    schilderkunst' Amsterdam 1929 (published by
    De Stijl, Paris, Leyden 1929)
'L'Esprit fondamental de l'architecture contempo-
    raine' Madrid, Barcelona 1930

Diaries and notebooks

1 Diary 3 May 1902–9. With separate summary,
   called 'Notes from my diary and impressions
   from my inner being and my outer environment 1908–1913'
2 Diary and letters II; 24 April–24 Sep. 1905
   (draft of previous diary)
3 Diary; 12 Jan.-18 Jan; 20 Jan.–27 Jan. 1915
4 Diary; 22 Sep. 1915
5 Diary; 17 Dec. 1920–April 1921. Including

'Tot Stijl'. 'Over de terminologie in kunst'.
'Reis naar Berlijn'. 'Bezoek aan het Bauhaus'.
'Reisnotities'
Diary: 29 Aug. 1930–1 Feb. 1931 (published in
De Stijl. last issue. Jan. 1932. as 'Journal

d'idées')
7   Diary: 2 April 1928–14 Feb. 1931
8   Ten single diary-sheets. marked A–J
Twenty-six notebooks. containing manuscripts of
   various articles and drafts of letters.

Selected writings on Theo van Doesburg

Books

Joost Baljeu *Mondrian or Miro* Amsterdam 1958
Reyner Banham *Theory and Design in the first
   Machine Age* London 1960
Stephen Bann *Experimental Painting* London 1970
Adolf Behne *Der moderne Zweckbau* Munich.
   Vienna. Berlin. 1926
Charles Biederman *Art as the Evolution of Visual
   Knowledge* Red Wing 1948
Peter Blake *Marcel Breuer. Architect and Designer*
   New York 1949
A. Boeken *Architectuur* Amsterdam 1956
Marcel Brion *Art Abstrait* Paris 1956
J. H. van den Broek *Creatieve Krachten in de
   Architectonische Conceptie* Delft 1948
Paul Bromberg *Architecture in The Netherlands*
   New York 1944
Theodore M. Brown *The Work of G. Rietveld
   Architect* Utrecht 1958
Paul Citroen *Palet* Amsterdam 1931
Dictionnaire de la Peinture Moderne Paris 1954
Alex. Dorner *Collection of the Société Anonyme*
   New Haven 1950
Karl Gerstner *Kalte Kunst?* Teufen 1957
S. Giedion *Space. Time and Architecture*
   Cambridge 1941
S. Giedion. R. J. Neutra *Europäer und Amerikaner*
   Zürich 1951
S. Giedion *Architektur und Gemeinschaft* Hamburg
   1956
C. Giedion-Welcker *Poètes a l'écart* Bern 1946
W. F. Gouwe *Ruimte* Rotterdam 1929

W. F. Gouwe *Vorm* Rotterdam 1932
Walter Gropius *Internationale Architektur*
   Munich 1925
Peggy Guggenheim *Art of this Century* New York
   1942
A. M. Hammacher *Stromingen en Persoonlijkheden*
   Amsterdam 1955
Henry Russell Hitchcock *Painting towards
   Architecture* New York 1948
Henry Russell Hitchcock *Architecture. Nineteen
   and Twentieth Centuries* London 1958
Fr. M. Huebner *Die Neue Malerei in Holland*
   Arnhem. Leipzig 1921
H. L. C. Jaffé *De Stijl 1917–1931* Amsterdam 1956
H. L. C. Jaffé *Piet Mondrian* New York n.d. 1971
H. L. C. Jaffé *Vordemberge Gildewart* Cologne 1971
Jurgen Joedicke *Geschichte der Modernen Archi-
   tektur* Teufen 1958
Philip C. Johnson *Mies van der Rohe* New York
   1947
Philip C. Johnson *Masters of Modern Art*
   New York 1954
Gyorgy Kepes *Language of Vision* Chicago 1944
Fr. Kiesler *Contemporary Art applied to the Store
   and its Display* New York 1930
   Konkrete Kunst, 50 Jahre Entwicklung Zürich
   1960
El Lissitzky and Hans Arp *Die Kunstismen*
   Zürich, Munich, Leipzig, 1925
J. B. van Loghem *Bouwen-Bauen-Bâtir-Building*
   Amsterdam 1932
L. Moholy-Nagy *Von Material zur Architektur*
   Munich 1929
L. Moholy-Nagy *The new Vision* New York 1947

L. Moholy-Nagy *Vision in Motion* Chicago 1947
Paul Overy *De Stijl* London 1969
Maurice Raynal *Peinture Moderne* Geneva 1953
George Rickey *Constructivism, Origins and Evolution* New York 1967
Paul Rodenko *Nieuwe Griffels, schone Leien* The Hague, Antwerp 1954
Kurt Schwitters, Theo van Doesburg and Dada *The Dada Painters and Poets* ed. R. Motherwell, New York 1951
Michel Seuphor *L'Art abstrait* Paris 1949
Michel Seuphor *Dictionnaire de la Peinture abstraite* Paris 1957
Michel Seuphor *Piet Mondrian, Life and Work* Amsterdam, New York n.d.
James Johnson Sweeney *Plastic Directions in Twentieth Century Painting* Chicago 1934
Jan Tschichold *Die neue Typographie* Berlin 1928
Giulia Veronesi *J. J. Pieter Oud* Milano 1953
J. V. Vriend *Nieuwere Architectuur* Amsterdam 1935
Gordon Washburn *Isms in Art since 1800* Providence 1949
K. Wiekart *J. J. P. Oud Ter Wille van een levende Bouwkunst* The Hague, Rotterdam 1962
Bruno Zevi *Architettura e Storiografia* Milan 1950
Bruno Zevi *Poetica dell'Architettura Neoplastica* Milan 1953

Articles

Agis, Maurice and Jones, Peter, 'Theo van Doesburg is of today' *Form*, no. 9, April 1969
Baljeu, Joost, 'Architecture and art' *Structure*, vol. I, 1958
Baljeu, Joost, 'De Stijl toen en J. J. P. Oud nu' *Forum*, 8, 1960–61
Baljeu, Joost, 'The content of the contemporary construction' *Structure*, series III 2, 1961
Baljeu, Joost, 'The problem of reality with Suprematism, Constructivism, Proun, Neoplasticism and Elementarism' *The Lugano Review* I 1, 1965
Baljeu, Joost, 'Theo van Doesburg en de oprichting van De Stijl' *Cobouw*, 139, 16 June 1967
Baljeu, Joost, 'De vierde dimensie' exhibition catalogue *Theo van Doesburg*, Eindhoven 1968
Baljeu, Joost, 'The fourth dimension' *Form*, 9, April 1969
Behne, Adolf, 'Von holländischer Kunst' *Das Feuer* II 5, 1921
Breijer, 'Theo van Doesburg' *Intérieur* XLVIII 280, 1931
Burchartz, M. 'Neue Gestaltung' *Thür. Landeszeitung* 1 Jan. 1924
Buys, H., 'De ontwikkelingsgang van Theo van Doesburg' *Bouwkundig Weekblad/Architectura* 19, 9 May 1936
'Theo van Doesburg' *Ma* July, 1922
'Theo van Doesburg' *Arquitectura* 4, 1931
'Theo van Doesburg, pintor y arquitecto' *A.C.* XI 5, 1931
Dexel, W., 'Theo van Doesburg' *Das neue Frankfurt* V 6, June 1931
Domela-Nieuwenhuis, Cesar, Contribution to last issue of *De Stijl* Jan. 1932
van Eesteren, C., Contribution to last issue of *De Stijl* Jan. 1932
Elzas, A., 'Atelier met woning te Meudon-Val-Fleury' *De Stijl* last issue, Jan. 1932
Elzas, A., 'Het nieuwe bouwen in Holland' *Opbouwen* IV 18, 15 Nov. 1934
Elzas, A., 'Theo van Doesburg' *De 8 en Opbouw* VI 17, 17 Aug. 1935
Elzas, A. 'Theo van Doesburg' *Kentiku Sekai* XXIX 10, 1935
Eyck, Aldo van, 'De bal kaatst terug' *Forum* 3, 1958
Faber, Hans, 'Theo van Doesburg' *A bis Z* 15, April 1931
Gerstner, K., 'Die Aubette als Beispiel integrierter Kunst' *Werk* 10, Oct. 1960
Giedion, S., 'Theo van Doesburg' *Cahiers d'art* VI 4, 1931
Giedion, S., 'Theo van Doesburg' *Frankfurter Zeitung* 29, March 1931
Gifreda, Marius, 'Theo van Doesburg' *Mirador* II 68, 15 May 1930
Graeff, Werner, 'Das Bauhaus und seine Krise um 1922' exhibition catalogue *Theo van Doesburg* Eindhoven 1968
Hedrick, Hannah, 'De droom van Does'

exhibition catalogue *Theo van Doesburg* Eindhoven 1968

Hedrick, Hannah, 'Van Doesburg's dream' *The Structurist* 9, 1969

Hedrick, Hannah, 'New translations of Van Doesburg's writings' ibid., 9, 1969

Hélion, Jean, 'Theo van Doesburg' *A bis Z* 15, April 1931

Hélion, Jean, Contribution to last issue of *De Stijl* Jan. 1932

Hess, Thomas B., 'The Dutch: this century' *Art News* Jan. 1953

Hoff, R. van 't, Contribution to last issue of *De Stijl* Jan. 1932

Hoste, Huib, 'Het vacantiehuis te Noordwijker-hout' *De Telegraaf* March 1919

Huebner, F. M., 'Die holländische Styl-gruppe' *Feuer* II 5, 1921

Jaffé, H. L. C., 'Groep "De Stijl" ' *Kroniek van Kunst en Kultuur*, June 1951

Jaffé, H. L. C., 'The De Stijl concept of space' *The Structurist* 8, 1968

Jaffé, H. L. C., 'The diagonal principle in the works of Van Doesburg and Mondrian', ibid., 9, 1969

Kelk, C. J., 'Klank- of waanbeelden?' *Het Getij* VI 2, 1921

Kelk, C. J., 'Het nieuwe in de poëzie' *Het Getij* VII 1, 1922

Kelk, C. J., 'Typographie en dichtkunst' ibid., VII 2, 1922

Kiesler, F., Contribution to the last issue of *De Stijl* Jan. 1932

Kok, Antony, Contribution to the last issue of *De Stijl* Jan. 1932

Leering, J., 'De architectuur en Van Doesburg' exhibition catalogue *Theo van Doesburg* Eindhoven 1968

Leering-van Moorsel, L., 'Notities bij de typografie van Theo van Doesburg' ibid., 1968

Lotz, W., 'Die Aubette in Strasburg' *Die Form* IV 2, 15 Jan. 1929

Een Manifest *De Opmerker* XLIII 48, n.d.

Markus, B., 'Theo van Doesburg' *Periszkop* June/July 1925

McNamee, D., 'Van Doesburg's cow: a crucial transition in the structure and reality of art', *The Structurist* 8, 1968

McNamee, D., 'Van Doesburg's Elementarism' ibid., 9, 1969

Meller, P., Niuwe architectuur in Europa' *CA* 2, 1926

Mieras, J. P., 'Manifest van "De Stijl"' *Bouwkundig Weekblad*, XL 2, Jan. 1919

Mondrian, P., Contribution to the last issue of *De Stijl* Jan. 1932

van Moorsel, C., 'Een Memento' *Het R. K. Bouwblad* II 19, 23 April 1931

De Ongerechte 'Holland op zijn rechts' *Architectura* XXVIII 10, 29 March 1924

Oud, J. J. P., 'Glas-in-lood van Theo van Doesburg' *Bouwkundig Weekblad* XXXIX 35, 31 Aug. 1918

Oud, J. J. P., 'Bouwkunst en kubisme' *De Bouwwereld* XXI 32, 9 Aug. 1922

Oud, J. J. P., Contribution to the last issue of *De Stijl* Jan. 1932

Ozenfant and Jeanneret, 'L'Angle droit' *L'esprit nouveau* 18, 1923

van Renssen, P., 'Cubisme' *Opgang* IV 3

Rinsema, Evert, Contribution to the last issue of *De Stijl* Jan. 1932

van Rossum, C. P., 'Surprises' *Haagsche Post* 12 June 1920

Sartoris, A., 'Elementarismo' *Belvedere* II 5, May 1930; 6, June 1930

Sartoris, A., 'Chronique de l'architecture. Ses rapports et l'élémentarisme hollandais' *Feuille d'avis* 17 March 1931

Sartoris, A., Contribution to the last issue of *De Stijl* Jan. 1932

Scheibe, Harry, 'Die Atmosphäre der neuen Architektur' *Die Form* I 15, Dec. 1926

Schuurman, K. E., 'Theo van Doesburg: Compositie 1919' *Museumjournaal* series VII 1, June 1961

Schwanhaüsser, Kurt, Contribution to the last issue of *De Stijl*, Jan. 1932

Schwitters, Kurt, 'Nachruf für Theo van Doesburg' *Volkswille* 15 April 1931

Schwitters, Kurt, Contribution to the last issue of *De Stijl*, Jan 1932

Seuphor, M., 'L'Aubette de Strasbourg' *Art d'Aujourd'hui* Dec. 1953

Seuphor, M., 'De Stijl' *L'Oeil* 22, Oct. 1956

Teige, K., 'De Stijl a Hollandska Moderna' *Stavba* III 2, 1924

Teige, K., 'Theo van Doesburg – Grundbegriffe der neuen gestaltenden Kunst' *Stavba* v 6, 1926

Torres-Garcia, J., 'Theo van Doesburg' *La vue de Cataluny* 1930

Vordemberge Gildewart, Fr., 'Zur Geschichte der Stijl-bewegung, *Werk* XXXVIII 11, Nov. 1951

Wils, Jan, 'In Memoriam Theo van Doesburg' *Binnenhuis* XIII 6, 12 March 1931; *Bouwbedrijf* VIII 6, 13 March 1931

van Woerkom, D., 'Architecture and motion' *Structure* II 2, 1960

van Woerkom, D., 'Architecture as an art' *Structure* IV 1, 1961

Wolf, N. H., 'Theo van Doesburg's werk' *De Kunst* XXVIII 1932, 16 May 1936

Xceron, J., 'Theo van Doesburg' *Chicago Sunday Tribune*, Paris edn., 28 April 1929

Zevi, Bruno, 'L'insegnamento critico di Théo van Doesburg' *Metron* VII 44, 1952

Notes

Introduction

1 *Brieven aan Bertha*, 1914/15. Part I, letter three, 18 Nov. 1914. Unpublished manuscript, Meudon

The brown period

1 *Quelques notices biographiques sur le peintre et architecte Theo van Doesburg*, 1928. Unpublished manuscript, Meudon

The blue period

1 'Futurisme', *Eenheid*, no. 127, 9 Nov. 1912

2 'Over moderne kunst', Kandinsky, *Eenheid*, no. 183, 6 Dec. 1913

3 'De ontwikkeling der moderne schilderkunst', *Eenheid*, no. 320, 22 July 1916

4 H. P. Berlage, *Studies over Bouwkunst Stijl en Samenleving*, Rotterdam, W. L. & J. Brusse, 1910

5 'Proeve tot nieuwe kunstkritiek', *Eenheid*, no. 111, 20 July; no. 112, 27 July; no. 113, 3 Aug; no. 115, 17 Aug. 1912

6 'Onafhankelijke bespiegelingen over de kunst', *De Avondpost*, 7 Feb. 1914

7 Umberto Boccioni, *Manifeste technique de la sculpture futuriste*, Point 7, Paris, 1912

8 'De nieuwe stijl in de schilderkunst', *De Avondpost*, 23 Jan. 1916

On active duty

1 'De ontwikkeling der moderne schilderkunst', *Eenheid*, several issues in 1916 (see bibliography) and in: *Drie voordrachten over de nieuwe beeldende kunst*, Amsterdam, Maatschappij voor goede en goedkoope lectuur, 1919

First contacts with Piet Mondrian and the architect J. J. P. Oud

1 Kunst-kritiek. Moderne kunst: Stedelijk Museum, Amsterdam, Expositie Mondrian, Leo Gestel, Sluiters, Schelfhout, Le Fauconnier, *Eenheid*, no. 283, 6 Nov. 1915

2 Piet Mondrian, Letter 20, Nov. 1915, to Theo van Doesburg; printed in part in Ex. Cat., no. 81, *De Stijl*: Stedelijk Museum, Amsterdam, 1951, p. 71

3 'Iets over schilderkunst als beeldende kunst', Ingezonden, *Nieuwe Courant*, 14 May 1916

The transition to Neo-plasticism

1 'De nieuwe stijl in de schilderkunst', *De Avondpost*, 2 May 1916

1917: Van Doesburg founds De Stijl

1 F. T. Marinetti, 'La nuova Religione-Morale della Velocità', Paris, 1916. Reprinted in: M. Drudi Gambillo and T. Fuiri, *Archivi del Futurismo*, Rome, De Luca, 1958, pp. 52–6

2 'De stijl der toekomst', lecture given publicly 1917. 'Drie voordrachten over de nieuwe beeldende kunst', Amsterdam, Maatschappij voor goede en goedkoope lectuur, 1919

3 Bart van der Leck, Letter 17 May, 1917, to Theo van Doesburg, Meudon

4 *De Stijl: Maandblad voor de moderne beeldende vakken*. Redactie Theo van Doesburg. Met medewerking van voorname binnen – en buitenlandse kunstenaars. (De Stijl: Monthly on modern plastic arts. Editor Theo van Doesburg. With the collaboration of important national and international artists.)

5 *De nieuwe beweging in de schilderkunst*, Delft, J. Waltman, 1917

6 'Grootmeesters der beeldende kunst: I', *Eenheid*, no. 357, 7 Apr. 1917

7 ibid., II, *Eenheid*, no. 392, 8 Dec. 1917

Dr M. H. J. Schoenmaekers and Neo-plastic theory

1 'Dr M. H. J. Schoenmaekers, Kunst en gedachte', *Het Getij*, Jan. 1918, p. 9

2 'Dr M. H. J. Schoenmaekers', *Beginselen der beeldende wiskunde*, Bussum, C. A. J. van Dishoeck, 1916, p. 54

3 'Schoonheids-en liefdemystiek: I', *Het Getij*, July 1918, pp. 180–90

4 'Denken-aanschouwen beelden', *De Stijl*, II 2, Dec. 1918, pp. 23–4

The problem of four-dimensionality

1 R. van 't Hoff, 'House and Country-house at Huis ter Heide', *De Stijl*, II 3, Jan. 1919, ill. 3, 5 and 6, p. 33; and no. 9, July, ill. 17

2 J. J. P. Oud, 'Architectonische beschouwing bij bijlage 8; Plattegrond woonhuis Fred. C. Robie door Frank Lloyd Wright', *De Stijl*, I 4, Feb. 1918, pp. 39–41

3 H. P. Berlage, *Amerikaansche Reisherinneringen*, Rotterdam, W. L. & J. Brusse, 1913

4 R. van 't Hoff, *De Stijl*, I 7, May 1918, ill. 11, *Plastic Stairpost*, undated

5 Piet Mondrian, Undated letter to Theo van Doesburg, written about March–Apr. 1918, Meudon

6 Bart van der Leck, Letter 8 Apr. 1918, to Theo van Doesburg, Meudon

7 'Aanteekeningen bij bijlage 12, De Zaag en de goudvischkom van P. Alma', *De Stijl*, I 8, June 1918, p. 93

I. K. Bonset: Van Doesburg as a Dadaist and poet

1 'La littérature. Manifeste II de *De Stijl*, 1920', *De Stijl*, III 6, Apr. 1920, pp. 49–54

2 'X-beelden' (Poems from the series 'Cubist poems', 1913–1919, *De Stijl*, III 7, May 1920, p. 57

3 I. K. Bonset (Pseud. Theo van Doesburg), *Nieuwe woordbeeldingen. Kubistische en expressionistische verzen, 1913–1920*, unpublished manuscript, Meudon

4 Letter to Tristan Tzara, 8 Dec. 1918, Meudon

5 Hugo Ball, *Flucht aus der Zeit*, Zürich, 1915

6 'Het andere gezicht', *De Stijl*, III 10, Aug. 1920, pp. 84–6

7 'Is een universeel beeldingsbegrip thans mogelijk?', *Bouwkundig Weekblad*, XLI 39, 1920, pp. 230–31

8 'De taak der nieuwe architectuur', *Bouwkundig Weekblad*, XLI 50, 1920, pp. 278–80; no. 51, pp. 281–85; XLII 1, 1921, pp. 8–10

The conflict with the Bauhaus

1 'Rondblik', *De Stijl*, II 9, July 1919, pp. 104–108

2 'Aanteekeningen bij de bijlagen (21. Lyonel Feininger: Vollersroda)', *De Stijl*, II 11, Sep. 1919 opposite p. 126

3 'Rondblik, Het expressionisme', *De Stijl*, II 12, Oct. 1919, pp. 140–42

4 'Overzichtelijke beschouwing bij de intrede van den derden jaargang', *De Stijl*, III 1, Nov. 1919, pp. 1–5

5 *Drie voordrachten over de nieuwe beeldende kunst*, Amsterdam, Maatschappij voor goede en goedkoepe lectuur, 1919

6 'Grondbegrippen der nieuwe beeldende kunst', *Tijdschrift voor wijsbegeerte*, XIII 1, 1919, pp. 30–49, 2 pp. 169–88

7 'Data en feiten (betreffende de invloedsontwikkeling van De Stijl in 't buitenland) die voor zich spreken', *De Stijl*, ser. XIV 79–84, 1927, p. 54

8 Walter Gropius, Letter 3 Nov. 1952, to Bruno Zevi, printed in part in: Bruni Zevi, *Poetica dell' architettura neo-plastica*, Milan, Libreria Editrice Politecna Tamburini, 1953, p. 161

9 Lothar Schreyer, *Erinnerungen an Sturm und Bauhaus*, Munich, Albert Langen-Georg Mueller, 1956, p. 237

10 Draft of letter to L. Moholy-Nagy, 1924, Meudon

11 Letter, 7 Jan. 1921, to Anthony Kok; printed in part in Ex. Cat., no. 81, *De Stijl*, Amsterdam, Stedelijk Museum, 1951, p. 45

12 Walter Gropius, preface to L. Moholy-Nagy, *The New Vision*, New York, Wittenborn, 1947, p. 5

Berlin and the rise of Functionalism

1 'De Beteekenis der mechanische esthetiek voor de architectuur en de andere vakken', *Bouwkundig Weekblad*, XLII 25, 1921, pp. 164–66; no. 28, pp. 179–83; no. 33, pp. 219–21

2 Also published in *Bouwkundig Weekblad*, and later as J. J. P. Oud, 'Uber die zukünftige Baukunst und ihre architektonische Möglichkeiten', *Holländische Architektur*, Bauhausbook, Munich, Albert Langen Verlag, 1926, pp. 63–76

3 Ill. 14, example of a colour-composition in an interior, 1919, with furniture by G. Rietveld, *De Stijl*, III 12, Dec., 1920, opposite p. 103

4 See note 1, The problem of Four-dimensionality

Aldo Camini: Van Doesburg as an anti-philosopher

1 G. Papini, *Il Discorso di Rima*, 1913; reprinted in *Archivi del Futurismo*, pp. 133–41

2 ibid., pp. 138, 140

3 'Caminoscopy. 'n Antiphylosophische levensbeschouwing zonder draad of systeem', *De Stijl*, IV 5, May 1921, pp. 65–71; no. 6, June, pp. 82–7; no. 7, July, pp. 97–9; no. 8, Aug., pp. 118–19, no. 12, Dec., pp. 180–82; v 6 June, 1922, pp. 86–8; VI 3/4 May/June, 1923, pp. 33–6; ser. XII 6/7, 1924, pp. 74–7

4 'Schoonheids- en liefdemystiek', I, *Het Getij*, July, 1918, p. 181

5 'Tristan Tzara, Manifesto of Mr Aa the anti-philosopher', *The Dada Painters and Poets*, New York, Wittenborn, 1951, pp. 83–6

6 F. T. Marinetti, *L'imagination sans fils et les mots en liberté*, Paris, 1913

7 C. Carrà, *La Pittura dei Suoni, Rumori e Odori*, 1913; reprinted in: M. Drudi Gambillo and T. Fuiro, *Archivi del Futurismo*, 1958, pp. 73–6

8 'Revue der avant-garde', *Het Getij*, VI 1, 2, 1921, pp. 109–12, 193–200

9 'Inleiding tot de nieuwe verskunst', *De Stijl*, IV 1, Jan., 1921, pp. 1–5; no. 2, Feb., pp. 24–6 (by I. K. Bonset)

10 F. T. Marinetti, *Manifeste technique de la litérature futuriste*, Paris, 1912

Constructivism in Western Europe

1 'Manifest III. Tot een nieuwe wereldbeelding', *De Stijl*, IV 8, Aug. 1921, pp. 123–6

2 'El Lissitzky and Elie Ehrenburg, Die Blockade Russlands geht ihrem Ende entgegen', *Ves* (Object, Gegenstand), no. 1–2, March–April, 1922, pp. 1–4

3 'R. Hausmann, Hans Arp, Iwan Puni and L. Moholy-Nagy, Aufruf zur elementaren Kunst', *De Stijl*, IV 10, Oct. 1921, p. 156

4 'Der Wille zum Stil. Neugestaltung von Leben, Kunst and Technik', *De Stijl*, v 2 Feb. 1922, pp. 23–32; no. 3, Mar., pp. 33–41

5 Piet Mondrian, 'De Realiseering van het Neo-plasticisme in verre toekomst en in de huidige architectuur', *De Stijl*, v 3, Mar. 1922, pp. 41–7; no. 5, May, pp. 65–70

6 J. J. P. Oud, 'Bouwkunst en Kubisme', *De Bouwwereld*, XXI 32, 9, Aug. 1922, p. 245

7 'Het kubisme voor 't laatst', *De Bouwwereld*, XXI 35, p. 270

8 'De consequentie van de pen en de teeken-haak', *De Stijl*, v 9, Sep. 1922, pp. 141–42

9 See J. J. P. Oud, *Mein Weg in De Stijl*, 's Gravenhage-Rotterdam, N. V. Uitgeverij Nijgh and Van Ditmar, N.D. (1961). See also J. Baljeu, De Stijl toen en J. J. P. Oud nu, *Forum*, XV 8, 1961, pp. 285–8

The International Congress of Progressive Artists, Dusseldorf, 1922

1 'Schöpferische Forderungen von De Stijl', *De Stijl*, v 4, Apr. 1922, p. 62

2 Theo van Doesburg, El Lissitzky and Hans Richter, 'Erklärung der Internationalen Fraktion der Konstruktivisten', *De Stijl*, v 4 Apr. 1922, pp. 61–4

3 ibid., p. 64

4 'El Lissitzky and Eli Ehrenburg, Deklaration an den ersten Kongress fortschrittlicher Künstler', Düsseldorf, *De Stijl*, v 4, Apr. 1922, pp. 56–7

5 See A. F. del Marle, 'Art, revolution, vie.

D'une conversation Lénine – Clara Zetkin. Réponse à Lénine', Vouloir, no. 23, Oct. 1926. See also Naum Gabo, 'On constructive realism', in: Katherine S. Dreier et al., *Three Lectures on Modern Art*, New York, The philosophical library, 1949, p. 69

6 Werner Graeff, 'Für das Neue', *De Stijl*, v 5 May 1922, p. 74

7 El Lissitzky, 'Proun', *De Stijl*, v 6, June 1922, pp. 81–5

8 Hans Richter, Film, *De Stijl*, v 6, June 1922, pp. 91–4

9 ' □ contre les artistes imitateurs', *De Stijl*, v 6 June 1922, pp. 95–7

10 L. Moholy-Nagy, 'Produktion-Reproduktion', *De Stijl*, v 7, July 1922, pp. 98–101

11 E. Prampolini, 'L'estetica della machina e l'introspezione meccanica nell' arte', *De Stijl*, v 7, July 1922, pp. 102–5

12 'Monumental art', (article in Russian), *Ves*, no. 1–2, March–April, 1922, pp. 14–15

13 'Az épitészet mint szintetikus muevészet', (article in Hungarian), *Ma, Aktivista Folyóirat*, no. 7, July 1922, p. 35

14 'Balans van het nieuwe', *De Stijl*, v 7 July 1922, p. 106; no. 9, Sep., pp. 130–35

15 'Konstruktivische Internationale Schöpferische Arbeitsgemeinschaft' (Proclamation in German, French and Dutch, signed by Theo van Doesburg, Hans Richter, El Lissitzky, Karel Maes and Max Burchartz), *De Stijl*, v 8, Aug. 1922, pp. 113–28

16 'Beeldend Rusland'. In the ser. Balans van het nieuwe, *De Stijl*, v 9, Sep. 1922, pp. 130–32

17 See note 7

The Weimar models, 1922

1 'De involoed van De Stijl-beweging in Duitschland', *Bouwkundig Weekblad*, XLIV 7, 1923,

pp. 80–84

2 Herbert Bayer, Walter Gropius and Ilse Gropius, *Bauhaus 1919–1928*, Teufen, Arthur Niggli and Willy Verkauf, 1955, p. 72

3 'Van de esthetiek naar het materiaal', *Bouwkundig Weekblad*, XLIII 38, 1922, pp. 372–5

4 J. P. Mieras, 'Prijskamp in de schoone bouw-kunst in 1921', *Bouwkundig Weekblad*, XLIII 1, Jan, 1922

5 From an interview of C. van Eesteren by the author

Mecano and other Dada activities

1 *Les feuilles libres*, April–May 1922

2 L. Moholy-Nagy, *Vision in Motion*, Chicago, Paul Theobald, 1947

3 I. K. Bonset (pseudo: Theo van Doesburg), 'Antikunstenzuivereredemanifest', *Mecano*, no. 1, yellow issue, 1922

4 Chroniek-Mecano, *Mecano*, no. 3, red issue, 1922

5 A. Kemeny and L. Moholy-Nagy, 'Dynamisch-konstruktives Kraftsystem', *Der Sturm*, XIII 12, Dec. 1922, p. 186

6 'Manifest Proletkunst' (signed by Theo van Doesburg, Kurt Schwitters, Hans Arp, Tristan Tzara and Chr. Spengemann), *Merz*, no. 2, Apr. 1923, pp. 24–5

7 'Anti-tendenzkunst', *De Stijl*, VI 2, Apr. 1923, pp. 17–19

De Stijl and Proun versus Functionalism

1 'Von der neuen Aesthetik zur materiellen Verwirklichung', *De Stijl*, VI 1, March, 1923, pp. 10–14

2 Mies van der Rohe, 'Bürohaus', G □, I, July 1923

3 Mies van der Rohe, 'Bauen', G □, II, Sep. 1923

4 Zur elementaren Gestaltung', G □, I, July 1923

5 Piet Mondrian, 'Moet de Schilderkunst minderwaardig zijn aan de bouwkunst', *De Stijl*, VI 5, 1923, pp. 62–4

6 El Lissitzky, 'Raum', G □, I, July 1923

7 'De beteekenis van de kleur in binnen- en buitenarchitectuur', *Bouwkundig weekblad*, XLIV 21, 1923, pp. 232–4

8 'Voorwaarden tot een nieuwe architectuur', *Architectura*, XXVII 27, Aug. 11, 1923, pp. 163–5

9 Dr W. Linder, *Ingenieurbauten*, Berlin, Wasmuth, 1923

10 Pariser Neuheiten. 'Motiv: nur', G □, II, Sep. 1923

The Paris models

1 From an interview with C. van Eesteren

2 Bruno Zevi, *Poetica dell' Architettura Neo-plastica*, Milan, Libreria Editrice Politecna Tamburini, 1953, ill. 33, 34, 35, 36 and 37

3 *Grundbegriffe der neuen gestaltenden Kunst*, Bauhausbook, Munich, Albert Langen Verlag, 1924, ill. 11 and 31

4 Theo van Doesburg and C. van Eesteren, 'Vers une construction collective', *De Stijl*, ser. XII 6/7, 1924, pp. 89–91

Le Corbusier's criticism of De Stijl

1 Ozenfant and Jeanneret (Le Corbusier), 'L'angle droit', *L'esprit nouveau*, no. 18, Oct. 1923

2 Ozenfant and Jeanneret, Pédagogie, *L'esprit nouveau*, no. 19, Nov. 1923

3 Le Corbusier, 'Le Salon d'automne. Déductions consécutives troublantes', *L'esprit nouveau*. no. 19, Nov. 1923

4 Piet Mondrian, 'Geen axioma maar beeldend principe', *De Stijl*, ser. XII 6/7, 1924, pp. 83–5

5 Die Kunst als Hemmung des Fortschrittes, incomplete MS of lecture, Meudon

6 Le Corbusier, 'L'exposition de l'Ecole spéciale d'architecture', *L'esprit nouveau*, no. 23, May 1924

7 Réponse à notre enquête: Où va la peinture moderne?', *Bulletin de l'effort moderne*, no. 3, Mar. 1924, pp. 7–8

8 Hans Richter, *L'esprit nouveau*, G. III, June 1924, p. 60

9 Hans Richter, *De Stijl*, G. III, June 1924, p. 58

10 'C'est le spirituel . . . ', G. III, June 1924, p. 38

Van Doesburg's architectural programme

1 'Tot een beeldende architectuur', *De Stijl*, ser. XII 6/7, 1924, pp. 78–83, and: 'De nieuwe architectuur', *Bouwkundig Weekblad*, MLV 20, 17 May 1924, pp. 200–201

2 El Lissitzky, 'Proun', *De Stijl*, v 6, June 1922, p. 83

3 El Lissitzky, Letter 22 Aug. 1924, to Theo van Doesburg, Meudon

4 Frank Lloyd Wright, *op cit.*, pp. 36, 33, 39 and 33 respectively

5 Frank Lloyd Wright, 'Ausgeführte Bauten und Entwürfe', Berlin, Wasmuth, 1910

6 Le Corbusier Saugnier *Vers une architecture*, Paris, Editions Crès 1923

7 Architectuur-diagnose, *Architectura*, XXVIII: 15, 17, May 1924, pp. 61–3

8 Theodore M. Brown, *The Work of G. Rietveld, Architect*, Utrecht, A. W. Bruna & Zoon, 1958.

9 Ex. Cat., no. 81: *De Stijl*, Amsterdam, Stedelijk Museum, 1951. See reproduction

10 *Kasimir Malevich*, Ex. Cat. Kunstverein Braunschweig, Haus Salve Hospes, 1958, ill. 47, 48 and 49

11 See text accompanying the ill. of an architectural model by Malevich, 1926, *De Stijl*, Jubilee-issue, ser. XIV 79/84, 1927, p. 65

12 'Vers une construction collective', *De Stijl*, ser. XII 6/7, 1924, pp. 89–91

13 '–□ + = R4', *De Stijl*, ser. XII 6/7, 1924, pp. 91–2

14 El Lissitzky, *Nasci*, Merz, no. 8/9, Apr., July 1924

15 'Die Entwicklung der modernen Architektur in Holland', unpublished MS., Meudon. This text is virtually the same as his article, 'Die neue Architektur und ihre Konsequenzen', unpublished MS., dated 1930, Meudon

16 See note 3 Paris models

17 See note 6 The conflict with the Bauhaus

Elementarism: another search for dynamics in painting

1 George Antheil, 'Manifest der Musico-mechanico', *De Stijl*, ser. XII 8, 1924, pp. 99–102

2 George Antheil, 'My ballet mecanique', *De Stijl*, ser. XII 12, 1924/5, pp. 141–4

3 'Surrealisme. Realistische samenspraak', *De Stijl*, ser. XII 8, 1924, pp. 103–6

4 See note 5 Mecano and other Dada activities

5 A. Kemeny, 'Das dynamische Prinzip der Welt-konstruktion in Zusammenhang mit der Funktionellen Bedeutung der konstruktiven Gestaltung', *Der Sturm*, XIV 4, Apr. 1923, pp. 62–4

6 A. Gleizes, *La peinture et ses lois. (Ce qui devait sortir du Cubisme)*, Paris, La Vie des Lettres, 1924, pp. 44–8, p. 53

7 Gino Severini, 'La peinture d'avant garde',

De Stijl, I 2, 3, 4, 5, 8, and 10, 1917/18

8   'De dood der modernismen. Diagnose van het
     Futurisme, Kubisme, Expressionisme,
     Purisme, Dadaisme, Constructivisme enz.',
     De Stijl, ser. XII 9, 1924/5, pp. 122–6

Mondrian leaves De Stijl

1   'Het einde der kunst', *De Stijl*, ser. XII 9,
     1924/25, pp. 135–6

2   See note 7 Le Corbusier's criticism of *De Stijl*

3   'Het fiasco van Holland op de expositie te
     Parijs in 1925', *De Stijl*, ser. XII 10/11, 1924/5,
     pp. 156–9

Van Doesburg's isolation in France

1   'El Lissitzky and Hans Arp', *Die Kunstismen
     1914–1924*, Erlenbach Zürich, Eugen
     Rentsch Verlag, 1925

2   El Lissitzky, 'K. und Pangeometrie', in the
     Europa-Almanach, Eds. Carl Einstein and
     Paul Westheim, Potsdam, Gustav Kiepen-
     heuer Verlag, 1925, p. 106

3   K. Malevich, *The non-objective world*
     (Introduction by L. Hilberseimer) Chicago,
     Paul Theobald, 1959, p. 8

4   Constantin Umansky, *Neue Kunst in Russland
     1914–1919* Potsdam, Gustav Kiepenheuer,
     1920, p. 22

5   Ibid., p. 15

6   See also Peter Lufft, Introduction to Ex. Cat.
     Malevich, Kunstverein Braunschweig, 1958;
     Franz Meyer, Ex. Cat. *Malevich*, Bern
     Kunsthalle, 1959; Horst Richter, El
     *Lissitzky, Sieg über die Sonne, zur Kunst des
     Konstruktivismus*, Cologne, Christopher
     Czwiklitzer, 1958, and W. Sandberg, 'Malevich
     en de datering van zijn werk', *Museum-
     journaal*, ser. III 5/6, Dec., 1957, pp. 113–14.
     In note 77 of this last publication, it is said
     that Malevich seems to have used the black
     square only once in 1913, on a theatre curtain

used in Petersburg for the opera 'Sieg über
die Sonne' by A. Krutchonjch. It there
served as a protest against the usual over-
decoration of theatre curtains. All sources
mentioned above unanimously agree that the
first Suprematist works of art do not appear
before 1915

7   El Lissitzky, 'K. und Pangeometrie', the
     Europa-Almanach, 1925, p. 108

8   'Le Corbusier, Architekturwende', the *Europa-
     Almanach*, pp. 166–7

9   J. J. P. Oud, 'Ja und nein', the *Europa-
     Almanach*, 1925, pp. 18–20

10   'Europäische Architektur', incomplete MS.,
     Meudon. The last page of this MS. was
     published in *De Stijl*, Ex. Cat. no. 81,
     Amsterdam, Stedelijk Museum, 1951, p. 120

11   I. K. Bonset, 'Het andere gezicht, Abstracte,
     sur-humanistische roman', *De Stijl*, ser. XIII
     77, 1926, pp. 66–70, and ff.

12   'Im Kampf um den neuen Stil', *Neue
     Schweizer Rundschau*, May, 1929, p. 377

13   *De Stijl*, ser. XII 10/11, 1924/25

14   'Piet Mondrian, L'architecture future
     néo-plasticienne', *L'architecture vivante*, (De
     Stijl-issue), III 9, 1925, pp. 11–13

15   'L'évolution de l'architecture moderne en
     Hollande', *L'architecture vivante*, (De Stijl-
     issue), III 9, pp. 14–20

16   Kurt Schwitters, Käte Steinitz and Theo van
     Doesburg, *Die Scheuche, Märchen*, Hanover,
     Apos Verlag, no. 3. 1925

De Stijl's dualism of mind and matter

1   Piet Mondrian, 'Art, pureté + abstraction',
     Vouloir, no. 19, Mar. 1926

2   'Vers un art élémentaire', *Vouloir*, no. 19,
     Mar. 1926

3   'Schilderkunst. Van Kompoisitie tot contra-

kompositie', *De Stijl*, ser. XII 73/74, 1926, pp. 17–28

4 'Schilderkunst en plastiek. Over contra-compositie en contra-plastiek, elementarisme, Manifest-fragment', *De Stijl*, ser. XIII 75/76, 1926, pp. 35–43

5 Hans Richter, 'Prinzipielles zur Bewegungs-kunst', *De Stijl*, IV 7, July 1921, pp. 109–12

6 Bart van der Leck, 'De plaats van het moderne schilderen in de architectuur', *De Stijl*, I 1, Oct. 1917, pp. 6–7

7 Bart van der Leck, Letter, 8 Apr. 1918, to Theo van Doesburg, Meudon

8 Auguste Joly, *Le futurisme et la philosophie*, Paris, 1912

9 'La situation de l'art moderne en Italie', unpublished MS., Aug. 1926, Meudon

10 'Beeldende constructie-leer in vier deelen. Eerste deel: De Kleur'. Texts in Dutch, German and French, unpublished MS., 1924–27, Meudon

11 Zijn, *De Stijl*, ser. XIII 75/76, 1926, p. 64

12 'Schilderkunst en plastiek. Elementarisme. Manifest-fragment', *De Stijl*, ser. XIII 78, 1927, pp. 82–7

13 W. T. Stace, *The Philosophy of Hegel* (Chpt. The philosophy of spirit, third division: absolute spirit), New York, Dover publications, p. 440

14 'Piet Mondrian, Natural reality and abstract reality'; in: M. Seuphor, *Piet Mondrian, life and work*, Amsterdam, Contact, p. 320

The Weissenhofsiedlung

1 Mies van der Rohe, *Die Form* (Introduction to a special issue dedicated to the Werkbund-exhibition 'Die Wohnung') II 9, Sep. 1927, p. 257

2 'Von der neuen Aesthetik zur materiellen Verwicklichung', *De Stijl*, VI 1, Mar. 1923, p. 10

3 *De Stijl*, ser. XV 85/86, 1928, pp. 123–6

4 'Uber das Verhältnis von malerischer und architektonischer Gestaltung' *Der Cicerone*, XIX 18, 2 Sep. 1927, pp. 564–70

5 'Architectuurvernieuwingen in het buitenland. De architectuurtentoonstelling "Die Wohnung" te Stuttgart', *Bouwbedrijf*, IV 24, 1927, pp. 556 and 558

De Stijl's jubilee issue

1 'Data en feiten (betreffende de invloedsontwikkeling van "De Stijl" in 't buitenland) die voor zich spreken', *De Stijl*, ser. XIV 79/84, 1927, pp. 53–71

2 Piet Mondrian, Letter 4, Dec. 1927, to Theo van Doesburg, Ex. Cat. no. 81, *De Stijl*, Amsterdam, Stedelijk Museum, 1951, p. 72

3 F. Kiesler, 'L'architecture élémentarisée', *De Stijl*, ser. XIV 79/84, 1927, p. 101

The Aubette, Strasbourg

1 'Notices sur l'Aubette à Strasbourg', *De Stijl*, ser. XV 87/89, 1928, p. 6

2 'Uit de dagboeknotities van Theo van Doesburhg, fragments of 1, May 1928 and 13, June 1928, *De Stijl* (last issue under the editorship of Petro van Doesburg), Jan. 1932, pp. 19–22

3 'L'élémentarisme et son orgine', *De Stijl*, ser. XV 87/89, 1928, pp. 20–5

4 ibid., p. 20

5 'Farben im Raum und Zeit', *De Stijl*, ser. XV 87/89, 1928, p. 34

6 ibid., p. 33

The Meudon house

1 From an interview with A. Elzas

2 'Die Verkehrsstadt', *Architektur der Gegenwart*, no. 3, 1929, pp. 4–10

Years of reflection

1 'Quelques notices biographiques sur le peintre et architecte Theo van Doesburg', unpublished MS., 1928/29, Meudon

2 'Der Kampf um den neuen Stil', *Neue Schweizer Rundschau*. no. 1, Jan. 1929; no. 3, Mar.; no. 5, May; no. 7, July; no. 8, Aug.

3 'L'importance de la 4me dimension dans la nouvelle plastique et la nouvelle architecture'; the title of this MS. was announced in *De Stijl*, last issue, Jan. 1932, p. 5 but had already appeared in *Neue Schweizer Rundschau*, no. 8, Aug. 1929

4 *Simultaneous Composition XXIV*, 1929, Collection Société Anonyme, Yale University, Art Gallery, New Haven, U.S.A.

5 W. T. Stace, *op. cit.*, p. 441

6 L. Moholy-Nagy, *Von Material zur Architektur*, Bauhausbook, Munich, Albert Langen Verlag, 1929

7 L. Moholy-Nagy, *The New Vision*, New York, Wittenborn, 1947. References in the text concern this English edition

8 ibid., p. 62

9 'Kunst–en architectuurvernieuwing in Italie', *Bouwbedrij*, VI 9, 1929, pp. 179–81

10 Fillia, 'Futurismo e Fascismo', *La Città Futurista*, I 1, Apr. 1929, p. 1

Art Concret

1 From a diary, observation entered during

May 1929, unpublished MS., Meudon

2 'Base de la peinture concrète: Manifesto', *Art concret*, Apr. 1930, p. 1

3 'Commentaire sur la base de la peinture concrète', *Art concret*, Apr. 1930, p. 2

4 ibid., section 2, p. 2

5 Dr M. H. J. Schoenmaekers, *Beginselen der beeldende wiskunde*, Bussum, C. A. J. van Dishoeck, 1916, pp. 196–7

6 ibid., p. 192

7 'De l'intuition à la certitude', *Réalités nouvelles*, no. 1, 1947

8 'Uit het Journal d'idées van Theo van Doesburg', *De Stijl*, Jan. 1932, last issue, pp. 24–5

9 J. H. de Groot, *Vormcomposite en centraliteit*, Amsterdam, with pub., 1922, p. 5

10 Dr M. H. J. Schoenmaekers, *op. cit.* pp. 204–5

Last activities

1 'Elémentarisme: Les éléments de la nouvelle peinture', *De Stijl*, Jan. 1932, last issue, pp. 15–6

2 Mondrian's essay, 'Art and Life', is found in H. L. C. Jaffé, *De Stijl 1917–1931*, London, Alec Tiranti, N. D. (1956), pp. 211–58

3 ibid., esp. pp. 220, 224, 228 and 242

4 ibid., pp. 212–13

5 ibid., p. 232

6 Letter of 9 Feb. 1931 to F. Kupka, Meudon

Index